Green Parties, Green Future

Green Parties, Green Future

From Local Groups to the International Stage

Per Gahrton

Foreword by Caroline Lucas

PlutoPress
www.plutobooks.com

First published 2015 by Pluto Press
345 Archway Road, London N6 5AA

www.plutobooks.com

Copyright © Per Gahrton 2015

British Library Cataloguing in Publication Data
A catalogue record for this book is available from the British Library

ISBN   978 0 7453 3345 8   Hardback
ISBN   978 0 7453 3339 7   Paperback
ISBN   978 1 7837 1508 4   PDF eBook
ISBN   978 1 7837 1510 7   Kindle eBook
ISBN   978 1 7837 1509 1   EPUB eBook

This book is printed on paper suitable for recycling and made from
fully managed and sustained forest sources. Logging, pulping and
manufacturing processes are expected to conform to the environmental
standards of the country of origin.

Typeset by Stanford DTP Services, Northampton, England
Text design by Melanie Patrick
Simultaneously printed by CPI Antony Rowe, Chippenham, UK
and Edwards Bros in the United States of America

CONTENTS

LIST OF FIGURES

PREFACE

It has been a thrilling journey full of despair and hope for those of us who began in the early 1980s (some a decade earlier) to establish Green parties and construct an international Green network. I myself initiated the Swedish Green Party after having failed (despite a period as a Liberal MP) in 'greening' the old Liberal Party. I was chosen as one of the first four co-secretaries of the European Greens in 1985. Since the beginning of the 1980s, I have visited Green parties in their home countries and at international Green congresses and gatherings all over the world. I met environmentalists in the crumbling Soviet Union around 1989–1990, visited Greens across the USA and Canada in 1990, reported in 1992 from the Earth Summit in Rio de Janeiro, and visited branches of Partido Verde from Manaus to Porto Alegre, including Brasilia where I was received by the first MP of Partido Verde, Sidney de Miguel, in the Chamber of the Parliament. As a Green Member of the European Parliament 1995–2004 I was present at events relevant for Green policy, such as the WTO meetings in Seattle 1999 and Doha 2001, the Johannesburg Rio +10 in 2002 and the Mumbai World Social Forum in 2004. I have participated in innumerable Green national campaigns and demonstrations, from Seville to Tirana, Venice to Tbilisi, Cairo to Baku. During my period as the chair of the China Delegation of the European Parliament 1997–2002, I met with environmentalists throughout China, and in 2006 I visited Japanese Greens in Fukuoka, Kyoto and Tokyo. I have, once or several times, visited at least half of the Green parties presented in this first global overview of Global Green politics. Furthermore, I have been present at all the Global Greens congresses, Canberra 2001, São Paolo 2008 and Dakar 2012, and at most of the major meetings of the European Greens, up until the EGP Council in Istanbul in November 2014.

The aim of this book is to give an overview of the growing global Green political movement, its thinking, ideology, world view, basic values, organisational structure and political strength. I don't claim to have produced a scientific treatise. However, I have made use of my capacity as PhD of Sociology, standing somewhere in between the analytical positivism of Emile Durkheim and the interpretative anti-positivism of Max Weber and George Simmel, in the sense that I reject the notion of social research as a branch of classical physics or mathematics, but still believe that quantitative methods are needed in order *to explain*, together with qualitative methods in order *to understand*. From this perspective I have chosen two types of approach. One is that of reporting as a *participant observer*, using my extensive notes and diaries from more than four decades as a Green activist and politician. Another is that of drawing on my experience not only as a sociologist but also as a reporting journalist, trying to act as an *external and critical observer*, using documents from Green parties and organisations, media reports, election results, interviews with Green actors and politicians, as well as research reports, memoirs of Green politicians and other relevant literature.

I am biased in favour of the Green political movement and the need for Green politics, but I hope not to be uncritical and blind to weaknesses, flaws, mistakes and hazards.

This book is my own project and does not in any way represent any Green party or organisation. All opinions are mine and the responsibility for the correctness of the thousands of details is mine alone. Nevertheless, it would not have been possible to produce this book without the support of some 30 dedicated Greens, from the international secretaries of individual parties to responsible persons in international Green bodies, from individual Greens with special knowledge to present and former Green Members of Parliaments and Governments.

I especially want to thank Anna-Karin Andersson, International Secretary of the Swedish Greens, for having checked the entire manuscript and contributed hundreds of corrections as well as recommendations for 'killing darlings'. I am also grateful to my wife, Drude Dahlerup, professor of political science at Stockholm University, who read parts of the manuscript from her professional point of view and made crucial recommendations. In addition warm thanks to the following Greens who have checked, corrected and commented on relevant sections: Rikiya Adachi (Japan), Liaquat Ali (Pakistan), Magda Alvoet, former minister (Belgium), Paolo Bergamaschi (Italy), Margret Blakers (Australia), Olzod Boum-Yalagch (Mongolia), Arnold Cassola, former secretary general of the European Greens (Malta), Jacqueline Cremers, former secretary general of the European Greens (Netherlands), Paty Doneau, coordinator of the Federation of American Greens (Mexico), Marina Dragomiretskaya (Bulgaria), Eva Goës, Green Forum (Sweden), Mayis Gulaliyev (Azerbaijan), Frank Habineza, president of the African Green Federation (Rwanda), Heidi Hautala, former minister (Finland), Jesus Hernandez Nicolou (Catalonia), Gerhard Jordan (Austria), Véronica Juzgado (executive secretary Global Greens), Ely Labro (Philippines), Benoît Lechat (Belgium), Lena Lindström (Sweden), Ralph Monö, former secretary general of the European Greens (Sweden), Suresh Nautiyal (India), Laura Nordström (Finland), Sara Parkin, former co-secretary of the Coordination of European Greens (England), Alfonso Pecaro Scanio, former minister (Italy), Liljana Popovska (Macedonia), Margot Soria Saravia (Bolivia), Erzsebet Schmuck (Hungary), Ji Seon (Korea), Mohamed Tounkara (Guinea), Ann Verheyen, European Green Party (Belgium), Ludger Volmer (Germany), Claire Waghorn-Lees, secretary of the Asia-Pacific Greens (New Zealand), Keli Yen, Asia-Pacific Greens Coordinator (Taiwan).

Some of the details in the book (especially in the Appendix) may become obsolete overnight, thanks to a parliamentary election, the decisions of a party congress, or a governmental reshuffle. It is my hope that relevant parts of the book will in due time be available on the web and continuously updated. Readers are welcome to send comments and information directly to me, per. gahrton@gmail.com.

Per Gahrton
Stockholm, Sweden, June 2015

FOREWORD

The extraordinary growth of Green parties around the globe is having a significant impact on the politics of an increasing number of countries, measured not just in terms of the number of votes won by Greens, but by way of their far-reaching influence on public opinion, the media, and indeed the established parties themselves.

From the formation of the first nationwide Green Party in the world, in New Zealand in 1972, to the foundation in recent years of Green Parties in Kenya, Benin, Brazil, Korea and Pakistan, Green influence has been widening and accelerating: more Green parties entering national parliaments, the Green Group in the European Parliament flourishing, and some 20 Green parties having taken part in coalition governments since the early 1990s.

Per Gahrton's compelling overview of the global Green political movement could therefore scarcely be more timely, offering both a unique assessment of progress so far, and valuable insights into how it might evolve in future.

It is a debate that has more than simply academic interest. It is no exaggeration to say that that the world is now in a state of crisis as never before – accelerating climate change, deforestation and over-exploitation of natural resources, together with growing inequality, and an increasingly precarious economic model.

We urgently need new thinking, a new sense of realism about the threats we face, and above all, a new way of working together in politics to tackle the things that really matter.

And as it becomes ever clearer that addressing the growing environmental crisis and avoiding catastrophic climate change will require far-reaching changes not just to our economy, but to all areas of policy making, so more people are turning to Green parties for hope and inspiration.

The challenge is to translate such concerns and aspirations into a widespread revolution in attitudes, and to turn fast-growing political support into practical programmes for government.

There seem to be a number of common factors which help determine the degree of electoral success enjoyed by the different Green parties, including the fairness of the electoral system in which they are operating, the existence of state funding for political parties, the level of environmental concern, and the prominence and historical development of other radical social and political movements. But it is also clear that each country provides a very different model for the development of Green politics.

For Greens in the UK, grappling with both a winner-takes-all voting system and no state funding, the challenges have been great – factors which make the recent so-called 'Green surge' all the more impressive. In the space of less than a year, membership of the Green Party of England and Wales has soared from a little over 12,000 to nearly 60,000, at the time of writing.

Analysis suggesting that this recent growth is driven at least in part by the Green Party's opposition to the politics of austerity raises critical questions that are still being worked through in many different countries and contexts: to what extent should today's Green parties explicitly identify themselves as parties of the left, and to what degree should they cooperate and work with established parties, either in temporary coalitions or via confidence and supply arrangements, in order to achieve at least some level of reform within the system?

Mainstream political parties lack the courage to adopt radical solutions to the social and environmental problems we face. More than that, they are often responsible for those problems in the first place. Parliamentary politics seems incapable of embracing the change that is so urgently needed. But protest, though vital, isn't enough. We need what Petra Kelly, one of the most famous Greens, has called an 'anti-party' – one that would seek power but never sacrifice morality; that would enter parliament but never become part of it; that would always remain, at heart, a party of the people.

It is a compelling ideal; and Petra Kelly helped to bring it to life as a co-founder of the Greens in Germany. As one of the first Green deputies to be elected to the Bundestag in March 1983, she entered the chamber in jeans, bearing armfuls of sunflowers, instantly bringing colour and life into the grey world of traditional politics. Though her political career was cut tragically short in 1992, she remains an inspiration for many in the Green movement and beyond.

And her challenge to us – to do politics differently – is more urgent than ever. With more and more people disillusioned with the political process, the opportunities for the Greens are great. This book, vital reading for both activists and observers, will help to make sure that such opportunities are grasped.

Caroline Lucas MP
Brighton, March 2015

INTRODUCTION: THE GREENS – TOWARDS HEGEMONY IN THE ANTHROPOCENE

The idea that humanity has recently entered a new epoch, the Anthropocene, having lived through the Holocene era for some 12,000 years, seems to be gathering increasing scientific support. A pivotal step in this direction was taken in January 2015 when a group of scientists defined the starting date of Anthropocene as the summer of 1945, when the use of the atomic bomb illustrated a new and highly dangerous capability of humans to change, and destroy, the basic prerequisites for life on Earth.[1] Even if humans have affected the environment since the beginning of the Holocene, and the first warnings were made already by classical Chinese and Greek philosophers several thousand years ago, the switch from the Holocene to the Anthropocene constitutes such a fundamental change that the need for completely new ideas about the effects of human activity appears to be more urgent than ever.

The Green political movement claims to be the carrier of these new ideas, of Green thinking or ecologism. It is hardly a coincidence that only a few years after the start of the Anthropocene, the first voices were raised questioning all earlier political ideologies, such as conservatism, liberalism and socialism, and that from the 1970s onwards many groups, organisations and political parties were established around demands for alternatives to the dominant models of thinking. As of January 2015 there were almost exactly 100 political parties (representing around 90 countries) affiliated to the Global Greens structure, through the four regional Green Federations: for Africa, the Americas, the Asia-Pacific Region and Europe. In addition there are dozens of other Green parties with the ambition to qualify for membership in the Global Greens structure. There are also parties that claim to be Green but have been denied affiliation to the Global Greens structure because they are considered either politically apart or artificial organisations set up by ruling elites for use against genuine Green efforts. Some of these parties are allowed to send representatives as informal observers at some Global Green meetings, which may encourage them to convert to genuine Green parties.

It is obvious that the Green label and a Green political identity are popular and considered assets in most parts of the world. There are Green parties in about 80% of the states of Europe, about 50% of the states of Africa and the

Americas, and about 20% of the states of the Asia-Pacific region. The trend is upwards, despite sometimes draconian countermeasures: if the power elite doesn't try to pre-empt a genuine Green party by creating a fake one, controlled by the ruling authorities, then new genuine Green parties in some countries are required to pay exorbitant deposits, prove the existence of an almost unreachable number of active members or, if there is nothing else to stop them, are hindered by hurdles in the election system. These types of obstacles, which have hit Greens hard even in countries which otherwise are considered good democracies (for example in Japan by deposits, in the UK, USA and other countries by the first-past-the-post election system), are sometimes defended as measures to guarantee political stability and avoid a devastating fractionalisation of the party system. But the most significant effect of all these factors is that they constitute a barrier against renewal in a time when a number of global crises illustrate that everywhere, even in the best of democracies, there is an urgent need for political renewal to cope with problems which the old parties and established ruling elites have so miserably failed to handle in adequate ways.

In an introduction to a book about the first 20 years of the European Greens, which I co-edited with Arnold Cassola in 2003, I had to admit that while I was sure that the Greens 'have a bright future', 'quite a few Greens from the first generation have difficulties recognising the Greens they fell in love with some 20 years ago'.[2] This is probably even more true to-day, some 50 years after the establishment of the first Green parties, in the UK and New Zealand. The major changes are both vertical – Green parties are entering parliaments and governments and taking part directly in the ruling of countries, regions and local assemblies – and horizontal – the number of Green parties is growing and spreading all over the world.

Some of the Green parties I have visited have been groups of enthusiasts without parliamentary representation, like in Peru, Egypt, Albania and Azerbaijan. Others have been large and growing mass-parties with tens of thousands of members, like in Germany, the United Kingdom, Brazil and my own Sweden. Some have consisted mostly of amateurs, others have already become professionals. But as I hope will be made clear in this book, most of the amateurs have the ambition to become more professional in order to be able to push Green issues more efficiently, while most of the professionals are aware that if they were to discard all vestiges of amateurism and grassroots democracy they would be cutting away the branch they are sitting on. And, most importantly, as I believe is proven in this book, most Greens, whether amateurs or professionals, share a very large number of values, principles, basic convictions and concrete proposals, to an extent that is unlikely to be found in any other 'political family' today. The many party programmes and platforms I studied for Chapter 4 are all nationally adapted variations upon one basic theme: We are one humanity, we are destroying the conditions for life on Earth, we must cooperate globally in order to stop the destruction of our common Gaia, and we must share the enormous richness of our Earth equitably to ensure that every living creature gets its fair share of the environmental space available.[3]

Chapter 1 gives an account of the background for and the process of the Green awakening in the 1960s and 1970s. Chapter 2 offers a presentation of and a discussion around Green philosophy. Chapter 3 gives a general overview of the emergence of Green parties. Chapter 4 presents and discusses several concrete Green proposals and policies, based upon an extensive analysis of Green programmes and platforms. In Chapter 5, the history of Green parties in government is related and analysed, based upon the relevant political science literature as well as interviews with former and present Green ministers. In Chapter 6 my vision of a Green future is outlined. In the Appendix some 100 Green parties from across the world are introduced, described and analysed.

Green ideas require testing and development. New and fledgling Green parties need support. This is already happening but could be developed much further. The Global Greens structure needs strengthening. In a world where a great deal of the real power has moved to global economic players, often operating outside democratic political systems, Greens must strive to secure positions of power in all democratically based institutions, from local communities to the United Nations.

1

THE GREEN AWAKENING

The 1960s was a turbulent decade. After a period of relative calm following the end of the Second World War everything began to change. Colonies fought for and achieved independence. The USA's aggressive attempts to contain communism with the mass bombing of Vietnam, isolation of Cuba, military interventions against progressive regimes and support for the fascist junta in Chile, mobilised enormous protests all over the world; the apartheid regimes of Southern Africa also triggered worldwide dismay and protest. At the same time socialism didn't have a much better reputation following the Soviet interventions in Hungary in 1956, Czechoslovakia in 1968, and Afghanistan in 1979. A 'new' left arose, still anti-imperialist, but without blinkers in relation to communist one-party dictatorships. Women's liberation advanced. Oppressed people everywhere rose to demand equal rights. Even in the assumed-to-be well-organised Western European welfare societies, discontent emerged and developed into political movements. The new generation demanded personal liberation from old traditions and superstitions. In Europe a 'sexual liberation' changed lifestyles and partly transformed into the student revolts of 1968. In some places, especially in France, links were made between student demands for more individual freedom and workers' and trade unionists' demands for improved working conditions, including 'industrial democracy'. A few years into the 1970s, however, some basic flaws of the 1968 movement could be observed: it was deeply split and had failed to organise into a powerful political organisation with leverage in the decision-making political system; despite its feminist rhetoric, it also remained predominantly male in its structures. Above all, it was driven by a materialist (often Marxist) outlook and was unable to understand and fight against the causes of the destruction of the environment and the quality of life.

Already in the 1970s many of the activists of the 1968 and similar protest movements became disillusioned with political slogans and other types of primarily verbal action. One alternative option was to define the enemy – be it the state, big business, the military-industrial complex, or just all those who held power – as deadly foes whom it would not be possible to affect or defeat by normal non-violent methods. Those who chose this option took up arms in what they considered a legitimate war of liberation. 'If it's right in Vietnam and Palestine, why not in Frankfurt, Paris and Stockholm?' One of the most well-known examples was the German Red Army Faction (or Baader-Meinhof Gang), but there were similar groups in other democracies: Action Direct in France, the Communist Combatant Cells in Belgium, the Red Brigades in Italy. Spain, Portugal and Greece, with their history of recent fascist dictatorship, also saw the emergence of violent groups. Even Northern Europe, with a reputation for stability, saw an eruption of terrorist violence. The Danish 'Blekinge Street Gang' (*Blekingegadebanden*) robbed banks in the 1970s and '80s, sometimes with deadly results, giving as a motive their wish to support the Palestinian resistance against the Israeli occupation.[1]

It is symbolic that the most well-known figure of the 1968 revolt, Daniel Cohn-Bendit – who later turned Green and was a member of the European Parliament from 1994 to 2014 – in a book commemorating the fortieth anniversary of the '68 revolt, already in the title urges readers to *Forget 68* (the book is in French, despite the English title).[2] When telling the story of the Greens, however, to forget '68 completely would be going too far. Undoubtedly some inspiration was taken from this upheaval by the Green pioneers in the 1970s, not least from the fact that quite a few of the activists who had been

Figure 1 A Green congress in Catalonia in 1985. One poster (far right) is a reminder of Green roots among peaceniks, feminists and other alternative movements. Another (far left), with text in six European languages, illustrates the limited expansion of Green parties in 1985 compared to 30 years later. At the microphone, Paul Staes, MEP of the Flemish Greens, Agalev. Photo: the author.

involved in the revolt switched to Green groups and parties. But perhaps it could be said that the main impact of '68 on the Green awakening came from its failure. The fledgling Greens in the 1970s had to realise that even if tough opposition to the existing political system was necessary, it was not enough; the Greens also had to propose alternatives and set the rules of the game, that is, participate in making political decisions on all levels.

EARLY WHISTLE-BLOWERS

One early whistle-blower was the Chinese thinker Meng Zi (Mencius), who lived 372–289 BC. He observed environmental destruction on a mountain, wrote about the causes of deforestation, and gave advice on the planting of new trees. Most of the early alarm-bells, however, come from the eighteenth and nineteenth centuries. Some lists of forerunners of Green thinking mention the Swedish biologist Carl von Linné (1707–1778) because he stated that animals have a soul. The French philosopher Jean-Jacques Rousseau (1712–1778) has also been interpreted as a Green pioneer for his belief that human beings are basically good: the evil of the world isn't the result of wickedness inherent in humans, but rather of their distance from a natural condition. Others mention Johann Wolfgang Goethe (1749–1832), because of the basic conflict in his major dramatic work, *Faust*, around civilisation and the meaning of life. The American Henry Thoreau (1817–1862), in his book *Walden, A Reflection Upon Simple Living in Natural Surroundings*, appears as a model for the 'green wave' people, who choose to withdraw into a more or less 'primitive' rural lifestyle.[3] Another example is the speech given in 1854 by the Native Indian Chief Seattle to a gathering of white settlers, demanding respect for the rights of indigenous people and their ecological way of living. Aldo Leopold (1887–1948) took a similar line in his posthumous bestseller *A Sand Country Almanac*, which has its place in Green history for its pioneering elaboration of an ecocentric and holistic ethic regarding Nature.[4] The Ukrainian biochemist Vladimir Vernadsky (1863–1945) is often mentioned as a founding father by ecologists in the former Soviet Union, because of his book *The Biosphere* and his theory of the noosphere (human cognition) as the third stage of the Earth's development, after the geosphere (inanimate matter) and the biosphere (life).[5] Just as the emergence of life has transformed the geosphere, the noosphere will, according to Vernadsky, transform the biosphere – which, it could be argued, is exactly what is going on at the beginning of the twenty-first century, with the shift from Holocene to Anthropocene.

FUTURE SHOCK AND GLOBAL CHALLENGE

In the period of the Green awakening a number of futurologists made dramatic predictions about a future that would be fundamentally different from the contemporary industrialised world. Even if not explicitly ecological, some of these forecasts influenced the Green awakening, two of which deserve mentioning.

The first is *Future Shock*, by the American futurologist Alvin Toffler, who claimed that humanity was in for 'too much change in too short a period of time', mainly because of the technological development. Industrialisation would become 'super-industrialisation' leading to an 'information overload'.[6] There is no doubt that technology has transformed the structure of production and the labour market profoundly, with far-reaching effects. In January 2015 it was reported that 400,000 jobs have disappeared from the Swedish industrial sector since 1980. Relocalisation away from the old high-cost industrial countries to new low-cost countries is not the only reason for this trend. Another is the dramatic increase in robotisation which makes human labour redundant. From a Green point of view this provides a strong argument for the shortening of working hours.

The second influential study is *Le defi mondiale* (The Global Challenge) by the French liberal journalist Jean-Jacques Servan-Schreiber (1924–2006), founder of *L'Express*.[7] One of his predictions was that computerisation would be more revolutionary for the poor parts of the world than for the rich, while new technology would create direct information links between poor peasants in Africa, Asia, Latin America and the rest of the world. This vision seemed far-fetched in 1980; in 2015 it is a reality. The fact that vast numbers of people now have an internet-linked, multi-information device in their pocket is not enough to ensure a fair globalisation from below, but it has changed the situation in a way that Greens must react to.

GREEN THINKING: ENVIRONMENTALISM OR ECOLOGISM?

In the foreword to the second edition of his seminal work, *Green Political Thought* Andrew Dobson wrote: 'In 1989 I knew of no textbook of this sort that included a chapter on ecological political thought, but now there are several.'[8] Still, he dates the birth of 'ecologism' to more than a decade earlier: 'The *Limits to Growth* report of 1972 is hard to beat as a symbol for the birth of ecologism in its fully contemporary guise.' That might be true, in hindsight. But Dobson is right in claiming that the real beginning of the use of ecologism as a label for the thinking of Green parties occurred around 1990. Acceptance of 'ecologism' as the acknowledged term for the ideology of Green parties is, however, not all-encompassing. The term is not to be found on the Encyclopaedia Britannica website, for example, where *environmentalism* is exhaustively defined as:

> a political and ethical movement that seeks to improve and protect the quality of the natural environment through changes to environmentally harmful human activities; through the adoption of forms of political, economic, and social organisation that are thought to be necessary for, or at least conducive to, the benign treatment of the environment by humans; and through a reassessment of humanity's relationship with nature.

Likewise, when searching for *ecologism* on the English Wikipedia site, one is redirected to *environmentalism*, which is here defined as:

> a broad philosophy, ideology and social movement regarding concerns for environmental protection and improvement of the health of the environment, particularly as the measure for this health seeks to incorporate the concerns of non-human elements.

Another Green encyclopaedia in which ecologism does not appear is John Button's *A Dictionary of Green Ideas* – neither among the 1,500 entries, nor in a three-page list of words starting with 'eco-'. Instead Button seems to use environmentalism to refer to what others call ecologism.[9] The broad and detailed definitions of environmentalism given by the Encyclopaedia Britannica, Button's Green dictionary, and the English Wikipedia give the impression that these sources have chosen to use environmentalism in place of ecologism – but only in English. The equivalent of ecologism is treated under that label on Wikipedia in several other languages: German: Ökologismus; Swedish: Ekologism; Danish: Økologisme; French: Écologisme; Dutch: Ecologisme. The reason why neither the Britannica, nor Button's dictionary, nor the English Wikipedia carry special articles on ecologism is difficult to understand, especially as most of the theoretical writing on ecologism as a political ideology has been done by authors writing in English. An example is Andrew Dobson, who underlines that it is very important to distinguish between environmentalism and ecologism, each of which he defines as follows:

> **Ecologism** holds that a sustainable and fulfilling existence presupposes radical changes in our relationship with the non-human natural world, and in our mode of social and political life.

Environmentalism argues for a managerial approach to environmental problems, secure in the belief that they can be solved without fundamental changes in the present values or patterns of production and consumption.

It is obvious that ecologism and environmentalism are rather close to two other important concepts used to describe different trends in Green thinking: *deep ecology* (= ecologism) and *shallow ecology* (= environmentalism). To some extent a third pair of concepts could also be seen as representing a similar divide: *fundi* (fundamentalist = ecologist) and *realo* (realist = environmentalist), although theoretically this dichotomy is of another dimension, as it was originally coined among the German Greens to distinguish between different strategies rather than ideological/philosophical trends, the fundis giving priority to maintaining the Greens as a radical counter-force against the centres of power, the realos advocating a strategy for securing executive power, including participating in only partly Green coalition governments.

In Dobson's view environmentalism is no ideology at all, while ecologism is an ideology based upon the 'twin condition of a belief in the limits to growth and a questioning of strong anthropocentrism'. He claims that 'many of the people and organisations whom we would want to include in the green movement are environmentalist rather than political-ecologist'. He emphasises that while ecologism emerged only in the 1960 and '70s, environmentalism is much older. This distinction between environmentalism and ecologism seems well-founded and makes an important contribution to an understanding of the differences between Green parties (which have an ecologist agenda) and a lot of other groups, including in the business world, which advocate all kinds of 'ecological' production and 'green' consumption, wildlife conservation, and so forth, which are merely environmentalist.

While environmentalism, as implied by the word, deals with the environment, Green political programmes are comprehensive, proposing alternative positions on every type of issue that might be the subject of political decision-making. To pretend that such a political platform is 'environmentalist' would give the wrong impression of a narrow, 'single-issue' political programme. But are the Green party programmes 'ecologist'? Some Greens would still prefer just to talk about 'green thinking'.

GREEN THINKING AND OTHER IDEOLOGIES

From a green perspective the great classical political ideologies – conservatism, liberalism and socialism – seem to have forgotten all other parts of existence than currently living human beings. Somewhat simplified, the essence of these ideologies could be summarised as follows: conservatism strives to maintain the supremacy of the upper class; liberalism wants to open up society for free competition between individuals irrespective of social class; socialism has the ambition of eradicating class differences and creating equality for everybody. The only relations taken into account are those between living people. There is no concern for other forms of life (animals, plants).

Some writers have claimed that conservatism is close to ecologism, because of its conservationist trend. But there is an important difference, as expressed by Dobson: 'Conservatism is interested in conserving and preserving the past, ecologism is interested in conserving and preserving for the future.' More important is that conservatism basically takes a position against the type of individual freedom that is important to Greens, such as free abortion and LGBT rights.[10] Another element of disagreement is the fact that most 'conservative' parties today pursue a neoliberal agenda on economics.

Some of the democratic and libertarian trends of Greens have their origins in liberalism, but liberalism is also the home of materialism, profit-seeking, market freedom, the anti-social myth of the invisible hand, and a valuing of competition instead of cooperation as lifestyle and social system.

While conservatism and liberalism, as the ruling ideologies globally and in most countries, pursue no agenda of major change, socialism, at least in principle, does. Like ecologism, socialism has a vision of a very different society compared to the existing one. As everyone knows, most socialist parties today seem to have capitulated to neoliberalism and no longer have much of a transformation agenda. This is not only a result of their conventional adaptation to the restraints of electoral politics, but has a deeper cause. To socialism the basic evil is capitalism, while to ecologists the basic evil is 'productivism'. While the rationale of Green scepticism about 'productivism' concerns its damaging effects upon nature, the rationale for the socialist struggle against capitalism has been of another order, one element being of course the unequal distribution of goods, but another having been the belief that capitalism is ineffective on its own terms and that a socialist economy would not only distribute goods more evenly but would also be more efficient in producing them.

Celebrating the sixtieth anniversary of Nikita Khrushchev's coming to power in the USSR (and the fiftieth anniversary of his losing it), a Russian newspaper recalled the fantastic story of the belief, held not only in the USSR, that the Soviet Union would soon produce more than the USA. Khrushchev once told a party meeting: 'The Americans are worried, they ask: When? I have told them: You can write in your notebook – in 1970 we will catch up with you (ovations by the public) and in 1980 we will produce twice as much as the USA (ovations by the public).'[11] But as the article reveals, the enormous production results reported to the Kremlin were empty balloons, managed by corrupt regional communist politruks. The balloons exploded, Khrushchev was toppled, and by the time the socialist system of the USSR should have been producing several times more than decadent US capitalism, the whole of the Soviet Union had collapsed.

HUMAN-MADE CATASTROPHES

Human societies and civilisations have destroyed their own living environment as long as there has been human civilisation. Jared Diamond has described how societies undermine their own existence by refusing to keep the exploitation of nature and environment inside the limits of what is possible, sometimes from lack of knowledge, sometimes from an incapability – due to competition, power struggles or other human vices – to do what is needed despite a rather good knowledge about what would be needed in order to secure the society for the future.[12] Diamond points to Easter Island as a frightening example of self-destruction. His examples are local or regional, however, and are bad enough at that scale. But only in modern times have human activities affected the environment to the extent that the future of humankind itself is put in doubt.

When reporting on the Mexican gulf oil spill in 2010, *Time* magazine also listed ten other man-made disasters since the Second World War. Especially fresh in the minds of those who started Green parties were the Seveso (Italy) dioxin cloud in 1976 and the Three Mile Island (USA) nuclear accident in 1979, which together represent two of the major threats: the uncontrolled chemicalisation of the total environment and the risks of radioactivity from nuclear installations, both military and civilian. In December 1984 came the Bhopal disaster, when a Union Carbide pesticide plant in India leaked enormous quantities of toxic chemicals, killing at least 2,259 people and damaging the health of hundreds of thousands. In 1986 the nuclear explosion at Chernobyl emitted radioactivity over large areas far outside the Soviet Union, and in 1989 the Exxon Valdez oil spill occurred. The death of the Aral Sea in Russia, due to overexploitation of water resources, the emissions from buried chemical waste at Love Canal, USA, as well as acid rain and the ongoing depletion of the ozone layer killing off northern forests, were other signs that humanity was not treating its living environment well.[13]

ENVIRONMENTALIST PROTESTS AND LOBBYING

The combination of the failure of the 1968 revolt, environmental catastrophes and a growing number of scientific alarm-bells inspired the founding of new environmental organisations, for example the World Wildlife Foundation in 1961, Friends of the Earth in 1969, and Greenpeace in 1971. Even more important was the growth of local environmental groups, sometimes focusing on a single local issue, such as stopping a new road or polluting factory from being built. These groups were often scornfully dismissed by decision-makers as instances of 'nimbyism' (not-in-my-back-yard), without any broader social and political outlook. But as a matter of fact what started as a 'single-issue-group' often developed into an organisation with a broad Green programme. According to an overview of environmental movements since 1945, the small groups of the 1950s have grown to millions; 'on a global level hundreds of millions of people engage in collective activity on behalf of the environment'.[14] The development from local protest to the establishment of a political party often follows a five-step track: First, grassroots movements/local protest actions. Second, membership movements, like the Sierra Club, and other pressure groups. Third, lobby groups/professional actions/theatre, Greenpeace, etc. What these first three steps have in common is that they all aim at changing the behaviour of those who hold the power. When environmentalists get fed up with not achieving their goals through protest and pressure, they may be tempted to try to build the society they wish for, to create their Green Utopia. This is step four, the construction of 'green alternative islands'. The fifth step is the creation of a political party.

GREEN ALTERNATIVE ISLANDS – INDISPENSABLE, BUT NOT ENOUGH

The most well-known contemporary blueprint for a Green Utopia, similar to Thomas More's *Utopia* (1516)[15] or Charles Fourier's (1772–1837) phalanstères,[16] is *Ecotopia* by Ernest Callenbach.[17] He depicted an ecological break-away community on the west coast of the USA, cut off from the rest of the world, where the citizens, under a woman-led government, seek a balance between humans and nature. Their establishment of their own autonomous mini-state is explained by their growing discontent with air pollution, chemical food, lunatic advertising and similar facts of mainstream life in the USA of the 1970s. The book was hailed by Ralph Nader, but dismissed in the British magazine *Peace News* as a 'shoddy amalgam of Swedish social democracy, Swiss neutrality and Yugoslav workers co-ops'.[18]

Since the publication of *Ecotopia* few, if any, similar visions of a Green future have been published, partly because Greens don't like to be ridiculed but also because they don't believe in fixed images of the Green future. Thus, it is not surprising that one of the most recent books about Green Utopias, *Green Utopianism: Perspectives, Politics and Micro-practices*, edited by the Swedish researchers Karin Bradley and Johan Hedrén,[19] makes no mention of Ernst Callenbach or his book. The authors explicitly discard any 'blueprint' for the Green future, referring to the sociologist Karl Mannheim, who stated that utopianism has nothing to do with detailed regulations but should be an open relation aiming at change.[20] In this vein the editors state that the purposes of contemporary utopianism are to explore alternatives, relativise the present, stimulate the will to change, and transgress current structures. They favour certain types of utopia, such as do-it-yourself cultures and alternative economies (local currencies, peer-to-peer exchange by internet, housing communities and urban commons/squatting). Bradley in her contribution, with the title 'Towards a Peer Economy', hopes that 'hackers, pirates, green consumers, corporate critics and ordinary citizens in peer-to-peer practices' will establish 'temporary autonomous zones', which will push development towards transformation. This sounds pretty similar to *Ecotopia*, even if more open and multifaceted. Thus, Green Utopianism four decades after *Ecotopia* remains strongly stuck on a concept coined by the economist Ernst Schumacher in the title of a work which, according to the *Times Literary Supplement*, is one of the hundred most influential books published since the Second World War – *Small is Beautiful*.[21]

An important contribution to the development of the Green thinking around 'small is beautiful' is *Localisation: A Global Manifesto*, by the British Green Colin Hines. His main point is that Green development is thwarted by the free flows of capital and goods, limiting the possibility of any local society introducing Green regulations, and pushing decision-making far away from those whom the decisions concern. Thus 'Green globalisation is an impossibility'. The alternative, proposed by Hines, is Green localisation, through ecological taxes, tariffs and controls to protect Green production, reduction of transportation, measures to ensure local food security, and local currency controls. The WTO should be replaced by the WLO (World Localisation Organisation) which should replace the GATT free trade rules with GAST – a General Agreement for Sustainable Trade.[22] Some years later two other British Greens, Michael Woodin and Caroline Lucas (the first MP of the UK Greens in 2010) further developed the Green concept of anti-globalisation and pro-localisation in *Green Alternatives to Globalisation*.[23] Like Hines they are critical of free trade globalisation, which they see as a threat to the environment which benefits the rich. Economic localisation, they maintain,

> is the antithesis to economic globalisation. It involves a better-your-neighbour supportive internationalism where the flow of ideas, technologies, information, culture, money and goods has, as its end goal, the rebuilding of truly sustainable national and local economies worldwide. Its emphasis is not on competition for the cheapest but on cooperation for the best.

Some of their policy proposals include a Tobin tax, local banks, checks on transnational corporations, GAST instead of GATT, and a Green Marshall plan with cancellation of 'conventional third world debt'.

The localisation ideology is one of the basic aspects of Green thinking. Most Greens, if awoken in the middle of the night and asked about the pillars of Green thinking would immediately mention 'decentralisation', 'local autonomy' or similar concepts. The question is how far localisation can be developed without losing the Green aspect of One World, according to which we are all interrelated in sharing the same Earth, which can only be saved through global consciousness and cooperation. Obviously one method of promoting an ecological lifestyle is to withdraw from the wider society and just create that lifestyle, here and now. But is this, in a globalised world, enough to realise the major change that is needed? Will a multitude of green islands do the job? Probably not, for one main reason: concrete Green alternatives may have some impact as illustrations of possibilities that are feasible and attractive, but the spreading effect is limited. Human history is full of ideological activists who created their own mini-societies, often, but not always, in the hope that their example would convince others to follow suit. Especially during its pioneer period, the USA was full of these 'islands', some of which still survive. But the 'big society' of the USA is neither Mormon nor Amish, and the fancy state of Callenbach's *Ecotopia* is obviously not supposed to change the surrounding world, being described as a very isolated entity when it is visited by a journalist from outside. It is hard to find any example where the establishment of model societies has had a strong enough impact to convince a whole country or nation to adopt the alternative model. Christianity became a world religion after a decision by a pagan Roman Emperor, Islam by jihad and mission, and communism spread by military conquests, to mention only a few examples. Slightly paraphrasing a famous expression of President Clinton's, it could be said: It's about politics, stupid! Without, in one way or the other, taking the executive, legislative power over a certain territory, no movement can impose its ideology over that territory and its population. Setting examples, constructing alternative models, creating Green islands, is a necessary prerequisite for a global transformation, but it is not enough. There is also a need to acquire the decisive political power, which, in a democratic and Green context, is equivalent to step number 5 in the development of the Greens: the establishing of political parties, fighting election campaigns to convince voters and win majorities, and in the end getting enough power from the people to participate in governments. The final goal is of course to create *fully Green governments*.

Maybe the famous Green slogan 'Think globally, act locally', coined by the French-American microbiologist René Dubos (1901–1982), should be reformulated as something like: 'Think and act both locally and globally'.[24] It is in the dialectical relation between the local and the global that Greens have their specific perspective: Genuine grassroots democracy is possible only locally; global democracy must be developed in quite other ways, probably along lines similar to the present UN general assembly.

Figure 2   A typical alternative, Green way of organising political discussions, here at the congress of the Catalonian Els Verds, in 1985. Photo: the author.

WHO ARE THE GREENS? A SOCIOLOGICAL APPROACH

According to polls, Green voters are most often female, younger and have a higher education than the average voter. However, there are also some sociological distinctions which are not based upon statistics but upon theoretical analysis.

The German sociologist Claus Offe has made a distinction between *Interessenten*, referring to interested parties such as enterprises, organisations and political parties, and *Betroffene*, referring to those who are concerned or affected by centralised decisions and actions, for example people living near a nuclear reactor or a noisy highway or a polluted river.[25] In this perspective it could be said that the *Greens are the concerned*.

The American sociologist Robert Merton has constructed a very enlightening scheme of the individual's relations to cultural goals and institutional norms, which in the case of Western capitalist society has the following shape (as slightly adapted from Merton):[26]

Cultural goal (to become rich)	**Institutional norm (to obey laws)**	
Reaction: yes	yes	= conformist
no	yes	= ritualist/bureaucrat
yes	no	= innovator, legal or criminal
no	no	= drop out, retreatist
no but new	no but new	= alternative creators

Conformists stick to goals and norms; ritualists give up goals and stick to norms; innovators (criminal and non-criminal) stick to goals but give up norms; drop-outs give up both goals and norms, alternative creators also give up both goals and norms, but try to create alternatives, new lifestyles, etc. In this perspective the *Greens are the creators of alternatives*.

The German sociologist Jürgen Habermas has emphasised that there is not only an economic crisis but also a crisis of rationality: decisions do not produce the intended results, leading to a crisis of legitimacy, which on the individual level takes the shape of a crisis of motivation.[27] In this context it could be said that the *Greens are the seekers of a new motivation*.

These schemes could be used to predict what Greens will do. As *the concerned*, they tend to struggle to stop the activities which have touched them in a negative way and made them into concerned. They adopt a *disruptive programme*, to stop or limit nuclear energy, poisonous emissions, private car pollution, etc. However as *alternative creators* they also want to initiate new activities, from cooperatives to biological farms, thereby adopting a *constructive programme*. What then do Greens do as *the seekers of a new motivation*? They search for a new type of quality of life, a new togetherness, which is a kind of *integrative programme*.

These three types of approaches logically draw the Greens into three types of action. The disruptive programme is best implemented on the *parliamentary level*, through laws which ban or restrict unwanted activities. The constructive programme, the actual construction of something new, is best implemented at the *grassroots level*. The integrative programme can only be realised on the *process level* – through gender balance, rotation, non-cumulation of positions and so on.

The relations between the levels could be expressed as follows: The relation between the parliamentary and grassroots levels is one of trial and error. Greens tend to know better what is wrong than what is right. The grassroots level initiates experiments and trials; the legislative level then intervenes by banning activities that are anti-Green and damaging to humans, life and the environment. The relation between the parliamentary and the process levels deals with efficiency. The Green process prevents the iron law of oligarchy from functioning with a detrimental effect. The encounter between the process and the grassroots levels is manifested through mini-pictures of the future, through people who act, and not only talk, in an alternative Green way, which enhances their level of credibility and strengthens their legitimacy.

This way of linking the Greens to a number of sociological theories of human behaviour can be summarised as follows: The Greens are a *counterforce* against economistic, conformist power groups with vested interests in the prolongation of Industrial Society – that is Big Business, the Big State and professional politicians. The Greens are the *concerned* and have a *disruptive* programme to stop and dismantle what is wrong, mainly on the parliamentary level. The Greens are also *alternative creators* who have a *constructive* programme to create alternative projects and structures, mainly through millions of initiatives at the grassroots level. The Greens are the *seekers of a new motivation* with an *integrative* programme designed to achieve a sense of emotional meaning, mainly by employing an integrative process. The Greens are convinced that human beings need a new lifestyle, which they are busy shaping through their political actions.

'THE PRIVATE IS POLITICAL'

During the 1970s the 'Reds' were a reading lot, establishing book cafés where Marxist-Socialist theories filled the shelves. Green activists did not read theoretical books; they studied organic farming or how to rebuild one's house to save energy. Like some of the feminists of that time – for example the Danish Red Stockings (*Rødstrømperne*) – the pioneer Greens were more interested in changing lifestyles than in searching for the mechanisms that have created the ecological mess we are all living in. For the Greens the *private is political*, a phrase which became the title of a book by the leading German Green, Claudia Roth.[28]

More so than other politicians, Greens are expected to 'live as they teach', a fact that has sometimes created problems for them, not only because of personal moral inadequacy, but also because it is not easy – in fact is often impossible – to live in a fully Green way in a non-Green environment.

NEITHER LEFT NOR RIGHT, BUT IN FRONT

During the early years of the Swedish Green Party I once met the Social Democratic Prime Minister Olof Palme (who was assassinated in 1986) in a TV debate. He said: 'The Swedish Greens are petty-bourgeois defectors from the Liberal Party (I had been an MP for the Liberals). The German Greens is quite another story. That is a genuine Left Wing party; with them Social Democrats might very well cooperate.' Some 30 years later, Swedish Conservative Prime Minister Fredrik Reinfeldt gave a different picture of the Green Party: 'Under the new leadership, the Green Party has returned to being the Siamese twin of the Left in Swedish politics; I can only regret this development' (Swedish Parliament, 13 June 2012). This schizophrenic attitude on the part of observers has its basic cause in the one-dimensional left-right distinction which has had and still has an overwhelming dominance in political discourse. While some Green parties have been caught in this quagmire and wasted time and strength on destructive infighting over their positioning to the right, the left or maybe in the middle, most Greens have denied the basic obligation to choose between left and right by declaring: We are in front! Sometimes this is described as a vertical line crossing the horizontal left-right scale, having at its end points 'material growth' and 'ecological balance'. In this two-dimensional scale, most traditional parties, from the left to the right, would be found close to the 'material growth' pole, while Greens would be rather alone close to the 'ecological balance' pole.

Figure 3   Press-briefing at the Stockholm Congress of the European Greens, 1987, with three leading female Greens: Petra Kelly (Germany), Freda Meissner-Blau (Austria), Sara Parkin (UK). Partly concealed by Meissner-Blau, Jakob von Uexkull, founder of the Right Livelihood Award (Alternative Nobel Prize). Photo: Ulla Lemberg.

GREEN PARTIES – TEMPORARY OR TRENDSETTERS OF THE TWENTY-FIRST CENTURY?

In August 1987, at the third congress of the European Greens in Stockholm, Hannes Alfvén (1908–1995) – Swedish Nobel Laureate for Physics and one of the most important scientists to support the 'no' option in the Swedish referendum on nuclear power in 1980 – launched the idea that every century gives birth to a great ideology which dominates the next; while the liberalism of the eighteenth century had dominated the nineteenth century and the socialist ideas of the latter had swept through the world in the twentieth century, we now saw the birth of a Green revolution which would be the trendsetter of the twenty-first century: the Green revolution, Alfvén said, 'is the societal answer to the dangers of existential destruction and to the new miseries of our time'.

Not everybody shared Alfvén's dramatic optimism about the Green future. Most political observers in the late 1980s and early 1990s looked upon the Green political phenomenon as a passing trend. When the German Greens failed to renew their parliamentary representation in 1990 and the same fate befell the Swedish Greens in 1991, several commentators felt sure this was the beginning of the end of Green political parties. In a book about the imminent decline of the Greens, the Oxford historian Anna Bramwell, working for the OECD in Eastern Europe, declared with delight that 'everyone likes environmental ideals, everyone sympathises with them, but practically nobody wants to vote for Green parties'. She predicted that the Greens would be 'further marginalized, possibly dissolving into disparate occultist matriarchal feminist and similar groups'. No doubt Bramwell was particularly disposed to foresee a Green decline, as she was overtly hostile and had written books claiming that Green thinking is basically fascist. But similar forecasts were made by others and could be heard as soon as a Green party got into trouble. Despite the fact that both the German and Swedish Greens had already made their comebacks by 1994, and dozens of Green parties since then have secured parliamentary representation all over the world, there is still a tendency to interpret a Green setback not as just that – a setback – but as the beginning of the end for that party.[29] It is true that some Green parties lost all their MPs during the two decades since the publication of Bramwell's book. However, most of them have recovered and on a worldwide scale the trend is clearly upwards. It is too early to judge whether this implies that Hannes Alfvén's dramatic forecast will come true, but it is a fairly credible prediction that Green political parties are here to stay on the global political scene.

2

GREEN PHILOSOPHY, SCIENCE
AND SOCIAL THEORY

Greens are sometimes accused of having a negative attitude towards hard facts and scientific knowledge. The truth is rather that Greens often refer to the hard facts of biology, chemistry and physics to argue for their positions. An overview of ecological thinking from 1945 to 2010 maintains that 'environmentalism has a strong scientific basis that sets it apart from other ideologies'.[1] At the same time there is sometimes discussion among Greens about the benefits of the practical results of science, for example new technologies. Many Greens are sceptical of what they pejoratively call 'technological fixes'. One example is the Swedish professor of Human Ecology, Alf Hornborg, who has dismissed the idea of technology as the saviour of our future as a myth.[2] In particular, he has dismissed the grandiose plans to provide Europe with solar energy from gigantic solar panels in the Sahara.[3]

An awkward example of the faith in technological fixes is provided by James Lovelock, the inventor of the holistic Gaia hypothesis. At the age of 87 Lovelock shocked his Green admirers when he proposed nuclear power as the only remedy against catastrophic climate change. He even mocks people who are afraid of radioactive radiation (offering to keep radioactive waste in his garden); worse still, this 'father' of ecological holism has forgotten that the ecological dangers cannot be avoided only through the use of technology, and that a shift of paradigm is required to adapt mankind to 'mother Gaia'.[4]

NEED FOR HOLISM

Holism is basic to Green thinking. A basic definition of the ecological perspective upon nature was given by George Herbert Mead (1863–1931): 'Nature is a system of systems and relationships; it is not a collection of particles or fragments which are actually separate.'[5] Later, one of the pioneers of modern ecologism, Barry Commoner (1917–2012), formulated four laws of ecology: 1) Everything is connected with everything else. 2) Everything must go nowhere. 3) Nature knows best. 4) There's no such thing as a free lunch.[6]

An important ecological concept is *sustainability*, which could be defined as the endurance of systems and processes. Closely connected to sustainability is *resilience*, connoting the ability of an ecosystem to respond to and recover from disturbance. If the system's resilience is good a sustainability that has been disturbed may be restored, if the resilience is less good, the damage may be irreparable.

Holism is also fundamental in another scientific source of Green thinking: the 'new physics', originally based upon Niels Bohr's and Werner Heisenberg's theories of interaction and uncertainty, which claim that the movements and relations of basic mini-units of matter are not so stable as supposed in classical physics, but often steered by probability rather than a classical cause-effect relation.[7] The importance of this for Green thinking has been developed by Fritjof Capra in his world bestseller *The Tao of Physics*, where he pleads for a kind of holism, which he argues has been lost in modern Western thinking, but can be found in Buddhism, Taoism, Hinduism – and in the new physics.[8]

ECOLOGICAL ECONOMICS

While Greens generally have a bad reputation and low credibility on economic matters, often being accused of basing proposals more on fantasy than on facts, the truth is that they have given a lot of attention to discussing and establishing a scientific basis for ecological economics. The director of the UK's Green Economics Institute, Miriam Kennet, has offered the following definition:

> Green Economics is the green movement's challenge to mainstream orthodoxy in economics and it is gaining ground globally and in the corridors of power as the best alternative to solving climate change, the credit crunch, poverty and biodiversity losses. It is about providing the practices and policies of economics, for all people everywhere, nature, other species, the planet and its systems. It is about provisioning for the needs, impacts, effects and responsibilities, for everyone and everything on the planet.[9]

Since Herman Daly coined the concept of a *steady-state economy*, defined as 'constant stocks of people and physical wealth maintained at some chosen, desirable level by a low rate of output', *ecological economics* has been established as an academic discipline, holding its first international meeting in Sweden in 1982.[10] In 1989 the International Society for Ecological Economics was founded and began to publish the journal *Ecological Economics*. Kenneth Boulding has urged humanity to shift from a 'cowboy' to a 'spaceman' economy – from an economy operating as if there were no limits to an economy where limits are inherent.[11] Hazel Henderson's book *The Politics of the Solar Age: Alternatives to*

Economics has also played a major role in Green thinking.[12] Most Greens would agree with her description of traditional economists as 'snake-oil salesmen'.

A couple of years ago I had the opportunity to participate in an international conference for ecological economists.[13] Over four days at the Boğaziçi University in Istanbul, 300 ecological economists presented papers and scientific reports on the ecological aspects of economic activity. Peter Söderbaum, a Swedish veteran of ecological economics, showed that indicators other than GDP can be constructed as objectively and scientifically as GDP. There was great frustration among the researchers at politicians' reluctance to consider well developed, scientifically constructed alternative indicators, despite their repeated commitments to the protection of the environment. In one paper Blake Alcott and Özlem Yazlik demonstrated that the ecological footprint of Turkey is about two thirds that of the European average.[14] Despite this, the subjectively perceived level of happiness among Turks is at least as high as among the inhabitants of richer countries. Does this mean that Turkey needs a higher material standard of living? Did any party in the recent Turkish election propose no increase in material consumption? No, affirmed several Turkish participants, such a party would not have received many votes. But yes, shouted a voice, which belonged to Professor Ahmet Atil Asici, a representative of the small Green party, which didn't participate in the elections. In his own comparative study of 213 countries he showed a clear correlation between growth and environmental destruction.[15]

LIMITS TO GROWTH

The most provocative difference between Green ecologism and other ideologies is the former's criticism of the quest for limitless, unqualified material growth. Greens neither believe in the possibility of nor feel an attraction for the dominant cornucopian[16] vision of futurologists like Herman Kahn (1922–1983) and Daniel Bell (1919–2011) – i.e. more of the same, business as usual.[17] They tend to agree with writers like Tim Jackson who offer a vision of *prosperity without growth*.[18] There are several reasons for this Green attitude:

1. *Limitless exploitation of resources is impossible.* Even if new technologies for extraction of non-renewable raw materials are developed to allow humanity to exploit sources previously unreachable, there will always be a physical limit: some resources will just be exhausted. In addition, the costs are increasing to the extent that some types of raw material will be economically unavailable even if not physically extinct. This perspective on growth was dramatically placed on the global agenda by the report of the Rome Club in 1972, *Limits to Growth*. Forty years later one of the authors of the report, Jorgen Randers,

estimated the development of major trends up to 2052: GDP growth will double; unemployment will remain stable; the increase in temperature will pass the critical 2 degrees and reach 2.8 degrees Celsius; the global sea level will be 36cm higher than in 2000; the ongoing sixth extinction of species will continue; untouched nature will remain only in some fenced parks; drought and extreme weather will hit the South, while the North, at least for a certain time, will have the benefit of warmer weather with an extended growing season. But this will be a vulnerable situation: the higher temperature may cause a meltdown of the gigantic 'tundra' releasing enormous amounts of methane gas, which may result in a vicious circle and chaos. According to Randers, it would take only 5% of current global GDP to make the world free of fossil fuels and solar-driven in 20 years. Why does this not happen? Randers himself indirectly accuses democracy as a system – in so far as its repeated elections promote short-sightedness among politicians.[19]

As a matter of fact several alternative indexes to GDP have been constructed by ecological economists and other scientists, among others: the Human Development Index (HDI); the Genuine Progress Indicator (GPI) or Index of Sustainable Economic Welfare (ISEW); the European Quality of Life Survey; Gross National Happiness; the Happy Planet Index (introduced by the New Economics Foundation in 2006); the OECD Better Life Index; the Future Orientation Index; the World Governance Index; and the Social Progress Index.

So why aren't these indexes used instead of GDP? According to Julien Morel, of the Stockholm Resilience Centre, the answer is that GDP is used culturally, to reconfirm the traditional material values of the growth society, operationally, for calculations in order to trigger conventional action, and politically, to serve as a 'pivotal reference' for motivating certain political actions.[20]

Sometimes decision-makers pay lip-service to the impossibility of limitless growth, but this is rarely followed by any change of policy. One example was a debate in the Swedish Parliament in 2011, when six out of eight parties agreed that there was a need to analyse the concept of GDP as a unit of measurement, because, it was said, it does not show the costs of growth for the environment, health and the climate. But while representatives of traditional growth parties may recognise that the GDP index is in some way flawed, politicians in general haven't stopped using GDP as the major sign of progress.

2. *Production is also destruction, total recycling is impossible.* According to the second law of thermodynamics, energy never disappears, but it loses quality with every transformation and becomes less usable, an effect that is called *entropy.* The pioneer in linking the second law of thermodynamics to the economic system was the Romanian-American economist Nicholas Georgescu-Roegen (1906–1994), in *The Entropy Law and the Economic Process.*[21] The law of entropy was introduced into modern ecologist thinking by Jeremy Rifkin,

in his book *Entropy*,[22] where he gives an illustrative example: A human being could live for a year by eating 300 trout, which need 90,000 frogs, which need 27 million grasshoppers, which need 1,000 tons of grass. Georgescu-Roegen, in a postscript to Rifkin's book, observes that it is obvious that it is impossible to retrieve rubber molecules from tyres or copper molecules from coins.

3. *High GDP doesn't guarantee happiness.* This insight is of course not new, it is present in several religions, especially Buddhism, and is scientifically proven by modern happiness research. A classical background was established by the French sociologist Émile Durkheim (1858–1917) with his theory of *anomie*, which located the cause of certain forms of 'deviant behaviour' or 'social disintegration' in the limitless quest for material richness. He was concerned about the dissolution and weakening of traditional cooperative structures, such as the church, because he claimed that humanity needs cooperation to feel happy, not only competition. He proposed new types of cooperative structures, adapted to modern society, some of which had similarities to trade unions, others to Green self-ruling cooperatives.[23]

The lack of correlation between GDP growth and happiness was established by Richard Easterlin and subsequently labelled the *Easterlin Paradox*.[24] In a worldwide overview of relations between growth and happiness 35 years later, Carol Graham found that growth causes less happiness in countries with rapid growth and incomes above the global average, and more happiness in poorer countries with slow growth. A conclusion is that 'the nature and pattern of economic growth and in particular instability and inequality issues can counterbalance the positive effects of higher income levels'.[25] After having received a lot of criticism, in 2010 Easterlin checked once more and found that his 'paradox' from 1974 was still valid.[26]

Graham's findings show that the main problem for happiness is not the material richness as such, but the quest to achieve it, and the associated rapid change, which illustrates the close relation between the ideology of growth and the ideology of competition. Even if competition is appropriate in sport and useful in promoting inventiveness and technological development, it can hardly be denied that every competition has winners and losers, and usually many more of the latter than the former. This is the basis of a key argument of Greens, who most often prefer cooperation to competition: a society full of losers, constantly striving to catch up with the winners, is less capable of taking the needs of nature and of future generations into consideration.

The ideology of cooperation seemed to take a major blow when Garret Hardin (1915–2003) presented his infamous theory of the 'tragedy of the commons', in which he showed that unregulated commons unavoidably degrade because the people having the right to use them give priority to their own interests.[27] However, the Nobel Prize winner Elinor Ostrom later demonstrated that if locally run cooperatives are established to run the commons such problems can be solved.[28] The lesson is of course that every collective alternative to the dictatorship of market competition cannot succeed without establishing the rules of the game.

While other countries seek to maximise their material production, or GDP, there is one – Bhutan – which has instead decided that the aim of government activity is to foster Gross National Happiness (GNH). The concept of GNH was introduced in 1972, initially by Bhutan's absolute monarch, but in 2008 it was included in the country's constitution by a democratically elected parliament. In 2011 the UN General Assembly endorsed a Bhutanese draft resolution entitled 'Happiness: towards a holistic approach to development'. In the capital Thimpu there is a special government committee which has the task of testing all legislative proposals against the GNH index. The Buddhist ethos of the country plays a part in this, but in Bhutan's official 2013 report *Happiness: Towards a New Development Paradigm*, the focus is on the shortcomings of GDP as a measure of progress.[29]

GREEN SOLIDARITY

Solidarity is an important concept for several ideologies. There are, however, different kinds of solidarity. Class or national solidarity is basically a kind of egocentrism, demanding that people feel solidarity with other people of their own type, social or national. Another type of solidarity, more liberal, is that between people of different types, for example, socially well-adapted persons and prisoners, or rich and poor. This type has often been looked upon with contempt by socialists, as a kind of paternalistic benevolence on the part of the upper class. In socialist thinking the poor shouldn't accept the benevolent support of the rich; they should join in class solidarity and fight for their rights. There may be some truth in the left-wing criticism of liberal solidarity, since there is the risk of it deteriorating into paternalistic charity. But at the same time it is not enough to show solidarity with people who are in a similar situation to oneself. As a matter of fact, if people understand solidarity only as a kind of common action with people of the same social or national group, then the world will be full of those who are left out, unable to enjoy any solidarity at all. This becomes more obvious when the perspective is broadened from an anthropocentric view of solidarity to a Green perspective. The Swedish Green Party calls for solidarity with three groups: 1) Animals, nature and the ecological system. 2) Future generations. 3) All humans in the world.

Sometimes of course, group solidarity is needed. Trade unions, for example, are important to a democratic society. Feminist solidarity among women may promote a higher degree of gender equality. Group solidarity between discriminated groups in pursuit of a common struggle for equal rights is of course commendable. However, this is not enough to create justice between human beings, still less to solve the huge ecological problems facing the world or to establish decent relations with other animals and nature. Nature cannot by itself stop the destructive forces of humanity before it is too late. In order for this to happen there must be a considerable number of human beings who feel a solidarity with nature.

ANTHROPOCENTRISM OR BIOCENTRISM?

Ecologists usually protest against the anthropocentric outlook, which assumes that humans are, in some way, outside nature and may exploit it for their own benefit. At the same time nature can appear to be very cruel to the weak, sick, deviant individuals of a species, and the balance between different species is maintained by a cruel struggle. The general degree of balance is a result of numerous imbalances at the individual level – the law of the jungle. It cannot be denied that most human societies have established measures to protect individuals. Ecologists often demand that we should live *with*, rather than *against* nature. But they usually don't demand that we should live *as* nature. There are no hospitals in nature, nor laws and courts to protect individuals against being killed and eaten.

Even if most Greens claim to have replaced the anthropocentric perspective with a biocentric or ecocentric perspective, they usually argue in a way that is far from free of all anthropocentrism. This issue has been at the centre of debates between the different schools of ecologism, leading to books with titles such as *The World Without Us*, where biocentrists of the most radical type come very close to arguing that because human beings constitute the single major threat to all other forms of life and nature, the best thing would be to get rid of them completely.[30] However, a political campaign promising voters that, if given power, the Greens will do their best to get rid of human beings, is, to put it mildly, hardly conceivable. Thus, while most Greens will dismiss traditional anthropocentrism given the damaging effects the reckless rule of humans has had upon nature and other life forms, without some consideration for the life and well-being of humans there would be no place for Green politics. What point would there be to Green politics if Charlene Spretnak and Fritjof Capra were right when they stated that 'Green politics rejects the anthropocentric orientation of humanism (which) posits that humans have the ability to confront and solve the many problems we face by applying human reason'?[31] If human beings had no ability at all to solve any of the problems we face, why should anybody spend time on Green politics and Green parties? Happily,

Andrew Dobson is of course right when he observes that a 'strong anthropocentric message comes through loud and clear in Green party manifestos'.[32]

It should also be remembered that even if human beings constitute the main threat to the biosphere, they are not outsiders, but parts of that biosphere just as much as other forms of life. This makes it ecologically legitimate not only from a tactical political point of view but also from a philosophical perspective to take human interests into account when analysing the state of the world.

GREEN VARIETIES

There are several different trends, schools and sub-theories within Green thinking. Here some of the Green sub-schools which have had an influence on Green party policies will be addressed.

Social ecology

Social ecology is a term coined by the US social philosopher, Murray Bookchin (1921–2006). In the Green internal debate, especially in the USA, it has often been presented as a *shallow ecology*, as the antithesis of *deep ecology*. Its main characteristic is that it takes social circumstances into consideration – in a way, so it claims, that deep ecology doesn't – both as part of the explanation of the ecological crisis and as part of the aim for Green movements. Some authors have observed three subgroups of social ecology:

Ecosocialism sees capitalism as the enemy of nature, socialism as its friend. Most Greens would agree that the basic elements of capitalism, like profit-seeking, promotion of consumption to increase profits, and the money-steered value system, contribute to environmental destruction. At the same time most Greens would doubt that socialism is much better. Experiences of the really existing socialism that existed in the Soviet Union and the communist bloc until the beginning of the 1990s are not good. Whatever distance eco-socialists may claim in relation to these bad examples, it is not easy to believe that an ideology which has failed so dramatically when in power – not only concerning democracy and human rights, but also concerning environmental protection – could be transformed into a genuinely ecologist way of thinking and acting.

Ecoanarchism, on the other hand, has undoubtedly contributed to Green thinking with its critique of hierarchy and authority, thereby promoting decentralisation, self-management and direct democracy, all of which are important (but not sufficient) prerequisites for ecological balance. Quite a few Greens would include the Russian 'Father of Anarchism', Pyotr Kropotkin (1842–1921), among the pioneers of Green thinking.

Ecofeminism as a concept was first introduced by the French feminist Françoise d'Eaubonne (1920–2005) in 1974.[33] Another influential ecofeminist is the American historian Carolyn Merchant, who has alleged that before the Enlightenment and the Scientific Revolution 'the female earth was central to organic cosmology ... for sixteenth-century Europeans the root metaphor binding together the self, society and the cosmos was that of an organism'.[34] This notion, that in the past there was a more organic and ecologic world, more or less ruled by women, is popular among some ecofeminists. But the truth is that if this world ever existed it was a very long time ago and certainly not in the Europe of Alexander the Great, the Roman Empire and the Christian Church, all very patriarchal and ecologically destructive types of society. The feminist ecological organic society may have existed thousands of years ago, or perhaps never. The main feature of ecofeminism is its linking of environmental destruction to the rule of patriarchy. Men, collectively, have failed miserably. Thus, the probability of women, as a collective, being able to realise the needed changes is considered far more likely than that of men being able to do so. Sometimes it is suggested that the fact that women generally are more ecologically minded is a result of a long history of culture and social impact, or of some biological traits inherent in women. The latter way of thinking is sometimes discarded as *essentialist*, even conservative and reactionary. It is noted that quite a few women are anti-ecological in their behaviour and thinking (and violent and criminal and materialist, and so on), and that quite a few men are very ecological, peaceful, collaborative and so on. The rejoinder of course is that the difference between women and men is an average with many individual exceptions; and if the cause is cultural or biological that may be of theoretical interest but has no practical implications. Whatever the causes of the 'original guilt' of men, no future can be built without them. Thus, to fancy a future in which roles have been reversed and humanity would live in matriarchies seems to be a distraction. Men cannot be excluded, but it is quite possible that women for some time will have to be in charge not only of half the power and responsibility, but of the larger part. Some of the most ecofeminist Green parties accordingly accept certain forms of overrepresentation of women, but would not do so for men.

Deep ecology

The term deep ecology was coined by the Norwegian philosopher *Arne Næss* (1912–2009). In his book *The Ecology of Wisdom*,[35] he states that 'the short time shallow ecology movement relies on technical fixes and pursues business as usual without any deep value questioning or long-range changes in practices and the system'. In contrast, deep ecology will 'engage in deep questioning and pursue alternative patterns of action' and displays a respect for the intrinsic worth of all beings. Næss also uses the concept of *ecosofy*, which he defines as 'a philosophy of ecological harmony or equilibrium'. Næss refers to the Dutch philosopher Baruch Spinoza (1632–1677), author of *Ethics*, as an ideological inspiration, and recalls that Spinoza said that 'animals have the same rights in relation to humans as humans have in relation to animals, but that humans have more rights'. Næss has listed eight basic principles of deep ecology, the second of which is 'biospherical egalitarianism in principle'. Why 'in principle'? Næss: 'Because any realistic praxis necessitates some killing, exploitation and suppression.' This alone demonstrates that Næss tried to be realistic in a way some of his admirers may not be aware of. That the overwhelming majority of human beings, including Greens, are of the opinion that they have the moral right to kill some living creatures – be they flies or mice – is a reality; at the same time most would agree that it is never morally acceptable to kill a gorilla. Murray Bookchin has claimed that 'rendering human beings and snails "equal" in terms of their "intrinsic worth" is simply frivolous'.[36] The dividing line lies somewhere between the fly and the gorilla, as Næss obviously realised. Does this pragmatic consideration diminish the value of Næss' principles of deep ecology? Andrew Dobson seems to think so; he claims that 'attempts to solve the difficulties with Næss' principle have ended by undermining the principle itself'.[37] However, it's not that easy. If it is always totally unethical to kill, should we prevent predators from killing – which means killing them? These types of theoretical deliberation are not generally mainstream among Green parties – and where they are so, could be looked upon as self-created stumbling blocks.

In any case, an important component of deep ecology and a biocentric world-view involves another attitude towards other life-forms, a radical form of which includes the principle of *animal rights*. The first call for animal rights was made by the British reformer, vegetarian and pacifist Henry Salt (1851–1939) in his book *Animals' Rights: Considered in Relation to Social Progress* (1894).[38] A well-known contemporary successor is the Australian philosopher Peter Singer, who in the 1970s published *Animal Liberation*.[39] He attacks *speciesism* and argues that distinctions between animals and humans are arbitrary. It is important to note that 'animal rights' is not the same as 'animal protection' or 'animal welfare', which are much weaker concepts. While some religions have always encouraged respect for animals (or certain animals at least), only a few laws against the cruel treatment of animals are known from the seventeenth century in Western Europe and the USA; the first steps towards a modern type of animal protection were taken in Great Britain in the nineteenth century, but still in the twenty-first century quite a few states have no or very weak rules in this respect. To many Greens, animal welfare, and even animal rights, are very important and basic to their thinking, even though Green platforms without anything to say on the subject can still be found.

Some critics have claimed that deep ecology is counterproductive because it 'will not secure widespread support'.[40] That may be true. However, deep ecology tests the limits of ecologism in a way that is important and productive even for a more social variant of Green thinking. Every ideology needs 'extreme' versions for its theoretical development, even if they are not well suited as guides to practical political activity.

OVERSHOOT AND FAIR ENVIRONMENTAL SPACE

The concept of *overshoot* was introduced by the American sociologist William Catton in his book, *Overshoot: The Ecological Basis of Revolutionary Change*.[41] The core implication of overshoot is that humanity is living with a 'deepening carrying capacity deficit'. Overshoot has the consequence that the *ecological footprint* is larger than the carrying capacity. It has been estimated that the ecological footprint of humanity is almost twice the available *environmental space*, a concept which is often extended into that of *fair environmental space* – coined by the Dutch environmental movement, used by Friends of the Earth at the UNCED in Rio 1992, and defined by J. B. Opschoor and D. F. Wetering as a concept that 'reflects that at any given point in time, there are limits to the amount of environmental pressure that the Earth's ecosystems can handle without irreversible damage to these systems or to the life support processes that they enable'.[42] The notion of environmental space has most often been used to indicate what space is available to humanity as a whole. With the addition of 'fair', however, it can also be used to tackle the different burdens and responsibilities of different communities, countries and regions, by indicating how much 'fair' space remains for certain entities and, conversely, how much others may have exceeded their 'fair' share of the common space. In relation to Europe as a whole, the Wuppertal institute has defined environmental space as 'the quantity of energy, water, land, non-renewable raw materials and wood that we can use in a sustainable fashion'.[43] A basic assumption is that the environmental space should be about the same for every human being, with consideration for local circumstances. All the research into this has, not surprisingly, demonstrated that the rich world is guilty of considerable overshoot. Thus, the rich world has a debt towards the poor world. This assumption, if accepted politically, has considerable consequences for the view of the financial debt most poor countries are considered to have to rich countries and/or international financial institutions. Also, international negotiations about global actions to ward off environmental threats to mankind are of course affected by the use of the concept of fair environmental space, which makes it one of the basic concepts for Green global policy.

GREEN SPIRITUALITY, NEW AGE

To Greens 'the private is political'; this means that for them lifestyle is of greater importance than it is in other political ideologies, which usually don't expect people to change their way of living. It is about living a greener life, consuming in a greener way, but also about post-material, non-material, even spiritual values as alternatives to the dominant materialist value system. In the countries where traditional religions were weak when Green parties were born, this created a space in and around Green parties for persons seeking spiritual alternatives. To a certain extent such trends were labelled New Age, which was also the title of a book by the American writer Mark Satin, who argues that we are living in a kind of thought prison with six sides: patriarchal attitudes, egocentricity, scientific single vision, nationalism/xenophobia, bureaucratic mentality and big city outlook. Thus, the solution is a radical shift of consciousness, something like a paradigm shift in our thinking.[44] Another book in the same vein published a few years later, *The Aquarian Conspiracy* by Marilyn Ferguson, argued in favour of personal responsibility and initiative.[45] While she referred to the French priest and philosopher Pierre Teilhard de Chardin (1881–1955), other New Age writers even mentioned the Swedish eighteenth-century mystic Emmanuel Swedenborg (1688–1772) as a source of inspiration. These New Age writings were characterised by a mixture of calls for a kind of 'moral revolution' and touches of spirituality close to religious mysticism. While the emphasis on individual responsibility to act for a better life directly, without waiting for central decision-makers to act, had a strong appeal among Greens, the more religious-like spirituality has been held to be outside Green party politics, regarded as a part of the private which is not political. However, elements of this mysticism have sometimes emerged close enough to Green contexts to give critics an opportunity to dismiss the Greens as a bunch of superstitious reactionaries with confused ideas. It is not popular to act and talk as if one considers one's own political group to have a higher morality than others. At the same time it should be obvious that without a change in the dominant value system there will be no change of the dominant social and economic system, and consequently no radical Green progress towards an ecologically sustainable society.

3

GREEN PARTIES
ALL OVER THE WORLD

When Sara Parkin compiled an international guide to Green Parties in 1989, only ten of its 335 pages dealt with Green parties outside of Western Europe, North America and Australasia.[1] And out of the half dozen countries in Eastern Europe, Africa, Asia and Latin America mentioned, only a few (Brazil, Japan, possibly Poland) hosted parties, rather than environmental movements. This picture has changed dramatically a quarter of a century later. There are now Green parties in all parts of the world and Green MPs in parliaments in all global regions.

Most of the oldest Green parties were founded in Europe during the first half of the 1980s. However, the very first party based upon Green thinking was the New Values Party of New Zealand, founded in 1972. The following year a party called People was founded in the UK; it very soon changed its name to the Ecology Party, and later to the Green Party of England and Wales. The next Green party to be formed was Agalev (short for Anders gaan leven/To live in another way), in 1979 in the Flemish-speaking part of Belgium. Also in 1979 the first Green MP in the world was elected, in Switzerland (albeit without a nationwide party yet having been established in the country). Over the following years Green parties were founded in several West European countries: in West Germany and French-speaking Belgium in 1980, in Sweden and Ireland in 1981, in Portugal in 1982, and in Luxemburg, the Netherlands and Switzerland in 1983. That same year two Finnish Greens were elected MPs, without the existence of a party. In 1984 several ecological political groups in France merged into Les Verts. In 1986 Greens in Austria came together to form Die Grüne Alternative. In the 1980s efforts to form Green parties were made also in most other West European countries, which either failed or bore fruit several years later (for example, in Denmark, Spain, Greece and Italy). At the end of the 1980s, with the fall of the Berlin wall, came a large number of Green parties in the former Soviet bloc, playing an important role during the first years of democracy, but losing support after a couple of years. Some, however, have later recovered.

It was also in the 1980s that the first Green parties in America were created, in 1983 in Canada, 1984 in the USA and 1986 in Brazil. Most of the Latin American Green parties, however, weren't formed until after 2000. Likewise in the Asia-Pacific region, apart from Australia and New Zealand, most Green parties are children of the third millennium, with one exception – the Mongolian Green Party, which was founded during the first year of democracy, 1990. The same goes for Africa, where the existence of Green parties is mostly a phenomenon of this century, with a few exceptions such as Egypt in 1990, Morocco in 1992 and Kenya in 1997.

THE INFLUENCE OF DIE GRÜNEN

The pioneer Green parties from the early 1970s, the New Values Party of New Zealand and the Ecology Party of the UK, were important sources of inspiration for other Green party creators; the fact that they worked in English simplified the transfer of information. Nevertheless, the most influential model was undoubtedly Die Grünen, for several reasons: 1) It was the first Green party to gain political influence in a large country. 2) It had a leading personality who became well-known throughout the world – Petra Kelly. 3) The politics of Die Grünen was the most radical antithesis to the previous dark twentieth-century history of Germany. 4) The party practised alternative and grassroots methods

Figure 4 A typical demonstration by Die Grünen, Germany (1980s). Photo: courtesy of Global Greens.

more radically than most other Greens. 5) It showed that Green thinking extends much further than environmentalism.

The New Values Party was too far away to have a similar influence, and the Ecology Party was too marginalised thanks to the British electoral system. Everybody interested in Green politics thus looked to Germany, if not for guidance, then for inspiration.

WHAT IS A GREEN PARTY?

The definition of a Green party used here is as follows: A Green party is a member of the Global Greens, through one of the four regional Green federations, covering Africa, America, Asia-Pacific and Europe. A number of other parties claiming to be Green also exist. Most of them have the ambition to qualify for membership in the Global Greens structure. Others have been denied membership because they are not considered politically Green, or judged to be 'fake' parties. Some of these will be mentioned in what follows, but the bulk of the presentation concerns parties that are affiliated to the Global Greens structure.

THE GLOBAL GREENS

The Global Greens (GG) is the worldwide association of Green parties. Already in connection with the Earth Summit in Rio de Janeiro in 1992 a Planetary Green meeting had been organised. In 1999 some 150 Greens from 24 countries participated in the Milenio Verde conference in Oaxaca, Mexico. Finally, in 2001, the Global Greens were founded at a congress in Canberra, Australia. A second congress was held in São Paolo, Brazil in 2008, which adopted 21 commitments for the twenty-first century. The third GG congress was held in Dakar, Senegal, in 2012. The fourth is scheduled for 2016 or 2017 in Europe.

The steering body of the GG is the Global Greens Coordination (GGC). Each of of the four federations elects three members to the GCC, plus three alternates who can stand in when needed. According to the founding resolution, the Global Greens Network is 'composed of two to three representatives from Green parties and movements identified in partnership with the relevant Federation'. The decisive authority as to which parties may become members, with the 'right' to identify as Green, lies with the regional federations.

According to an end-of-year report by its Convener, Margret Blakers, the Global Greens in 2014 have consolidated, with over 5,000 people receiving Global Greens News, and have issued statements on, among other issues, nuclear disarmament, the conflict in Ukraine, climate change, whaling, and

Figure 5   A Global Greens conference at the UN Climate Conference, COP20, in Lima, December 2014. From the left: Elizabeth May, leader of the Green Party of Canada; Christine Milne, leader of the Australian Greens; Veronica Juzgado, coordinator of the Global Greens; Yujin Lee, South Korean Greens; Stina Bergström, Swedish Greens. Photo: courtesy of Global Greens.

the Gaza conflict. Veronica Juzgado has replaced Alice Rosmi as Global Greens Secretary. The members of the Global Green Coordination at the beginning of 2015 were as follows:

African Greens Federation
Frank Habineza (Democratic Green Party of Rwanda), May 2008–present
Adamou Garba (Niger Parti Vert), May 2008–present
Fatima Alaoui (Parti Vert Morocco), June 2014–present
alternate Saraha Georget (Madagascar), June 2014–present
alternate Badono Daigou (Chad), June 2014–present
alternate Robinah K. Nanyunja (Uganda), June 2014–present

Asia-Pacific Greens Federation
Keli Yen (Green Party Taiwan), October 2011–present
Liaquat Ali (Pakistan Green Party), May 2010–present
Suresh Nautiyal (Uttarakhand Parivartan Party, India), May 2010–present
alternate Masaya Koriyama (Midori no To, Greens Japan), October 2012–
    present

alternate Ballav Timalsina (Nepali Green Party), March 2014–present

European Green Party
Steve Emmott (Green Party of England and Wales), November 2009–present
Merja Kähkönen (Vihreät–De Gröna, Finnish Greens), May 2013–present
Jean Rossiaud (Les Verts/Die Grünen, Switzerland), May 2013–present
alternate Saraswati Matthieu (Groen, Belgium), November 2012- present
alternate Eva Goës (Miljöpartiet de Gröna, Sweden), November 2009–present
alternate Felix Deist (Bündnis 90/Die Grünen)

Federación de Partidos Verdes de las Américas
Fabiano Carnevale, (Partido Verde Brazil), November 2013–present
José Antolin Polanco (Green Party of Dominican Republic), 2014–present
Patricia O. Maldonado (Green Party of United Mexican States), August 2014–
    present

The Global Green Charter, adopted in 2001 in Canberra and revised in Dakar in 2012, can be considered a statement of Green Basic Principles. In the preamble the Global Greens recognise

> that the dominant patterns of human production and consumption, based on the dogma of economic growth at any cost and the excessive and wasteful use of natural resources without considering Earth's carrying capacity, are causing extreme deterioration in the environment and a massive extinction of species ... that developed countries through their pursuit of economic and political goals have contributed to the degradation of the environment and of human dignity ... that without equality between men and women, no real democracy can be achieved ... that future generations have the same right as the present generation to natural and cultural benefits.[2]

The Global Greens declare that their politics is based upon six basic principles: ecological wisdom, social justice, participatory democracy, non-violence, sustainability and respect for diversity. More than 100 policy proposals are made, some of which follow here in an abbreviated and compressed version: support of grassroots movements, democratisation of gender relations, access to official information and to free and independent media, increase of government aid to developing countries, rapid transition to zero carbon economies, phase out of nuclear power, moratorium on new fossil fuel exploration, an end to the patenting and merchandising of life, public ownership of the essentials of life such as water, creation of a World Environment Organisation, serious reform of the World Bank and IMF and the WTO, a Tobin-Henderson Tax or Financial Transactions Tax, the right of women to make their own decisions, including the control of their fertility, support for the UN Declaration on the Rights of Indigenous Peoples, death penalty to be abolished worldwide, treatment of asylum-seekers in accordance with the 1951 Geneva Convention on the Rights to Asylum, decriminalisation of homosexuality, support for organic agriculture, ban on the commercial growing of genetically modified crops, phase-out of all persistent and bio-accumulative man-made chemicals, animal welfare, increasing well-being rather than GDP, strengthening of the role of the UN as a global organisation of conflict management and peacekeeping, support for the International Criminal Court, curtailment of the power of the military-industrial-financial complex, elimination of the international arms trade.

GREENS IN AFRICA – GROWING RAPIDLY
(For details on the African Green parties, see the Appendix)

At the beginning of the 1990s, as a result of the move to multiparty systems in many African states, quite a few parties with Green or environmentalist ambitions were founded on the continent. During the 1990s Green parties were started in Cameroon, Egypt, Guinea, Ivory Coast, Kenya, Mauritius, Mali, Morocco, Mozambique, Niger, Burkina Faso, Senegal and South Africa.[3] However, several of these parties didn't survive, and their relation to present-day Green parties is obscure. The majority of the present African Green parties have been founded – or re-founded – in the twenty-first century. A Federation of Green Parties in Africa was established in Kenya in May 1998 but did not survive. A new African Green Federation (AGF) was established in Kampala, Uganda, on 17 April 2010. The founding congress elected an executive of nine persons with Frank Habineza as president: three of the nine were women, including the second vice president, Saraha Georget Rabeharisoa of Madagascar. Furthermore, the six regions (South, West, Central, North, East and Ocean Islands) elected one representative each, four men and two women. There had been, however, several types of African Green cooperation before the establishment of AGF. Among these was the first African Green University in Rabat, Morocco, in March 2009, where 50 African Greens from Morocco, Nigeria, Rwanda, Burundi, Niger, Mali and Guinea-Conakry discussed themes such as 'Can ecology save Africa?' and 'What role will African Green Parties play?'[4]

In October 2010 the AGF presented a report on African Greens to the Global Greens meeting in Tallinn, where it was reported that new Green parties had been established in Uganda, Zambia, Rwanda and Somalia. In 2011 the African Greens Academy in Burkina Faso brought 13 countries together. According to an AGF report, 'the Green Ideology needs always to be analysed and be put in the African Continental politics context, so that we become relevant to voters and our countries'.

Figure 6   African Greens, Dakar 2012. From the left: Frank Habineza, president of the African Green Federation, Robinah K Nanyunja, president of the Ecological Party of Uganda and Bob Brown, co-founder, long-time senator and key figure in the Australian Greens. Photo: the author.

AGF MEMBERS: STATUS IN NOVEMBER 2014

In many African countries several parties claiming to be Green exist, but the AGF has found that some of them don't live up to the standards of a 'real' Green party. Frank Habineza, president of the AGF, has provided some information of interest:[5]

> In Tunisia the former regime sponsored another green party (Parti des verts pour le progress) to sabotage the real one (Tunisie Verte). After the fall of Ben Ali, the AGF-party was registered and thus Tunisia has two green parties, but AGF accepts only one … Ivory Coast pulled out after their party split up. Those inside the country accused the party leader of always living in France … They created a new party which is in final phases of being registered.

All AGF members (except Ivory Coast) were classified during 2014 as being in 'good' or 'bad standing'. The criteria are given by Habineza as follows:

Good standing means, members who have paid up their membership fees (100 USD) and annual subscription (50 USD) from 2010 to-date and equally those who have paid up Global Greens annual membership fees, 20 Euros, two years, and 30 Euros last year. Those who have not paid up are in *bad standing* and will lose their membership status.

There were 18 parties from 18 countries in 'good standing' in November 2014; the same parties had attended the AGF congress in Madagascar in June 2014. Tunisia however, having been classified as in 'bad standing' in March 2014, was also present. Another 10 were adjudged in bad standing, while Ivory Coast was not classified. From May 2015 the AGF home page lists 22 member parties, some of which are indicated as associated members.

Burkina Faso: Rassemblement Des Ecologistes du Burkina
Burundi: Burundi Green Movement – Associate Member
Chad: Union des Ecologistes Tchadiens
Congo: Parti Ecologiste Congolais (DRC)
Egypt: Egyptian Green Party
Gabon: Green Party of Gabon – Associate Member
Guinea: Parti des Ecologistes Guineens
Kenya: Mazingira Greens Party of Kenya
Madagascar: Parti Vert Hasin'I Madagasikara
Mali: Parti Ecologiste du Mali
Mauritius: Les Verts Fraternels
Morrocco: Parti des Verts Pour le Développement du Maroc
Niger: Rassemblement pour un Sahel Vert/Parti Vert du Niger
Rwanda: Democratic Green Party of Rwanda
Senegal: Fédération Démocratique des Ecologistes du Sénégal
Sierra Leone: Green Movement/Green Watch – Associate Member
Somalia: Somalia Green Party – Associate Member
South Africa: Ecological movement of South Africa – Associate Member
Togo: Afrique Togo Ecologie (ATE)
Uganda: Ecological party of Uganda
Zambia: Green Party of Zambia
Zimbabwe: Green Party of Zimbabwe – Associate Member

Other Green parties in contact with AGF

Angola: Partido Nacional Ecológico de Angola
Benin: Parti Vert du Benin/Benin Green Party
Burkina Faso: Parti Ecologiste pour le Développement du Burkina
Central African Republic: Mouvement des Verts de Centrafrique
Ghana: Ghana Green Movement

Ivory Coast: Parti Écologique Ivoirien
Mozambique: Ecological Party-Movement of Earth
Nigeria: Nigerian Green Movement
Tunisia: Parti Tunisie Verte

Habineza also provided information about other African countries not currently on the membership list:

> Mauretania: no recent news. Algeria: They supported a coup d'etat and we lost track of them. Cameroon: The leader has been staying in Belgium for over 10 years and the party is non-existent. Congo Brazzaville: There is a new party which has been accepted in the Central African Federation. Guinea-Bissau: It's not active, the leader died. Reunion: No information. Sudan: Still in the process of becoming party.

The fact that the third congress of the Global Greens (29 March–1 April 2012) was held in Africa (Dakar, Senegal) was a strong encouragement for the African Greens. One newspaper carried the headline 'The African Greens display their first success' and reported that 47 African countries were represented among the participants. The appointment of the leader of the Greens of the host nation Senegal, Haïdar El Ali, as Minister of Environment just two days after the congress 'confirms the institutionalisation of ecological politics on the African continent'.[6] Among the environmental problems raised at the congress by African delegates were poisonous waste, overfishing, overexploitation of forests, and land grabbing. However, one delegate warned that if the Green parties were to start checking the environmental effects of mining and oil extraction they would be subject to repression from their respective governments.

AGF CONGRESS IN MADAGASCAR 2014

At the AGF congress in Madagascar in June 2014 representatives of 17 African Green parties participated. According to Per Inge Lidén – an observer from the Swedish Green Forum, which contributes financially to the development of Green parties in Africa – the AGF has developed organisationally, with fewer personal conflicts and a more efficient process. Political differences between African Green parties do, however, exist, in terms of their positioning on the left-right spectrum, and policies on gender balance and drugs (the Zambian Green Party struggles for the legalisation of cannabis). Generally, it is difficult for an outside observer to determine how strong the African Green parties really are. Most of them cannot boast any significant election results, which of course is due partly to the sometimes chaotic situation in some African states.

The goals discussed at the congress included strengthening local branches, merging parties into one Green party, further development of Green thinking about food, water, energy, and sustainable society, and increased contacts between MPs from different countries. A new executive was also elected, consisting of president Frank Habineza (Rwanda); first vice president Adama Sere (Burkina Faso); second vice president Sarah Georget (Madagascar); secretary general Papa Dessa Dieng (Senegal); cashier Robina Nanyunja (Uganda); responsible for communication (new) Adamou Garba (Niger); representatives of regions: North – Mohamed Awad (Egypt); West – Napo Nissau Irenee (Togo); South – Kelvin Kaunda (Zambia), East – Charles Maringo (Kenya), Central – Didace Pembe (Congo-Kinshasa, RDC); Ocean – Silvio Michel (Mauritius). (Ten men, two women.)

The general evaluation was that the congress was well organised, but that the participation of women should be increased. The next congress of the AGF is planned for 2016 or 2017 in Kinshasa.[7]

THE SIX REGIONS OF THE AGF

The AGF is divided into six partly independent regions, with their own structure and leadership:

The *Eastern Region* has an office in Kampala. The East Africa Greens Federation congress of November 2013 brought together representatives of Green parties from Rwanda, Uganda, Kenya and Burundi in Kigali, Rwanda. Robinah K. Nanyunja, President of EPU (Uganda), was elected as secretary general. In total six women and three men were elected to lead the EAGF.[8]

The *Central Region*: the Central African Greens Federation (Federation des Ecologistes et Verts d'Afrique Centrale – FEVAC) was established in Kinshasa, Democratic Republic of Congo at a congress in November 2014, which elected Didace Pembe Bokiaga from DRC as president, supported by three more men.

The *Ocean Region* consists of Mauritius and Madagascar. At the AGF congress in Madagascar in June 2014, the executive of the AGF had proposed to merge the Southern and Ocean regions, but this was opposed by Madagascar and Mauritius who preferred to try to get more members from other African islands; the congress decided to reject the proposal by the executive.

The *Western Region* has a new executive and an office in Niamey and has held seminars about Green economics in Ougadougou. At a congress in Niamey, in October 2012, the Federation of Ecological and Green Parties in West Africa elected as president Irénée Nissao Napo, Togo, who is supported by three men and one woman.

The *Northern Region* was formally established as the North African Greens Federation in June 2013 with headquarters in Cairo, and has as its members the Greens from Egypt, Tunisia and Morocco. Mohamed Awad, Egypt, was elected president, supported by two women and one man. Green participants in the meeting were received by the Speaker of the Shura (Upper House) and the Sheikh of al-Azhar.[9]

The *Southern Region:* Greens from Zambia, Mozambique, South Africa, Lesotho and Zimbabwe met in Maputo, Mozambique in May 2013 and set up the Southern Africa Greens Federation (SAGF) with headquarters in Lusaka, Zambia. Four men and three women were elected to the committee, with Patrick Sindane, South Africa, as president.

Figure 7 Participants at the meeting of the Federation of American Greens in Lima, 2014. From the left: Carla Piranda, National Secretary of the Organization of the Greens of Brazil; Francoise Alamartine, International Relations of the Greens of France; Julia Duppré, delegate from Brazil Greens to the FPVA and Youth Commission of FPVA; Flor de María Hurtado, General Secretary of the Greens of Peru and Ombudsperson of the FPVA; Verónica Juzgado, Secretary of Global Greens; Rosy Guzman, delegate from Peru Greens to the FPVA; Elizabeth May, Canadian Parliamentary Green Party; Margot Soria, President, Greens of Bolivia; Matilde Baján, leader of the Greens of Guatemala; Sanda Everette, delegate from the US Greens to the FPVA. Photo: courtesy of Global Greens.

THE AMERICAS – SOME OF THE STRONGEST GREEN PARTIES
(For details on the Green parties of the Americas, see the Appendix)

Several Green parties were established in the Americas in the 1980s, in countries like the USA, Canada, Brazil and Mexico, and have survived and grown stronger.[10] In other countries, however, the early Green parties didn't survive. In some cases their emergence in America was inspired by developments in Europe, sometimes by individuals who had spent time in exile from Latin American dictatorships, for example Fernando Gabeira, the prominent co-founder of Partido Verde, Brazil, who for some time in the 1970s sold tickets in the Stockholm subway. But in most cases the decision to establish a Green party was a result of the devastation of the nature and the environment by the neoliberal regimes which followed after the fall of the dictators, as well as the inadequacy not only of neoliberalism but also of traditional socialism to solve the social and economic problems of the region. A distinct feature of several Latin American Green programmes is their ambition to stimulate people to adopt a more 'moral' attitude towards politics and society. One reason for this is of course the high levels of local corruption. Some parties also display a sympathy for 'spirituality'. At the same time some Latin American Greens have taken a strong position in favour of equality for LGBT people, for example the Partido Verde in Brazil. In principle all American Greens believe in gender balance, and they are usually progressive on social issues. Some Green parties in the region identify as 'left' (e.g. in Bolivia), others as centre or centre-right (Venezuela, Mexico). Among the American Greens there are also strong feelings in favour of the indigenous populations, which are numerous in several countries.

LA FEDERACIÓN DE PARTIDOS VERDES DE LAS AMÉRICAS, FPVA (THE FEDERATION OF GREEN PARTIES IN AMERICA)

According to the FPVA, the Greens of the following countries were members as of autumn 2014: Argentina, Brazil, Bolivia, Canada, Chile, Colombia, Dominican Republic, Mexico, Peru, the USA and Venezuela. Among the observers waiting to fulfil certain requirements in order to become full members are Costa Rica and Guatemala. Guyana is a permanent observer. The FPVA was established in December 1997 in Mexico City; its founding members were Greens from Argentina, Brazil, Canada, Chile, Colombia, Dominican Republic, Mexico, Nicaragua, Peru, Venezuela and the USA. According to its statutes, FPVA aims to solve environmental problems through participation in governments. It hopes to unite movements which adopt and practice solidarity, cooperation and love and respect for all manifestations of life, through a programme of environmentally sustainable development. The FPVA only accepts one party from each country and only parties from independent states; thus Guyana and Puerto Rico can only be accepted as observers. At least a dozen Latin American and Caribbean states have no Green party that is a member of the FPVA.

At its Annual General Assembly in La Paz, Bolivia, in the autumn of 2013, the Federation elected its new executive committee, with ten persons, including three co-presidents: Patricia Maldonado of Mexico, Antolin Polanco of Dominican Republic and Fabiano Carnevale of Brazil. Out of the ten members four are women. Since 2002 FPVA has held annual meetings.

GREEN PARTIES IN THE ASIA-PACIFIC REGION

The Asia-Pacific Green Federation (APGF) held its first congress in 2005 in Kyoto, Japan, following an Asia-Pacific Green Politics Workshop in Brisbane in 2000 and the Global Greens Congress in Canberra in 2001. In a report from the second congress in Tapei, 30 April–2 May 2010, it is stated that over 200 people attended, including representatives from 17 Asia-Pacific countries. Nineteen of the 22 organisations from 15 countries that have gone through the process of applying for and being accepted as Members, Associates or Friends of the APGF were present. According to a report from the Australian Greens in 2012, APGF had 18 member parties from 13 countries;[11] in 2015 the number of full members is 11. However, there are several Asian countries in which Green parties have emerged only to disappear. Non-member Green parties exist or have existed in Syria, Jordan, Lebanon, Iraq, Yemen, Palestine, Kurdistan, Iran, Palestine, Bangladesh and Kyrgyzstan. In Israel a Green party has participated in Knesset elections since 1999, but has never received more than 1.5% of the vote, not enough to secure a seat (in 2013 the percentage plummeted to 0.2%, and in March 2015 the result was only 0.07%). Some countries have had parties as members of APGF, but these have either disappeared or deteriorated: Sri Lanka, Hong Kong, Papua New Guinea, the Solomon Islands. The Greens of Vanuatu (who got 3 out of 52 seats in the parliament in 2012 and held the position of prime minister from March 2013 to May 2014) have an unclear relation to the APGF, which is being investigated. The People's Republic of China is a special case, where it is not possible to establish a normal Green party. However, thousands of legally registered local environmental groups, and an unknown number of non-registered ones, do exist and are rather free to act, so long as they do not try to establish a nationwide structure. As a matter of fact, the APGF has several contacts with Chinese groups and individuals, both in China and in exile.

In Thailand, according to one report, the king has been encouraging a well-managed environment and initiated many ecological projects: 'it is clear that a green party can maximise this chance where they can get support from the king, if they know how to use it'.[12] Some of the Asia-Pacific Green parties are old and strong and play a significant role in the political life of their countries, for example in Australia and New Zealand; the Mongolian Greens have also been successful and even participated in governments. Some parties are undoubtedly advancing and have won seats at local and/or regional levels, such as in Japan and Taiwan. The Korean Green Party also seems to be progressing. In those countries closely aligned with the West (Australia, New Zealand, Japan), Greens often take a position against the involvement of their countries in military interventions by Western troops. In some cases Green parties in the region have raised issues which might be perceived as sensitive from a traditional point of view, such as the right to abortion and the rights of LGBT persons.

There is a degree of male dominance in most of the Asia-Pacific Green parties. Out of the 11 member parties, three have gender-balanced co-presidents (Japan, New Zealand and Taiwan), one has a female president (Australia) and seven have a traditional one-man presidency. However, even the male-dominated parties adhere to principles of gender equality and admit that the imbalance is a problem they must take action to resolve.

As of 2015, the committee of the APGF consists of eight members (five men and three women): Keli Yen (Taiwan, also Secretary), Suresh Nautiyal (India), Anna Reynolds (Australia), Rikiya Adachi (Japan), Robin Winkler (Taiwan), Ballav Timalsina (Nepal), Bob Hale (Australia) and Claire Waghorn-Lees (New Zealand). The APGF has its headquarters in New Zealand and is planning to hold its third congress in June 2015.

GREENS IN EUROPE – PIONEERS AND VETERANS
(For details on the European Green parties, see the Appendix)

Even if Green political activities began quite early outside Europe, the ecological awakening that resulted in the emergence of Green parties was strongest in Europe during the 1970s and 1980s. Already in 1979 an attempt to establish cooperation between European Green parties was made, with the Coordination of European Green and Radical Parties. However, the differences between Greens and Radicals proved too great to overcome. The Radicals were more libertarian and less social than the Greens, and dependent on a male guru, the Italian Marco Pannella (such a dependency not being a feature of Green parties).

TOWARDS ORGANISED EUROPEAN GREEN COOPERATION

In March 1983 Agalev organised a meeting in Brussels with Die Grünen, the Irish Greens, the Ecology Party of the UK, Ecolo and several French groups. Dirk Janssens, of Agalev, was appointed secretary. The Irish Greens demanded that Esperanto should be adopted as the common language of Greens, which was not accepted. Instead simultaneous translation between the major languages was provided voluntarily by trainee interpreters. A major breakthrough for European Green cooperation was a Joint Declaration, signed in March 1984 by Les Verts, the Ecology Party of the UK, the Ecology Party of Ireland, Agalev, Ecolo, Miljöpartiet (Sweden), Alternative Liste Österreich and De Groenen (the Netherlands). Die Grünen supported the Joint Declaration but did not join the new Coordination of European Greens (CoEG). The reluctance of Die Grünen to join a purely Green body remained a headache for the CoEG during the following years. The Joint Declaration highlighted several points which have remained basic principles of green thinking: 'Stop those who in pursuit of continued economic and industrial growth are undermining the basis of life itself.' European cooperation should 'take disunity into account and consist of regions rather than nation states'. The declaration took a position against the 'accumulation of weapons' in favour of 'civilian based non-violent defence', against excessive consumption, nuclear energy and artificial needs, in favour of 'community based self-reliance', a reduction of work hours and the redistribution of income and resources. Later a Common Programme for the election to the European parliament, *Towards a Green Europe*, was adopted: 'We reject a new military superpower and want a Europe of regions.' Many Green demands were listed: disarmament, elimination of military blocs, civilian defence; a halt to nuclear power, renunciation of Euratom; sustainable development; recycling; support of local and regional units; cooperatives; taxes to prevent waste; agriculture in balance with nature.

FIRST GREEN CONGRESS AND EUROPEAN ELECTIONS, 1984

The first major gathering of European Greens was the Green congress in Liège, 30 March–1 April 1984, which prepared for the European elections in June of the same year. The election result was a step forward for the Greens: Die Grünen (8.2%/7 MEPs), Agalev (4.3%/1 MEP), Ecolo (3.9%/1 MEP), Groen Progressief Akkoord (5.6%/3 MEPs). The 12 Green MEPs, together with others, formed *GRAEL*, the Green-Alternative European Link. GRAEL cooperated with Danish critics of the EC and Belgian and Italian regionalists to form the Rainbow Group.

GRAEL agreed on a Declaration of Paris, which called for 'an alternative, neutral and decentralized Europe with self-administered regions maintaining their individual cultural independence'. In November 1984 the CoEG had eight member parties: the UK Ecology Party, Miljöpartiet, Comhaontas Glas, Ecolo, Agalev, Les Verts, Dei Greng and Alternative Liste.

SECOND CONGRESS IN DOVER, 1985: CONFRONTATION BETWEEN UK GREENS AND DIE GRÜNEN

The Second European Green Congress was held in Dover, UK, 21–24 March 1985. The *Guardian* carried the headline 'European ecologists try to knit an alliance' and *The Times* reported that 'the Western world's youngest and, it says, fastest growing political movement gathered delegates from twelve European countries, the USA, Canada, Australia and Japan'.[13] Sara Parkin of the UK Greens stated that Greens reject nuclear power, both military and civilian, stand for neutrality, reject the economic and political concentration of power, Western hegemony over the third world, male domination and violence, and support human rights. Petra Kelly of Die Grünen attacked the British majority election system and the dominant male chauvinism. A special feature of the Dover congress was that every session began with a minute of silence and meditation, which had the purpose of 'promoting agreement by having us all on the same wave-length'. At a CoEG meeting, Ali Schmeissner (Die Grünen) scornfully dismissed the Dover congress as 'Sara Parkin's private show', thereby highlighting the confrontation between Schmeissner's left-wing position and Parkins 'green-green' approach. It was also reported that Dei Greng (Luxemburg) had split, that there were several Green lists in Italy, that a new system for local elections in France gave Les Verts a better chance, and that the two infighting Green parties in Austria were going to meet. The Green landscape was fluid and evolving in a somewhat chaotic way.

THE COEG GROWS AND STRENGTHENS ITS STRUCTURE

In late September 1985 four co-secretaries were elected (replacing the one-man work of Dirk Janssens, Agalev): Sara Parkin, UK, Bruno Boissière, France, Dirk Janssens, Belgium, and Per Gahrton, Sweden. Parkin, Boissière and Gahrton remained in office until 1989, but Janssens was replaced by Leo Cox and Willy de Backer, both from Belgium. In January 1986 there were ten member parties of the CoEG: ALÖ, Agalev, Ecolo, De Grønne (Denmark), Comhaontas Glas, Les Verts, Dei Greng, De Groenen, Miljöpartiet, and the UK Green Party.

One controversial issue in 1986 concerned unanimity versus qualified majority. Some, including Miljöpartiet, didn't like the risk of having to accept political decisions with which the party couldn't agree. A compromise proposed by Willy de Bakker was adopted: if there was no consensus, then a decision should be postponed and a working group set up; there should also always be a blocking possibility, which could be used after the critical party has sounded an alarm-bell. In a paper on 'Basic democracy and Green party organisation', presented to the CoEG meeting in September 1986, Sara Parkin said it was now time to 'debunk a few myths about alternative systems'. She was sceptical about horizontal structures or webs. 'I would also be pleased to hear of one organisational web that doesn't have a big spider at its centre.' Parkin was touching very sensitive nerves among Greens when she pointed out the conflict between the Green ideals of a flat, grassroots structure and political efficacy. In January 2015 Parkin stated that her experience in the women's movement in the 1970s had convinced her that 'lack of structure opened up the organisation to fragmentation and powerlessness'.[14] She was right, but her warnings were premature. Green parties didn't try to reach a viable compromise on strategy and organisation until about a decade later – but by then Sara had turned to other types of Green activity.

On 28 April 1986 the CoEG undertook a joint action against the military blocs by placing pieces of ice outside the Soviet and US embassies in Brussels. On being invited into the Soviet embassy the Eurogreens noticed that the

Figure 8 The co-secretaries of the Coordination of European Greens (from left: the author, Bruno Boissère, France, Sara Parkin, UK) together with Antoine Waechter, presidential candidate for Les Verts in 1988. Waechter represented the 'neither-left-nor-right' current. He left Les Verts in 1994, but returned to the fold 15 years later after having failed to establish his own movement. Photo: Ulla Lemberg.

diplomats were in an awkward mood. Some hours later the world was informed of the Chernobyl nuclear disaster; it became another proof of the validity of basic Green attitudes, in this case of their anti-nuclear position.[15]

DIE GRÜNEN JOIN THE COEG

One of the main conflicts inside the CoEG had been about the Dutch representation therein. A 'green-green' party, De Groenen, had been accepted, but Die Grünen (without yet themselves being full members) demanded that a red-green coalition, Groen Progressief Akkoord (GPA), should be permitted to join. In a letter to the CoEG of 12 June 1984, De Groenen objected to GPA membership because it might lead to communists taking part in the Green fraction of the European Parliament. The minutes from a CoEG meeting in Barcelona on 23 February 1985 quote the representative of Die Grünen, Ali Schmeissner, as asserting that 'Die Grünen would only join if GPA was allowed to join'. Sara Parkin rejected 'the blackmailing by Die Grünen'. In January 2015 she emphasised that she feared that people like Schmeissner were aiming at the destruction of the CoEG.[16] She was probably right, because some German fundis didn't believe in an independent Green political dimension.

The process which led to Die Grünen joining the CoEG started with a letter in December 1986 from a member of the Central Board (Bundesvorstand), Norbert Kostede, to some 30 Green, alternative and left-wing parties about the International Cooperation of the Greens.[17] Kostede wanted very broad cooperation, but admitted that the CoEG should not be dismissed. The leading personality of the Austrian Greens, Freda Meissner-Blau, wrote to Kostede[18] proposing Vienna as the headquarters for a 'Green International' with an office and a magazine. Finally, a decision was made on 14–15 February 1987 by the Bundeshauptausschuss (BHA)[19] of Die Grünen, and at the CoEG meeting of 7–9 March 1987 Die Grünen applied for membership, 'in the hope that better cooperation between green and alternative movements worldwide would be possible ... (but) the European Greens cannot have the function of a green international'. The application for membership by Die Grünen was accepted unanimously. Norbert Kostede, however, still pleaded for a broader international.[20] The apprehensions inside Die Grünen about membership of the CoEG were underscored when the federal working group on international relations made a proposal[21] to the party congress of 1–3 May 1987 in Duisburg to revoke the decision to join the CoEG. However, Die Grünen remained a member, even though the German Greens maintained their ambition to cooperate not only with 'pure' Greens but also with left-wing parties. At the CoEG meeting of 13–14 June 1987, Jürgen Maier, of Die Grünen, repeated that the party wanted 'cooperation with all groups and other parties involved in the movement'. Sara Parkin replied that the 'role of CoEG is to promote Green politics'. Several speakers agreed. The present author stated that 'we need a green identity'. Osmo Soininvaara (Finland) asked if 'Die Grünen really is a Green party or just a coalition'. In the autumn of 1988 Die Grünen once more caused consternation by distributing an address list of 'Green-alternative and progressive parties in Europe'[22] which contained party addresses from 18 Western European countries. Apart from the members of the CoEG some of the parties were considered rather awkward bedfellows by most Greens, for example the Italian Democrazia Proletaria; the Greek Communist Party Interior and the Party of the Greek Left; the Norwegian Socialistisk Venstreparti; the Danish Venstresocialistisk parti/Socialist left party; the French Partie socialiste unifié and Les renovateur communists, and not least the Irish Sinn Féin. Most Greens felt that CoEG must wait for the development of genuine Green parties and not consider any left-wing group with some environmental points to make as a Green party.

STOCKHOLM CONGRESS, 1987: TOWARDS A GREEN TWENTY-FIRST CENTURY

The third European Green congress was held in Stockholm, 28–30 August 1987. Three hundred Greens from 20 countries participated. It was reported that there were now Green MPs in Austria, Belgium, Finland, Italy, Luxemburg, Portugal, Switzerland and West Germany. In a keynote speech, Hannes Alfvén, the Swedish Nobel Prize winner for physics, called for a 'Green revolution'. In a debate on 'Does a green ideology exist?', the Italian Sergio Adreis said he preferred 'theory' to 'ideology': 'Greens are characterised by pragmatism, the capacity to mobilise citizens around a single issue.' Other speakers were Freda Meissner-Blau of Austria, Osmo Soininvaara of Finland, Solange Fernex of France, Paul Staes of Agalev, and Sara Parkin and Petra Kelly. Joschka Fischer was also invited, but sent a letter of regret, giving as a motive that 'at the same time there will take place a meeting of the Green Realos, at which I absolutely must participate'.[23] To Fischer, the power struggle inside Die Grünen was more important than the construction of an international Green movement.

Some media attention was given to a fierce attack upon Die Grünen by the Belgian MEP Paul Staes, in which he accused the party of 'cultural imperialism or ideological colonialism'.[24] Petra Kelly also criticised Die Grünen. Three members of the central executive of Die Grünen complained after the congress that 'the others look upon us a big brother, but want our money'. However, they reported that Agalev had apologised for the attack by Staes and that the Swedish organisers were astonished that Kelly had used her speaking time to criticise her own party.

The international media attention was considerable. *Frankfurter Allgemeine Zeitung* judged that a first step towards a Green International had been taken,[25] although another Frankfurt newspaper, *Frankfurter Rundschau*, was of the opposite opinion.[26] The Dutch *NRC Handelsblad* had the impression that the Greens were divided over strategy,[27] while the *Guardian* reported that 'internal feuding threatens Greens' West German future'.[28] In an interview with the *Guardian*, Petra Kelly admitted she was afraid that the feuding between realos and fundis would destroy Die Grünen, but saw hopes in other countries. The semi-official magazine of the German Greens[29] was adamant: there could be no Green International, since the development of the national alternative parties is too different.

In a final remark on behalf of the Swedish hosts, the present author summarised the situation: 'We have reached the end of this congress, but not the end of the green revolution, proclaimed by Hannes Alfvén when he opened the congress. Not even the beginning of the end, but maybe the green movement is now close to the end of its beginning.' A survey among participants at the congress revealed some interesting results:[30] 83% said they believed that Green politics was a coherent political way of thinking; 82% could imagine Greens in governments; and 72% agreed that Greens are neither left nor right.

EU ELECTIONS 1989: JUST BEFORE THE FALL OF THE BERLIN WALL

At a meeting on 11–12 March 1989 the CoEG adopted a Common Programme for the upcoming European election. The idea of a 'Europe of autonomous regions without borders', as an alternative to the European Community, was mentioned in the preamble. The programme also took a position against military alliances and in favour of a 'common house of Europe' (after an expression by the Soviet leader Mikhail Gorbachev), which would not be possible 'neither in a bloc-divided Europe nor in a Western European Superstate, nor with the existing north-south economic gap'. The great project of the European Community, a single market since 1992, was described as 'profoundly unecological'. It was emphasised that 'we understand the opposition within the European Community as in Denmark and reject the unilateral harmonisation with the EEC undertaken by countries like Austria, Sweden, Finland and Switzerland'. The programme explicitly declared 'support for the Green parties in these countries in their opposition to joining the EEC'.

In the spring of 1989 Die Grünen still demanded 'an alliance of green, alternative and regionalist parties and groups as broad as possible in a joint rainbow group in the European Parliament'.[31] In connection with the fifth European Greens Congress in Paris,[32] *Le Monde* asked if the Greens were right-wing or left-wing, concluding that they include two trends, one anti-militarist, anti-nuclear, libertarian, and close to the left, the other naturalist and apolitical. The paper commended the Greens for their struggle 'for environment, disarmament and the moralisation of public life', and concluded that nobody can avoid them.[33]

At a CoEG meeting at the end of June[34] the results of the European elections were discussed, which gave a somewhat chaotic picture of the situation. In Spain there had been four 'Green' parties, none gaining any seat. A representative of the Irish Comhaontas Glas accused Die Grünen to have caused them to miss out on a seat with Petra Kelly's open support for a non-Green candidate. In Luxemburg, despite more than 10% of the vote going to Greens, there was no Green MEP elected because the votes were divided between two competing Green parties. The Italian Greens were also split, but both parties won seats, Verdi three and Arcobaleno two. Even Les Verts, despite securing 10.6% of the vote and nine MEPs, reported problems because Dorothée Piermont, number 1 on the German ballot paper, had been in France supporting the New Left list. The UK Greens, with Sara Parkin having a leading profile, had striking success with 15% of the vote, but no seats. The UK Greens complained that Die Grünen had openly supported two Labour candidates, which created confusion. The Ecologist Alternative of Greece claimed that they lost out on a seat to a fascist party because of another competing ecological party. A lengthy discussion about the future parliamentary group followed. Should it be only Green or alternative and left-wing?

After this relative success in the elections, with Green MEPs from eight countries, a Green parliamentary group, the Green Group in the European parliament (GGEP), was established, with the following members: Agalev 1, Ecolo 2, Die Grünen 8, Les Verts 8, Verdi 3, Arcobaleno 2, GroenLinks 2, Os Verdes 1, plus three non-Greens: Democrazia proletaria 1, Lega Antiproibizionista 1 and Euskadiko Ezkerra, Basque country, 1, comprising altogether 30 MEPs. In a press release it was stated that the Greens in the European Parliament would work according to 'the political base programme of the Eurogreens, March 12, 1989, which takes a stand in favour of a Europe of autonomous regions, without frontiers or military alliances, for an ecological, social and democratic development, and against the non-ecological character of the Single Market'. Even some non-EC Green parties, including the Swedish Greens, signed the agreement, which also gave special status to a representative of the Green Party of England and Wales as a member of the group with full voting rights, in defiance of the British electoral system. There was also a common platform with the regionalists and the Danish anti-EC movement. However, this was not enough for one of the left-minded German MEPs, Dorothée Piermont, who decided to resign from the GGEP and rejoin the Rainbow Group. In a CoEG-meeting on 30 September 1989 the eternal issue of the Green Left of the Netherlands was settled with acceptance of their membership.

In January 1990 the CoEG had 19 member parties from 17 countries: Austria: Grüne Alternative; Belgium: Agalev and Ecolo; Denmark: De Grønne; Ireland: Comhaontas Glas; Finland: Vihreä Liitto (Green Alliance); France: Les Verts; Italy: I Verdi; Luxemburg: Dei Greng; Portugal: Os Verdes and MDP; Spain: Los Verdes; Sweden: Miljöpartiet; Switzerland: Parti Ecologique/Grüne Partei; UK: Green Party; Germany: Die Grünen; Estonia: Estonian Green Movement. There also were observer parties from Spain, Norway and Greece. From the autumn of 1989 five new co-secretaries took over: Heidi Hautala, Finland; Gerhard Jordan, Austria; Pierre Jonckheer, Belgium – Ecolo; Paolo Bergamaschi, Italy; Isabel Castro, Portugal.

GREEN MPS, NEUTRAL GREENS, EFTA GREENS

In February 1990 (16–19) the Swedish Greens organised in the Swedish Parliament the first conference for Green members of parliament. In the invitation it was noted that 'there are now Green MPs in 16 European national parliaments, including the European Parliament in Strasbourg and the People's congress in Moscow'. A follow-up conference was arranged later the same year in Vienna, but since then special conferences for Green MPs have been replaced by meetings in connection with congresses of the European Federation of Green Parties (EFGP) or the European Green Party (EGP) or the EU parliamentary group.

On 19 February 1989 a special meeting for Greens from neutral countries was held in Innsbruck, with representatives from Sweden, Finland, Ireland, Switzerland and Austria. A common statement was adopted, insisting that a 'credible neutrality is not compatible with EC membership'. At the same time the present author, representing Miljöpartiet, stated that 'we must accept that the Green parties of the EC countries, except Denmark, are not in favour of the exit of their countries'. Also the EFTA Greens met once or twice, but when several of them joined the EU in 1994 this came to an end.

FROM COORDINATION TO FEDERATION

In June 1993 at a congress in Finland the Coordination of European Greens was transformed into the European Federation of Green Parties (EFGP). In 1996, when the EFGP held its first congress, in Vienna, 21–23 May, there were 28 member parties from 26 countries: Belgium, Bulgaria, Netherlands, Luxemburg, Germany, Estonia, Greece, Malta, Ireland, Denmark, Austria, Italy, Georgia, UK, France, Norway, Portugal, Switzerland, Hungary, Russia, Spain, Sweden, Scotland, Finland, Ukraine, Slovakia. Among the speakers at the Vienna congress were the informal leader of Die Grünen, Joschka Fischer, the Green Minister of Environment from Georgia, Nino Chkhobadze, and representatives of Greens from the USA, Cameroon and Palestine. The Green political movement was growing from being mainly West European (together with the USA, Australia and New Zealand) into a global phenomenon.

FROM FEDERATION TO EUROPEAN PARTY (EGP)

At a congress in Rome, 20–22 February 2004, the Eurogreens once more transformed themselves, this time into a European Green Party (EGP). Among the speakers at the founding meeting of the EGP were German Minister of Foreign Affairs, Joschka Fischer, and the Prime Minister of Georgia, Zurab Zhvania. Several participants observed that Fischer's contribution was less Green, and contained more conventional power politics, than Zhvania's contribution, despite the fact that Zhvania had left the Georgian Green Party ten years earlier. Grazia Francescato, the EFGP spokesperson, boasted that the Greens were now 'a pan-European party that will contribute to shape the new enlarged Europe as a "green civic power".'[35]

A Charter of the European Greens was adopted at the second EGP congress in Geneva, 13–14 October 2006. The charter states that 'Greens stand for social justice, for gender equity, for justice between generations, and for justice at the global level ... Greens want to see less military interventions and the implementation of the concept of a civil foreign and security policy.' Recourse to military means is only legitimate with an explicit mandate from the UN Security Council. The Greens favour that the EU, provided it is open for further enlargements, transforms into a truly democratic institution, reorients its priorities towards an environmentally and socially sustainable model of development, and assumes its global responsibilities, under the UN and in cooperation with the OSCE and the Council of Europe. Or, in a nutshell: the EU is the right instrument to achieve Green cooperation across Europe, provided the EU transforms itself into a mainly Green body.

Before the European elections of May 2014 the EGP adopted a common manifesto, with the title *Change Europe, Vote Green*. It emphasised that 'Europe is our common home' (where Europe, according to information given to the author by the EGP Secretariat, must be understood as the entire area covered by the Council of Europe, i.e. considerably larger than the European Union). It also demanded a 'fundamental political reorientation and democratic renewal of the European Union' in the direction of 'fair economic cooperation that respects our ecological responsibilities'. It protested against 'neoliberal austerity and short-term greed' and asserted that 'our economic model is not sustainable'.

In a Political Evaluation of the 2014 Common Election Campaign adopted at the Istanbul EGP Council in November 2014 it was declared that 'the EU has to change'. It was deplored that 'anti-Europeans, chauvinists and right-wing extremists gained in the elections', while the Green result was mixed, with setbacks in France, Belgium, Greece and Germany, signs of recovery in Ireland and the Czech Republic and clear victories in Austria, Croatia, Hungary, Sweden and the UK. Of special interest is the observation that 'part of our success with our campaign came from the fact that we did not get bogged down in an abstract pro-EU/anti-EU conversation, but were able to position ourselves as the one party among the pro-Europeans that clearly insists on major change, and the one party among change advocates that reliably defends the European project'.

The Political Evaluation affirmed that this was the third common Green campaign for a European election. That was true in the sense that it was the third common campaign of the EGP; it also was the first time Greens across the EU had participated in the nomination of a gender-balanced pair of top candidates, Ska Keller (Germany) and José Bové (France). However, common Green programmes for European elections have been adopted since 1984, by the Coordination of European Greens and the European Federation of European Greens. Participation of Greens in campaigns in EU countries other than their own was also common for decades before the establishment of the EGP. This is not to deny that cooperation and mutual support has steadily increased, or that the EGP secretariat was correct to claim that the 2014 campaign was the most transnational ever.

Some European Greens like to see the shift from the EFGP to the EGP as a step based upon increased ideological support among European Greens for the supranational aspect of European cooperation. However, the determining reason for the switch was the introduction by the EU of new regulations in 2003, giving organisational, administrative and financial advantages to European 'parties', established according to several detailed requirements. Thus, the first European 'parties', including the EGP, were established in 2004. In 2014 there were 13 recognised European 'parties', the EGP being the fifth largest, receiving almost 2 million euros annually from the EU.

EU election campaigns are and will for a long time remain 28 (or more) national campaigns with an increasing element of common positions, statements and manifestations, as well as mutual support, especially among Greens. The Green mission is global and must have a strong transboundary and international aspect. But the Green parties are also rooted in grassroots democracy. To pretend that the European Green 'Party' is a party similar to those that conform to the common use of the concept is not only factually wrong, but politically counterproductive, because it creates a false image of Greens as adherents of centralised superstructures.

It is commendable that the European Greens manage to cooperate more in election campaigns and other transboundary activities than other political families. But it is also promising that the flawed admiration among some Greens for centrally managed supranational structures (in the name of Europe), according to the 2014 Manifesto as well as the Political Evaluation, has been superseded by a well-balanced compromise between the two unavoidable dimensions of Green thinking, the global and the local.

GREENS AND THE EEC/EU: FROM OPPOSITION TO JUBILATION TO HESITATION

In the 1980s opposition to the European Economic Community was almost without exception a feature of European Green ideology. The EEC (from 1992, the European Union) was considered to be an anti-ecological and militaristic project (as shown in several of the statements by the European Greens quoted above). Everywhere in countries that were not yet members of the EEC/EU, Green parties were campaigning against membership, especially vehemently in Sweden, Norway and Austria, but also in Switzerland and Finland. The EEC/EU Green parties criticised the 'superpower' ambition of the EEC/EU and put forward the Europe of Regions as an alternative. Some examples of anti-EC statements: In 1988 the Swiss Greens said no to the Internal Market, which was reported in Swiss newspapers.[36] In December the co-secretaries of the CoEG in a statement commenting on an EEC-summit in Rhodes (1 December 1988) accused EEC leaders of 'insulting the citizens of Europe'. 'Mounting public concern over the real effects of the 1992 process cannot be smoothed away by any "glossy and impressive" but meaningless common statement issued over the week-end.' Before the European elections of 1989, Die Grünen demanded: 'Superpower Western Europe – no! Cooperation, yes, this single market – no!'

In the mid 1990s the different attitudes among European Greens towards the EU could still be observed. The Scottish Greens in their manifesto for the European elections of 1994 underlined: 'This manifesto will explain why we are still opposed to the EU.' And when the EFGP adopted a resolution on the ongoing Inter-Governmental Conference (IGC) on a new treaty for the EU, in Turin (11 February 1996), Swedish, Norwegian, English and Irish Greens expressed reservations about the Common Foreign and Security Policy (CFSP), the monetary union (EMU) and the Third Pillar (legal and police cooperation) because of centralist tendencies in the proposals. However, other more 'federalist' minded parties (Germany, Austria and Luxemburg) also expressed reservations about the majority position that armed interventions by the EU could only be made after a mandate from the UN or the OSCE. At the same time the common Green position on the IGC clearly stated that 'achieving a peace oriented CFSP and giving the European Parliament more rights are important steps towards demilitarising Europe and dissolving NATO'.

In 2006 the Swiss Greens dropped their opposition to Swiss membership of the EU, demanding that Switzerland should join in order to transform the EU into a Green body.[37] The Swedish Greens followed a similar path two years later, when the members decided, with 55.6% in favour and 44.4% against, to drop the demand that Sweden should quit the EU.

One reason for giving up the radical resistance to the EU was its subsequent enlargement, especially when in 2004 it grew from 15 to 25 members, which made the EU 'the only show in town' for European Cooperation. Another reason was that despite its bleak record on the environment, the 'greening' of the EU appears to be the main way of obliging Europe to shoulder its international ecological responsibilities. A third reason was the fact that, having been a Red-Green position in the 1970s and 1980s, the negative attitude towards the EU had been taken over from the 1990s onwards by xenophobic right-wing parties. Still, there are clearly distinguishable differences in the attitudes among Greens towards the EU. A revealing example was a debate in the early 2000s in the Green Group in the EP between Paul Lannoye (Ecolo) and Dany Cohn-Bendit (Die Grünen and Les Verts), both well-known as pro-EU. But in a quarrel Lannoye exclaimed: 'I am pro-European, I am not "Europeanist", I want to use the EU for Green purposes, but I don't see the EU as an end in itself.'

In a report in 2011 by the Green European Foundation about the future of the European Union, some 50 experts agreed that the EU must become more competent, at the expense of national sovereignty. But they also underlined that more democracy and citizen's participation is needed to overcome the crisis of confidence which has followed the euro and debt crises.[38] While most Greens want to strengthen virtually all other decision-making levels (local, regional, European, global), some Greens seem to have bad feelings towards nation-state democracy. One reason for this is of course the link between nationalism and nation states. But it is not easy to see the logic in siding with Scottish and Catalonian aspirations for national sovereignty while protesting against demands in small countries, such as Sweden, Norway or Denmark, for the retention of power at the national level instead of transferring it to the EU.

A GREEN KEYNES: GREEN NEW DEAL

For some years the notion of a 'Green New Deal' (GND) has been popular among European Greens. Basically it is a Green version of the New Deal of the 1930s, which was based upon Keynes' conviction that there is no way out of an economic depression via austerity. *Le Monde diplomatique*[39] has observed that the concept of a Green New Deal was not invented by Greens but by UNEP (the United Nations Environmental Programme) in 2008. An example of Green use of the concept is a book by French Green economist Alain Lipietz.[40] His approach is rather far from advocating de-growth; he proposes substantial investments to facilitate Green transformation, partly through a federal EU budget and common EU taxes. He claims that new jobs will be created, for example, if 4.5 million jobs disappear in the car industry, they would be replaced by 8.5 million jobs in the public transport sector. Likewise, a switch to biological agriculture would create millions of new jobs. At the same time he predicts a need for fewer working hours. The reviewer in *Le Monde diplomatique*, Aurélien Bernier, notes that Lipietz is still angry with those who voted against the European constitution in the French referendum in 2005, but recalls that two decades earlier Lipietz pleaded for a unilateral French approach with devaluation and 'intelligent protectionism'.[41] Why is that model outdated? Why has the original Green vision of a Europe of Regions turned into calls for more centralised power for the EU? Why has the decentralisation of powers become almost anathema among leading European Greens? Lipietz is one of the most inventive of contemporary Green economists. However, the Greens today need a balanced combination of his current federalist position and his more localised approach of 1984.

EAST EUROPEAN GREEN AWAKENING

Already before the fall of the Berlin Wall the Paris Green Congress (April 1989) received a message from Baltic Greens blaming the USSR for ecological destruction directed against Baltic peoples, and underlined that the Baltic states were occupied, not legal parts of the USSR. The statement was signed by T. Frey, of the Estonian Green Movement, A. Ulme, of the VAK/Latvian Environmental Protection Club, and Z. Vaisvila, of the Lithuanian Greens.

In December 1989 the CoEG organised a debate about the new situation with Green representatives from Hungary, Bulgaria, Poland, the German Democratic Republic and Estonia. A statement was made in which the European Greens expressed a hope that 'people in East Europe will achieve complete freedom, for instance Estonia, Lithuania, Latvia, Georgia. The German question must be resolved in a European framework; the process of unification between the two states is a historical process, which should be oriented in an ecological and democratic direction.' With the liberalisation that followed Mikhail Gorbachev's becoming the leader of the Soviet Union in 1985 it was possible to start environmental groups that were relatively independent. Quite a lot of the frustration was then channelled through Green groups. In several countries this brought Green parties good results in the first multiparty elections. Greens entered parliaments and even governments. However, this initial upsurge petered out after the collapse of the Soviet Union in December 1991, which was followed by a raw, unregulated form of capitalism. The Greens lost ground, sometimes split, and wasted time infighting.

The structure of the Eastern European Green parties was usually traditional, with no gender balance and one male president. Their policies were more environmentalist than ecologist. As a result of their bad experience of socialism the Eastern Greens were often naively pro-capitalist. Many had difficulties with the Western Greens' peace policy and saw NATO as a liberator, not as an imperialist warmonger. A problem in some countries has been that rich oligarchs have tried, and sometimes managed, to buy weak and inexperienced Green parties. Despite this, Green parties steadily developed throughout Eastern and Central Europe, and after some time drew close enough to the Western Green way of thinking to be accepted as members of the Eurogreens. The CoEG, EFGP and EGP have held many Council meetings in Eastern and Central European countries: Budapest in 1990, Sofia in 1991, Budapest in 1995, Bratislava in 1999, Budapest in 2001, Riga and Kiev in 2005, Ljubljana in 2008, and Tallin in 2010.[42]

For many years the Dutch GroenLinks has organised a Green East-West Dialogue. During these meetings a rapprochement of opinions has been observed, particularly since most of the Eastern and Central European countries have become members of the EU. The 'casino capitalism' following the collapse of the USSR convinced most Eastern Greens of the flaws of the market economy. Women's liberation has reached Eastward (Pussy Riot, Femen). And lately new types of Green parties have emerged, such as LMP Hungary, Zelenite Bulgaria, SMS Slovenia and DOM Macedonia.

EGP STRUCTURE

The Congress of the EGP is made up of 400 delegates from the member parties, proportionally, based upon their latest election results in national or EP elections. Every member party is entitled to at least four delegates. The Congress adopts basic programmes and platforms. It is convened at least every five years.

The *Council* of the EGP normally meets twice a year and consists of around 110 representatives of the member parties, with adjusted proportional representation based upon the latest national or EU election; however, every member party is entitled to at least two delegates (and every party delegation must be gender balanced). The council elects the committee and handles applications for membership; it also decides on organisational matters and makes political statements on current affairs.

The EGP Committee is elected by the Council and consists of nine members, including two spokespersons (male/female), a secretary general and a treasurer. The term for the committee members is three years. The committee members from Spring 2015 are co-chairs Monica Frassoni (Italy) and Reinhard Bütikofer (Germany); Gwendoline Delbos-Corfield (France), Steve Emmott (UK), Panu Laturi (Finland), Lena Lindström (Sweden), Saraswasti Matthieu (Belgium), Maria Peteinaki (Greece) and Mar Garcia Sanz (Spain/Catalonia), who in 2014 was elected as secretary general, replacing Jacqueline Cremers (Netherlands). Thus there is a female majority; there is also, however, a strong dominance of North Western Greens.

There are a number of networks and working groups affiliated to the EGP, including a Gender network and a network for Green seniors. There are also regional networks, such as the Balkan Greens, Baltic Greens, etc. The liveliest of the affiliated organisations of the European Green cooperation is probably the Federation of Young European Greens, FYEG. Originally most Green parties hesitated to start youth branches, because it was assumed that everybody, irrespective of sex, age, etc, should work together. But it soon became clear that teenagers can have apprehensions about working politically in the same structures as their parents. Some parties allowed youth groups, and in 1988 the FYEG was established. It now has 44 member organisations and a lively programme.

The CoEG has held five congresses: Liège in 1984, Dover in 1985, Stockholm in 1987, Antwerpen in 1988 and Paris in 1989. There have been nine secretary generals of the EFGP and the EGP: Leo Cox Belgium (1993-94); Anne de Boer, the Netherlands (1994); Ralph Monö, Sweden (1994-99), Marian Coyne, Scotland (1999), Niki Körtvelyessy, UK (1999), Arnold Cassola, Malta (1999-2006), Juan Behrend, Germany (2006-9), Jacqueline Cremers, the Netherlands (2010-2014), and Mar Garcia Sanz, Spain (2015-present).

The EFGP held 15 Council meetings between 1994 and 2003, and four congresses: founding congress in Majvik, Finland, 18-20 June 1993, first congress in Vienna, 21-23 June 1996, second congress in Paris, 26-28 February 1999, and third congress Berlin, 17-19 May 2002.

The EGP held 22 Council meetings between 2004 and May 2015, and four congresses: founding congress in Rome, 20-22 February 2004, second congress in Geneva, 13-14 October 2006, third congress in Brussels, 27-28 March 2009, and fourh congress in Paris, 11-13 November 2011.

The Green European Foundation (GEF) is an independent body based upon national Green foundations and think-tanks, financed by the European Union. GEF produces many reports, arranges seminars, and publishes the *Green European Journal*.[43]

As of January 2015 EGP has 39 full member parties in 34 countries (with two members in five countries), associate members in three countries (one of which also has a full member party), and candidate members in three countries (one of which also has a full member). Thus there are 45 Green parties from 38 European countries affiliated to the EGP. In addition there are Green or semi-Green parties in another nine countries, most of which have the ambition of becoming EGP members (for details of the parties, see the Appendix). Thus, out of the 47 member states of the Council of Europe (CoE), only one has no Green or semi-Green party (San Marino), while the non-CoE-member Kosovo has a Green party. If only the parties with some formal affiliation to EGP are taken into consideration, it can be concluded that there are Green parties in 80% of the states of Europe (defined as member states of the CoE). If the other Green parties are taken into consideration the European coverage increases to close to 100%.

Figure 9   Green members of the European Parliament on a street demonstration, 1998. From the left: The author, Heidi Hautala (Finland), Magda Alvoet (Belgium), Wolfgang Kreissl-Dörfler (Germany), Johannes Voggenhuber (Austria), Wolfgang Ullman (Germany). Photo: unknown assistant of the Greens in the European Parliament.

THE GREENS IN THE EUROPEAN PARLIAMENT

Since 1984 there have always been Greens in the European Parliament, usually around 40, plus some independents or others to make up a parliamentary group. Following the election of 2014, the Green/EFA group currently has 50 members, out of which seven belong to the regionalist group EFA/European Free Alliance, while five are independent. Thirty-eight are elected as members of Green parties. There are Green MPs in 23 European national parliaments (including Catalonia, Scotland and Northern Ireland). The strongest parties, when their number of MEPs is estimated as percentage of the total number of MEPs from their country, are:

1. Miljöpartiet, Sweden, 20%.
2. Die Grünen, Austria, 16.7%.

3. Dei Greng, Luxemburg, 16.6%.
4. Die Grünen, Germany, 11.4%.
5. EELV, France, 8.1%.

If instead the percentage of national MPs (out of the total number of seats in respective parliaments) is estimated, the rank order looks a little different:

1. Die Grünen, Austria, 13.1%.
2. Dei Greng, Luxemburg, 10%.
3. Die Grünen, Germany, 9.9%.
4. Miljöpartiet, Sweden, 7.1%.
5. Socialist People's Party, Denmark, 6.7%.

Some countries such as the UK and France are hampered by their majority election system when it comes to this type of estimation.

THE IMPACT OF THE EUROPEAN GREENS

For at least 25 years political scientists have followed and tried to understand the Green political phenomenon, mostly based upon studies of European Green parties. One of the most knowledgeable researchers on Green parties, Wolfgang Rüdig, has reacted against the unwillingness among many of his colleagues to perceive the Greens as something more than just another type of protest against the power elite. Already in 1990 he suggested that the main engine driving the Greens is what they say it is – the new 'ecological cleavages'.[44] One more traditional researcher, Russell J. Dalton, after having talked to Green representatives in a dozen European countries at the beginning of the 1990s, drew the conclusion that 'we think it unlikely that ecologists will be agents for rapid or radical social change ... rather than transforming political systems they will reform them'.[45] At the end of the '90s Elizabeth Blomberg was slightly more positive, noting that the 'greening of politics is now an established phenomenon of Western European political systems', but she also claimed that 'as a group working together the success of the Greens has been strictly limited'.[46] In the early 2000s, John Burchell made a comparative analysis of the Swedish Miljöpartiet, the French Les Verts, the German Die Grünen and the UK Greens.[47] His general conclusion was that where the 1980s had been formative, the 1990s had seen a setback:

> Green parties have clearly changed their organisational structures and, in some cases, have taken on board more 'traditional' approaches. As with the German Greens, all three parties have become more 'professional-

ised' in certain respects, such as those concerning spokespersons and the weakening of the rotation principle. However the Green parties still maintain a distinctive approach to party organisation, participation and democracy.

Burchell, like all other researchers, finds that despite adaptive moves there is no 'evidence for assimilation of the Greens into established party frameworks'. 'The party organisations still attempt to incorporate the values and ideas of the "new politics" such as decentralisation, anti-professionalism and participation'.

Finally, a major study in 2008 of 13 Green parties in Western Europe, the USA, Australia and New Zealand, comes to the conclusion that while there is no doubt most of the parties studied have gone through an adaption process, this 'has not killed grass-roots democracy'. While the report admits that the 'system' has partly succeeded in transforming the Green parties, they have managed to

cling to some specific grass-roots democratic and power-sharing traits, albeit moderating them: collective leadership – even though it is now reduced to more concentrated versions, such as a pair of (male and female) party 'co-presidents' – direct intervention of rank-and-file members at the national level, limitations on simultaneous position-holding and of salaries for apparatus leaders as for MPs. Thus they now find themselves in some sort of intermediate, or perhaps even 'schizophrenic' position – we used the image of 'centaurs', with professional-electoral, efficiency-seeking heads, but still amateur-activist, participation-seeking bodies.

The overall conclusion of this research report is that 'Green parties will likely remain a case apart for quite a while.'[48]

THE GREEN IMPACT WORLDWIDE

Even the most critical observer would probably have to agree that Greens worldwide have had an impact in at least the following aspects:

1. The most obvious and important impact has of course had to do with *environmental considerations*. Every type of pollution and destruction of the environment in countries with a Green party will now not only be met by demonstrations and protests but will also carry the risk that the politicians responsible may lose votes in the subsequent election. Scores of environmental laws have been passed either under pressure from Green parties or directly pushed through by Green ministers.

2. The insight that *fossil fuels must be replaced by renewables, not by nuclear energy*, has been strengthened by the presence of Green parties. Out of 17 European countries with nuclear power, only five had any new reactor under construction in August 2014. Out of the majority of states without nuclear energy, only Belarus had a reactor under construction. Nobody can deny that the presence of Green parties has contributed to stopping plans in countries like Austria and Italy for the introduction of nuclear energy. In Germany the Greens were the original driving force behind the ongoing total dismantling of nuclear energy. In Finland the Greens, by twice quitting governments over decisions to build new reactors, have guaranteed that the issue isn't buried under the silence of the traditional power elite. In France and Belgium and several other countries Greens are also guaranteeing that the nuclear issue remains a political issue. In Sweden the Greens have succeeded in halting plans to reopen new reactors, and in Switzerland and the Netherlands similar plans have been shelved because of the existence of Green parties in parliaments.

3. The *practical implementation by Greens of feminist values and gender balance* establishes a model that others are tempted by or find it difficult to avoid. Compared to other political groupings, females are generally in the majority among the Greens. However, there are differences between the world regions. In Western Europe, 12 parties are led by co-presidents (in one case, Switzerland, by two women), six have a female chair, seven a male chair. Among the former communist states of Eastern and Central Europe only four parties are led by co-chairs, three by a female chair, 13 by a male chair. The Latvian Green Party is probably the most male dominated, with two male chair persons and no woman either as MP or as member of the Board. However, according to the Rule book of the EGP (#23.1) 'The European Green Party promotes and encourages female and male participation on all political levels. As long as female participation has not reached 50% the European Green Party will make an extra effort to achieve equal gender balance throughout the Party and the bodies of the Party.'

In the Asia-Pacific Region there are three parties with gender-balanced co-chairs, one with a female chair, and 11 with male chairpersons. In Africa and Latin America the system of gender-balanced co-chairs seems to be rare. With the exception of a few cases with prominent female leaders, as in Madagascar, Mali, Morocco, Uganda and Bolivia, the leadership of Green parties is dominated by men. However, in the AGF structure, including the six regions, as well as the in the FPVA, the level of gender balance is high.

4. In several countries Greens have acted as a *brake on other parties tempted to cooperate politically with xenophobic populist parties*. The Belgian Greens refused to include xenophobes in government negotiations; the GroenLinks has, despite a tough environment, remained the most pro-immigration party in the Netherlands; Die Grünen were the promoters of new citizenship legislation

which benefits immigrants; in Switzerland the Greens stand strong against xenophobic populist trends; and in Sweden Miljöpartiet made an important agreement with the right-wing government on liberalised immigration rules in order to keep the xenophobic Sweden Democrats from having any influence on immigration policy.

5. Greens have been active in enhancing *equal rights for sexual minorities*. This has been especially important in less secularised countries where Greens have taken considerable risks in defending the rights of LGBT people. In France a Green MP administered the first gay wedding. There are also a high number of Green MPs present at Pride parades, enhancing the legitimacy of such events to the extent that sometimes even mainstream politicians dare to take part.

THE GREENS ARE BECOMING GLOBAL

Green party politics is becoming less dominated by European Green parties. The growth of Green parties in other parts of the world has accelerated in the third millennium. If this century is to be a Green one, as predicted by Hannes Alfvén at the Stockholm Congress in 1987, it must be globally Green.

4

GREEN POLICIES: BUILDING STONES OF A GREEN IDEOLOGY

What do Greens have in common?[1] Do they have anything important in common that differentiates them from other types of political parties? Do they have the same values, the same kind of proposals on how to solve problems? The following answer is partly based upon a reading of some 50 Green platforms and programmes.[2] But other documents have also been consulted in order to enlarge the analysis of some pivotal Green issues.

THE WORLD ACCORDING TO THE GREENS

Environmental catastrophe

Almost unanimously Greens have a rather bleak perception of the state of the world. Primarily they see all kinds of environmental threats towards mankind and all life on Earth. It is the relationship between Nature/Life/Ecosystem and human activities that are the focus. There is no difference in this respect between parties from rich developed countries and parties from poor developing countries. In particular a text from the Somali Greens disproves the notion that considering environmental problems should be some kind of luxury for the rich:

> One unfortunate anguish that will face Somalis long after a solution is found for the current political crisis is the damage that has been done to the environment of the nation ... people have turned to all kinds of illegal and damaging activities [such as] the burning of trees and forests for charcoal, the poaching of wild animals for leather, and the export of all kinds of animals for foreign currency. Some of the current environmental problems that Somalia faces are: the use of contaminated water which contributes to health problems; deforestation; overgrazing; soil erosion; desertification; merciless poaching of wildlife; recurring droughts; and frequent dust storms over the northern and eastern plains in summer. Somalia is also one of the

uppermost nations listed as a site for the dumping of hazardous nuclear and chemical waste by industrialized nations.

The most common Green description of the present situation of the world and human life is that it is full of hazards due to climate change, radiation, pesticides, desertification, the manipulation of genes, etc. The Bulgarian Greens put it dramatically: 'Extinction or reform!' The message is clear: Life itself is threatened. This leads to an important question: Whose life?

Population explosion

Population explosion has sometimes been a sensitive issue for Greens. Does it in fact exist? Around 1800 there were 1 billion human beings. It took another 123 years to reach the second billion. Since then the increase has been rapid, and the UN forecast for 2050 is 9 billion. The most well-known dystopia based upon an uncontrolled increase in the world population is Paul Ehrlich's *Population Bomb*.[3] It is full of predictions which have not come true, such as the disappearance of the United Kingdom, and global famines. Despite such snags Ehrlich still keeps to his basic conviction, while opponents ridicule him by asking if he is hungry.[4] In any case, it appears obvious that the more humans there are the more environmental space will be needed. As we are already overexploiting Mother Earth, it is correct to say that population increase is per se anti-ecological. At the same time, having children is a basic human right and an important aspect of the quality of life. Thus the Green response cannot involve anything as extreme as forced sterilisation, nor even imposed limitations of the number of children a family is entitled to have.

In a Green manifesto from 1988, Sandy Irvine and Alec Ponton stated that 'There is a happy relation between women's liberation and population control.'[5] And indeed, women's liberation is the only lasting method for keeping the population stable. But the manifesto also proposes a number of additional measures, some of which are positive, for example free family planning, more research into new methods of contraception, the right to free abortion; however, there are other proposals that must be rejected, for example, a bonus for not giving birth or for sterilisation, tax benefits for those with fewer than two children, withdrawal of benefits for a third child, a ban on infertility treatment or surrogate motherhood. These proposals are inhuman and also unnecessary. Some of those countries where women's liberation has won major victories are countries with no natural increase of the population.

Humanity as starting point

The Austrian Greens state that Greens have a non-anthropocentric perspective, in which the wider ecosystem is the starting point rather than human beings.

Quite a few parties mention other threatened 'groups' like animals. Most Greens mention the need for animal 'protection', and only a few use the terminology of 'animal rights' (such as the Swedish and Norwegian Greens and the Green Left of Netherlands) or 'respect for animals' (Catalonian Greens). Despite strong biocentric feelings among Greens, an idea that appears in some versions of 'deep ecology', claiming that human beings are 'only' one life-form among others, has not been taken on board by Green parties. On the contrary, Green parties in their practical politics usually adopt a humanity-centred outlook: *We are threatened when the Ecosystem is threatened. That is why we must reform.* (See also the paragraph on *deep ecology* in Chapter 2).

Scarcity of justice, solidarity, equality, democracy

While offering more or less elaborate or apocalyptic descriptions of the environmental hazards that surround us, Green programmes are usually less direct in describing the social, economic, cultural, democratic, judicial and other aspects of their countries or the world. An exception may be the Moldavian Greens, who take as their starting point the fact that Moldavia has the lowest score on the UNDP Human Development Index of all European countries. Most Greens, however, have clear ideas about the state of affairs in political fields other than the environment and ecology. But this is treated more by proposals to solve existing problems than by direct descriptions of the situation that needs to be changed. When the Colombian Greens present an ethical code for politicians as a major demand it is easy to infer that ethics is a rare commodity in Colombian politics. The requirements that are listed – the primacy of general interest over individual, altruism in political activity, honesty in public service, moral responsibility of the political leader – imply that exactly these characteristics are lacking in Colombia. And when almost every Green party explicitly demands 'social justice' and 'global solidarity' it must be inferred that the Green perception is that social justice and global solidarity do not exist to an acceptable extent in our present world.

Almost all parties have gender equality as a main demand, but it is the Scandinavian parties that use the toughest language in demanding 'feminist' policies, despite the fact that women in the Nordic countries are hardly the most discriminated against. Many programmes (though far from all) also include sexuality among the aspects where diversity must be promoted. But the strongest and most explicit wordings about the rights of gays and lesbians are found in some European, American and Pacific Green programmes, while African and Asian Greens more often keep silent. At the same time no Green party explicitly expresses anything against equal rights for homosexuals; and gender equality can be found in Green programmes in all regions.

Environment and ecology first

It is obvious that almost all Green parties are rooted in an awareness of the environmental threats against humanity and life. Greens are also aware of huge social injustice globally and nationally. Very often they have doubts about the quality of democracy in their countries. Concerning the formulation of what are the main problems of humanity today, there is a rather coherent and common outlook among Greens from all over the world. The Greens are absolutely not 'single issue' parties. Some parties are keen to emphasise this even in their slogans, like Belgian Ecolo: 'A greener earth, a more just world.' The Chilean Greens begin their programme with the statement that 'the ecologist is anybody who supports a socio-cultural-economic organisation that permits human beings to fulfil themselves in harmonious balance with their fellow beings in a responsible relation with the environment they live in'.

But the starting point and the priority is, almost without exception, the environmental crisis in all its aspects. As the Canadian Greens explain: 'Putting environment first in our platform makes sense, because our environment is at the heart of our well-being.' Belgian Groen promises their voters: 'Towards an ecological change.' The German Grünen say that 'the environment makes the difference'. Some new and smaller parties have not developed much beyond this 'environmentalist' one-dimensionality. All established Green parties, though, have fully-fledged programmes with detailed proposals concerning everything from maternity leave to foreign policy.

Whom do Greens blame?

In general, Green programmes can be weak in explanations. Instead of analysis very often there is a kind of 'blaming', pointing at somebody or rather something, an activity or a trend, which is accused of being guilty. Seven major 'scapegoats' have been constructed on the basis of Green programmes. Number one is growth/industrial society/productivism, which means the dominant concentration upon the maximum production of material commodities. The Italian Greens put it bluntly: 'A Green is someone who sees in economic growth the original cause of the degradation of our planet'.

The second most frequently identified 'scapegoat' is closely related to the first: economic globalisation/neoliberalism. The texts of the French Greens in particular are full of rhetoric against these phenomena. The Turkish Greens demand a 'global struggle against capitalism and neoliberalism'. And the Russian Greens blame the extreme neoliberalism of the 1990s for many of the problems facing their country. The Norwegian Miljøpartiet goes rather a long way in demanding 'decapitalisation of the means of production   in a way that transfers the right of property into forms where it cannot be sold or bought'. The

Philippine Greens are also far-reaching when they state that 'all land belongs to the community occupying it, never to individuals'. Most Green parties explicitly accept private ownership and the market economy – less as a matter of principle, more because such an economy is considered the least bad system known. And almost all Greens emphasise that the market must not be totally free, but must be subject to tight controls and restrictions. Only among some of the Eastern European Greens can a more explicitly positive evaluation of basic aspects of liberal economy be observed, such as the Ukrainian Greens who state that 'Private property is the ground for democracy, the basis for economic progress and citizens' social protection.'

The third 'scapegoat' is again related: big business/transnational corporations. The Swiss Greens demand that the secretive banking system of their country should be abolished: 'End to the hunt for maximum profits!'

Many Green parties, of course, blame humanity as such, like the UK Greens who state that 'It is human activity more than anything else which is threatening the well-being of the environment on which we depend.' Other more or less frequently invoked scapegoats, directly or indirectly mentioned in Green programmes, are commercialism/consumerism, colonialism, and central state abuses.

This reveals, despite some variations, a unified Green outlook concerning the causes of the major problems facing our world. Humanity is to blame – not the 'naked ape' but the human being in his or her capacity as a greedy and materialistic producer and consumer who seems to appreciate only those things that can be valued in terms of money. This type of system – involving neoliberalism, capitalism, economic globalisation, unrestricted markets, profit-seeking, productivism – not only causes an ecological collapse, it even fails to give human beings what they want – happiness, security, health, satisfaction. But Greens don't believe that the alternative is some kind of traditional socialism. Most imply this without saying so explicitly in their programmes. The Brazilian Partido Verde, however, says it clearly: 'PV does not accept the narrow polarisation between left and right, we are in front.'

Are there common Green values?

Green programmes don't usually start with descriptions of problems and analyses of causes, but with values. Some Green parties are very explicit about this. The basic principles of the Mexican Greens have a special attraction: 'Amor, Justicia, Libertad' (Love, Justice, Freedom). Short, efficient and to the point! The Swedish Miljöpartiet has tried to concentrate its programme in three 'solidarities': with animals, nature and the ecosystem; with future generations; and with all the other people in the world. New Zealand Greens have four basic values: ecological wisdom, social responsibility, appropriate decision-making and non-violence. Die Grünen of Austria have six basic principles: ecology, solidarity, self-rule, grassroots democracy, non-violence and feminism. Dei Greng of Luxemburg adheres to the same basics as the Austrian Greens, adding another three: structural change of the economy, equal participation of immigrants, and the promotion of an ecological and social Europe. And the US Greens have their ten key values: grassroots democracy, social justice and equal opportunity, ecological wisdom, non-violence, decentralisation, community-based economy, feminism and gender equity, respect for diversity, personal and global responsibility, future focus and sustainability. The Global Greens and the European Greens have adopted similar catalogues of basic values. Based upon all these programmes and platforms 14 basic Green principles have been extracted. They are listed in order of their frequency in the documents studied by the present author, but no exact figures are given because it is sometimes difficult to judge if a value is present when the exact word is not mentioned:

1. Sustainability/circulation economy
2. Gender equality/feminism
3. Non-violence
4. Ecological wisdom
5. Social justice
6. Participatory/grassroots democracy
7. International cooperation
8. Global solidarity
9. Life quality, not quantity
10. Human rights/freedom
11. Biodiversity
12. Cultural diversity
13. Fair trade
14. Self-reliance

WHAT DO GREENS PROPOSE?

There is, then, a rather widely shared value base among Greens. But what about policies? Here, rather randomly, one or several policy issues for each of the 14 basic principles have been chosen for further elaboration, sometimes based upon additional documentation.

Sustainability/circulation economy

a) *Nuclear/fossil fuel/renewable energy.* Not one of the programmes studied even covertly hints that nuclear energy might be acceptable as a replacement for fossil fuels. Several parties also have fixed dates for an exit from the oil dependence. The Czech Greens put rejection of oil as one of their very first priorities for the modernisation of Czech society. All Greens demand a switch towards renewable energy.

In Germany nuclear power is being phased out by a non-socialist government. Following Fukushima, even conservative politicians who were previously pro-nuclear power are recognising that it is an impossible form of energy in a democratic society. Indeed, even within German industry, insight into the unacceptable risks of nuclear power has led to a reappraisal. The head of Siemens has announced his company's decision 'to completely abandon nuclear power'.[6] However, in several EU countries (and elsewhere) the ruling elites have reacted as if the German decision does not affect them. But why should Germans accept that some states, like Finland, are expanding their nuclear power, thereby exposing the whole of the EU to risks?

b) *Organic agriculture/food quality.* This issue is very close to the hearts of most Greens. Some relate it to a revival of rural cultures and lifestyles. Several Greens are fond of the concept of *permaculture*, which is an integrated system of permanent agriculture, designed to enrich rather than destroy local ecosystems.

c) *Reduced transport.* Most Greens demand a shift of emphasis from road to rail. But some consider that transport as such causes the basic problem and must be reduced even when it becomes less polluting. Greens from countries where a lack of transportation is a major problem are more nuanced, such as the Benin Greens: 'To be able to travel in all Africa, locally as well as internationally, the Beninians should be able to dream about bicycles, normal trains, express trains or air planes, under comfortable and secure conditions.'

d) *Enviromental taxes/polluter pays principle.* Such demands are present in most Green programmes and policies.

Gender equality/feminism

a) *Right to abortion.* Most parties are in favour, none openly against. However some are silent on the matter. In connection with the EGP 2014 Election Manifesto the following remark is found on the EGP homepage: 'Please note, the Irish Green Party/Comhaontas Glas was unable to agree to, and Alternattiva Demokratika registered their objection to, the following: "Sexual and reproductive rights are essential elements of human dignity. We Greens defend the right of self-determination over our own bodies." It is noteworthy, in these times of allegations that Islam is more intolerant and reactionary than other religions, for example Christianity, that the necessity to betray basic principles of women's rights by such a concession to traditionalist and religious feelings was not felt by any of the EGP-affiliated parties working in overwhelmingly Muslim countries – Albania, Azerbaijan and Turkey – but by two old and relatively well-established parties in countries with Catholic populations.

b) *Prostitution.* Everybody wants to fight against trafficking, but some Greens (Netherlands, Germany) are in favour of the 'legalisation' of prostitution as such, in order to transform it into a regular profession. They believe that prostitutes will thereby become free of the mafia and obtain more social security. Others (like Miljöpartiet) on the contrary support the Swedish law (1999) criminalising the buyers of sexual services (most often men), but not the sellers (most often women). In 2009 Iceland and Norway introduced similar legislation and discussions about doing so are ongoing in several countries, for example France.

Non-violence

a) *Disarmament.* Almost all Greens are in favour of disarmament globally and nationally. Most are also in favour of abolishing general conscription.

b) *Military intervention only with a UN mandate.* Most parties accept this principle. However the Serbian Greens in their programme of 2001 draw attention to the fact that 'the position of Greens in FRY [Federal Republic of Yugoslavia] during the second half of 1999 and during all of 2000 was additionally complicated by being unconsciously connected by citizens of FRY with those European Greens that voted in favour of military intervention of NATO against FRY'.

c) *Restrictions on arms exports.* All parties are either in favour or silent. EU Greens want the EU code to have a stronger legal force.[7]

d) *No to military alliance/NATO.* Most Greens in NATO countries seem to accept the status quo, while Norwegian and Portuguese Greens consider leaving the pact. Greek Greens demand the 'cessation of dependence of the EU on NATO'. Croatian Greens say 'No to NATO, no to military alliances'. Greens from neutral countries (Sweden, Finland, Austria, Ukraine, Switzerland, Malta) reject joining NATO. The Georgian Greens also reject NATO membership. Australian and Brazilian Greens question their countries' military relations to the USA, but some Greens in new NATO countries, like Latvia, were in favour of their country joining.

One of the origins of the Green parties was the peace movement. Many Greens were pacifists, refusing to serve in the military. Today some Greens have accepted military interventions and consider terrorism to be a new phenomenon which can only be contained by violent military means. Is there then any difference between the Green position and the position of any ruling elite? We can check by asking a series of questions:

1. Is it legitimate to respond violently if one's country is attacked by the military forces of another country?
2. Is it legitimate, after a terrorist attack, to attack another country suspected of harboring those responsible for the deed?
3. Is it legitimate to use armed force in a struggle of national liberation?
4. Is it legitimate to use armed force while resisting a foreign occupation?
5. Is it legitimate to intervene in sovereign states by force to prevent them from attacking other states?
6. Is it legitimate to intervene by force to protect an oppressed population against oppression by its own rulers?
7. Is it legitimate to intervene by force against a sovereign, non-democratic state in order to effect 'regime change' and install democracy?
8. Is it legitimate to support, with arms or military personnel, a legitimate struggle of liberation or resistance?

A traditional radical pacifist would answer no to all questions. A classical left-winger would probably reply yes to 1, 3, 4 and 8, possibly also 6, and no to the rest. A traditional right-winger would reply yes to all, except 3, 4 and 8. What about the Green reaction? The Green replies most in line with original pacifist Green ideals would probably be something like the following:

1. Yes, in the unlikely event of an outright attack by the military forces of another state, it would be legitimate to respond with military force. But not only violently. There should also be a pre-planned strategy for civil resistance.
2. No, not with military force or an attack upon other countries. A terror attack is a crime and should be dealt with by police not military means.
3. It depends – every case must be dealt with separately. ETA's violence was not legitimate, because in Spain it was possible to work for the independence of the Basque country through peaceful, democratic methods. What about an armed liberation struggle in Tibet? It may come, but it would be a pity if the radical pacifism of the Dalai Lama doesn't achieve a result by itself.
4. Yes, armed resistance against an occupation is legitimate, but this doesn't mean that it is always appropriate. In France, Norway, etc., it was legitimate to conduct an armed struggle against the Nazi occupation. The Palestinians have the same right in resisting the illegal Israeli occupation; despite this, the internationally acknowledged organisation of all Palestinians, the PLO, has chosen a non-violent liberation strategy. The choice is up to the occupied people.
5. No, not without a mandate from the UN. No state may start a 'preventive' war unilaterally.

6. Yes, given that the UN-adopted responsibility to protect may make a 'humanitarian' intervention legitimate, but only with specific UN mandate.

7. No, real democracy can only by established by the people themselves. The experience of Afghanistan is devastating.

8. Yes. To give one example: the Swedish Greens, as part of the government, have supported the deployment of Swedish military instructors in Kurdistan to assist the Kurdish forces fighting Islamic State in Syria and Iraq. Unfortunately nothing indicates that any non-violent approach would be efficient against the brutal and murderous methods of IS.

Ecological wisdom

This value is the most important basis for most Green policies. Here we will mention only two important principles:

a) *A total ban or restrictions on genetically manipulated organisms (GMOs), permanent chemicals, hormones and antibiotics in meat.* Such demands exist in some form in most programmes.

b) *Precautionary principle.* This is included in most programmes.

Social justice

a) *Basic income.* Greens generally dismiss the 'work moralism' which is strong in traditional parties. The basic Green belief is that everybody has a right to a reasonable standard of living, irrespective not only of sex, race, etc., but also irrespective of work. Hence the idea of a general basic income as a right for everybody. Several parties demand (or have demanded) some form of basic income, including Brazil (*imposta negativa*), Germany (*Grüne Grundsicherung*), Norway (*samfunnslønn*), Finland and Sweden (*medborgarlön*).

One of several proposals for a basic income was put forward by the French economist André Gorz.[8] It has been argued that a kind of basic income exists in welfare states, where everybody is guaranteed a minimum standard. But then usually an application must be made and control by the social authorities must be accepted. The radical idea of a basic income is that everybody, as a basic right without any conditions or controls, should receive a certain amount every month. The counter-arguments are well-known: basic income will cause an enormous circulation of money, from taxpayers, via the state, back to the citizens, most of whom will neither gain nor lose. Why then not concentrate on making the rich pay higher taxes in order to develop the social welfare system for the poor and those in need?

Osmo Soininvaara, Finnish Minister of Health 2000–2002 and leader of the Finnish Greens 2001–2005, has been champion of basic income, writing a book on the subject[9] and introducing a citizen's initiative. According to the proposal all other transfer payments would be unnecessary, because every person would automatically receive enough to cover basic living expenses. The exact amount has been much debated. The Finnish Greens have suggested 440 euros per month. The finance tycoon Björn Wahlroos, who has come out in favour of basic income, has calculated that to completely eliminate poverty, everyone should receive 1,166 euros monthly.[10]

A Basic Income Earth Network was established in 1986 to support the idea of basic income and exchange of ideas.[11]

b) *Public ownership of social essentials*. Some Green parties maintain that social essentials should be publicly owned or controlled. In the 1990s, the Swedish Greens actively campaigned for 'private alternatives', like cooperative 'free schools' and healthcare centres, to be financed by taxpayer's money. However, having seen such reforms being usurped by risk capitalists and schools and healthcare centres being transformed into objects of financial speculation, the party repented, publicly apologised for having been naive, and is now demanding an end to profit-making from publicly supported schools and healthcare centres. This demonstrates how difficult it is for local initiatives to remain clean, idealistic and ecological, when not defended by a strong welfare state against the efforts of speculative capitalism to distort and exploit whatever can be transformed into a profit-making business. In a report by the Green European Foundation it is shown that the entry of profit-making companies into the welfare and education sectors has increased all over Europe. Most Green parties oppose this development, but in different ways.[12]

Participatory/direct/grassroots democracy

Most Greens are dissatisfied with representative democracy, and would like more *direct democracy*. Nevertheless, parliamentary democracy is accepted and reforms are proposed, such as *proportional representation* (where it is not already in place), more *referenda*, a *lowering of the voting age* (16 or 17 years), and *ethical rules* for politicians. One aspect of direct democracy is *civil disobedience*, which some Greens want to legalise under certain conditions.

International cooperation

a) *A stronger, more federal, and greener EU*. Several European Greens express general satisfaction with the EU, like the German Greens who say that the EU 'is a success that has brought us 50 years of peace, security and welfare'. Others, like the French Greens, want a stronger EU, but on condition that it makes possible a more social and ecological Europe. Irish Greens oppose the militarisation of the EU. Greek Greens demand a 'new beginning for a Constitutional Treaty without the neo-libertarian suppressive, militaristic, anti-environmental clauses of the previous plan'. (See also 'Greens and EEC/EU: from opposition to jubilation to hesitation' in Chapter 3).

b) *A stronger, reformed UN*. Unanimously Greens are in favour.

Global solidarity

Global solidarity is basic to most of the Green programmes. Several parties from the developed countries demand a *Tobin tax*, increased *assistance to developing countries*, and the *cancelling of debts*.

All Green parties from immigrant countries have a basically *positive attitude towards immigration*, expressed by the Canadian Greens when they talk about the 'incredible human potential that 300,000 new Canadians bring to the country each year'.

Life quality, not quantity

a) *Restrictive or liberal drug policy?* Most programmes don't mention this issue, but those that do are profoundly split. Though all programmes emphasise taking a humanitarian approach towards drug-abusing individuals, there is a deep division concerning the availability of drugs. Some parties (e.g. in Scandinavia) advocate restrictions, such as a ban on all narcotics (including cannabis) and limits on the sale of alcohol. Others (Netherlands, Austria, France, etc.) advocate legalisation of 'soft' narcotics in order to break the power of mafias, but 'freedom' arguments are also presented. A special case is Zambia where the Greens demand the legalisation of cannabis for its potential to generate export incomes.

b) *An alternative index to GDP*. All Greens are dissatisfied with GDP as an index and several parties mention the need for other ways to measure 'progress' and development (see Chapter 2, 'Ecological economics').

c) *Shorter working hours*. This is central to several Green programmes, all of which agree with the Albanian Green formulation: 'To work less so that all can work.' The French Greens secured shorter working hours during their first period in the government. There are two main reasons for decreasing work time: 1) To make room for more people to find work – according to a report from the Green European Foundation 'no European country managed to achieve a rate of unemployment below 6% without having a mix of at least 25% part-time workers, with average working hours not exceeding 21 hours …

if we reject both massive part-time work and unemployment, the solution is to reduce full-time working hours'.[13] 2) To increase quality of life. The Swedish Greens managed to introduce a right for anyone to a paid for 'free year' if an unemployed replacement could be found. It was very popular, but was abolished after the right-wing victory in the elections of 2006. Belgian Groen has proposed something similar in the form of a time-insurance policy (tijdverzekering).

d) *Anti-commercialism, publicity tax, Green consumerism.* Demands for a curb on advertising were strong in the infancy of Green parties, and several Green programmes still contain demands for limitations on publicity, especially for certain commodities like tobacco, or products directed at children. Some Greens demand the introduction or augmentation of taxation on advertising. However, it is also claimed that any intervention into free publicity is tantamount to a limitation on freedom of expression. Some put their faith in 'Green consumerism', partly inspired by the classic *Green Consumer Guide*,[14] and no doubt ecologically conscious consumers play an important role and are increasing in number. An early argument against Green consumerism was that to be a perfect consumer 'a shopper should have to be free to spend all day going from one shop to the other'.[15] Green consumerism may help by steering production towards less damaging products, but as long as the total amount of consumption increases, it is hard to believe that the pressure on the environmental space can be curbed only by an increase of ecologically conscious consumption.

Human rights/freedom

Most Green programmes elaborate on all kinds of threats to personal freedom, old and new, not least the technological controls that threaten individual integrity. But only about a third of the programmes studied explicitly mention *equal rights for homosexuals*. For some parties this is a very important issue, such as Verds d'Andorra, whose programme has a special chapter on 'sexual freedoms'. Others are silent. But no Green party demands any kind of discrimination against homosexuals.

While most Greens emphasise the importance of *media pluralism*, without restrictions imposed by the government, some also warn against other kinds of threat to real freedom of expression, like the Polish Greens who state that democracy is 'threatened by manipulation of public opinion by media control by interest groups, political populism and corruption'.

Biodiversity

a) *No patenting of life.* This is a demand in most Green programmes.

b) *Animal rights*. Animal 'protection' is a common demand, but animal 'rights' are mentioned in only a few programmes. (See also Chapter 2, 'Deep ecology'.)

c) *Considerate hunting*. Most Green programmes don't mention hunting at all. Those that do are split. Some are in favour of 'sustainable and environmentally friendly hunting' (Latvia), while others are critical of hunting lobbies (France) and demand more restrictions (Malta). In some parts of Sweden local popular opinion would prefer to annihilate all wolves, because they eat the elks and kill hunting dogs, while Greens want to maintain a sufficient number to guarantee survival without inbreeding.

Cultural diversity

a) *Special policy for national minorities*. All parties with considerable national minorities demand more rights and services for them (New Zealand/Maoris, Australia/Aborigines, Canada/Aborigines, Czech Republic/Roma, Norway/Sami, Brazil/Aborigines, etc.).

b) *Integration for new minorities*. Most Green programmes talk about diversity and demand that cultural differences must be respected. At the same time human rights must be upheld. Some parties want to ban 'forced marriages' and 'veils'. The Dutch Green Left says 'live together, go to school together', and demands that children of all religions and ethnic groups should meet at school, while other Greens (like the Swedish Miljöpartiet) accept separate schools on religious and linguistic bases as a policy of cultural pluralism.

Fair trade

a) *Abolish or reform the International Monetary Fund, the World Bank and the World Trade Organisation?* Some Greens want to abolish one or all of these organisations, while others are satisfied to demand radical reforms. Most Greens have a sceptical attitude towards completely 'free' trade and support environmentally and socially motivated restrictions.

b) *No to the Transatlantic Trade and Investment Partnership (TTIP)*. The Greens in the European parliament have taken a position against the proposed EU-US trade and investment partnership, for reasons outlined in January 2015 by Green MEP Yannick Jadot: 'It is an opaque procedure, which can and is used by multinational corporations to whittle away EU standards and regulations across a range of policies from the environment to food safety to social protection.' Thus, from a Green perspective TTIP threatens both the environment and democracy. The investor-state dispute settlement mechanism (ISDS) may, according to the Greens, give commercial interests priority over democratic decisions made by the European and other parliaments.

Local autonomy/self-reliance

The local level is close to most Green hearts (see also Chapter 1, 'Green islands'). A special variety is *bioregionalism*, which is based upon the belief that policies should be worked out and implemented taking into account the ecological integrity of bioregions (for example areas connected by a water system). The main promoter of bioregionalism, the American writer Kirkpatrick Sale has, however, astonished many Greens by arguing that, in the name of diversity, there could be not only democratic bioregions, but also theocratic, aristocratic, oligarchical, even old-fashioned principalities.[16] Most Greens would argue that a bioregion that is not democratic has no place in the Green vision.

Andrew Dobson has made a distinction between *self-sufficiency* (a state of absolute economic independence) and *self-reliance* (a state of relative independence). He has put forward arguments against self-sufficiency, and, to a lesser extent, against self-reliance: 1) Not everything can be produced locally. 2) The solution to environmental problems requires coordination and planning. 3) Redistribution/social justice requires a central administration. Dobson remarks: 'If the market is to be fettered, who is to do the fettering?' and refers to Rousseau who in the *The Social Contract* (1762) came to the conclusion that a better society requires a Lawgiver to 'change human nature'.[17] Perhaps the aim shouldn't be to 'change human nature', which sounds like brainwashing, but in every society that takes the ecological challenge seriously it must be an aim to promote the responsible/altruistic/future-oriented aspect of humans, against their irresponsible, egoistic and short-sighted aspect.

a) *Local money.* One aspect of local self-reliance is local money. As illustrated by the ongoing euro crisis, there is an intimate relation between currency and self-determination. The recognition that adoption of the euro would entail some loss of national sovereignty was a major reason for the decisions by the UK, Denmark and Sweden not to join the Economic and Monetary Union of the EU. Since the 'no' victories in the Danish (2000) and Swedish (2003) referenda on the subject, several of the economic authorities who campaigned for a yes vote have admitted that they were wrong. While Greens in non-euro EU countries mostly reject joining the EMU, most Greens in euro countries want to keep the currency. Some believe that a common currency and local currencies can survive together. Several thousand kinds of local money are in use throughout the world. One alternative currency, not local but digital, is *bitcoin*. An aim, alongside increasing local power, is to undermine the dominance of the speculative banking and money-systems which created fictive riches out of nothing. In Greece local currencies have been established to avoid the influence of the euro. Something similar happened in Argentina in 2001, when provinces introduced their own currency in order to bypass the banks. Another example is

LETS – Local Exchange Trading Systems, which exist in many countries all over the world.[18] One argument for these local alternatives is that they allow for local economic activity despite the failure of the wider society; another is that they keep a local community's money away from the speculations of finance capital.

From a Green point of view it is obvious that the existing money-system is at the core of the ecological problem; and the euro is by no means a solution, as some believe. It may be true that a common currency abolishes the possibility of speculative trading exploiting the differences between national currencies. But the euro, like the dollar, is at the same time part of a distorted money-system that has made speculative profits possible. Local and alternative currencies are competing with the major destructive systems. The more different currencies there are, the more difficult it is for big capital to secure total control.

b) *No interest on borrowing.* This is an old demand from some 'alternative' economists, who maintain that the possibility of being paid just for owning money is a basic evil of the anti-ecological system. Quite a few systems have been established where borrowing is possible without paying a fixed percentage as interest, but sometimes other systems for 'paying' the lenders are then invented to ensure these alternative systems survive. Islamic banks have a long experience of these problems. Most Green parties don't include this type of issue in their programmes; some have done so, but then removed it after finding the practical difficulties to be considerable.[19]

TOWARDS A COMMON GREEN THINKING

As has been shown, on some points Green parties have contradictory opinions; on other issues several parties have no clear or declared position. Emphases are placed differently, and the age, size and place in the political system of each Green party will often play a role in the choice of policy. All the same, overall there is a very wide sphere of common Green thinking among political parties from places as different as Sweden and Somalia, Russia and Brazil, Taiwan and Benin. When the present author was a member of the Green group of the European Parliament (1995–2004), critics noted our differences on the issues of drugs, prostitution and the federal structure of the EU. These were real, but statistics showed that on the whole no other political grouping in the European Parliament voted together to such an extent as did the Greens.

In every democratic political group, party or movement there will be differences of opinion on certain issues. Nevertheless, there is a Green way of thinking that has proven strong enough to keep together hundreds of parties and groups, hundreds of thousands of political activists all over the globe, in a common struggle for an ecologically balanced world.

5

GREENS IN GOVERNMENTS

In some Green parties the question of whether or not to become part of a government was hot in the 1980s.[1] The most well-known example was Die Grünen, where one faction – the fundis – rejected participation in government on the grounds that Greens should not administrate an immoral system, while the other faction – the realos – actively sought government power. However, in most countries Green participation in government in the 1980s seemed utterly hypothetical.

Nonetheless, from the early 1990s up to 2015, European Green Parties have participated in government in 21 countries: Belgium, Bulgaria, Czech Republic, Denmark, Estonia, Finland, France, Georgia, Germany, Greece, Ireland, Italy, Latvia, Lithuania, Luxemburg, Poland, Romania, Slovakia, Slovenia, Sweden and Ukraine. As of January 2015 there were Green representatives in the governments of Greece, Latvia, Luxemburg and Sweden. Green Parties have also participated in governments outside Europe, for example in Burkina Faso, Senegal, Guinea-Bissau, Mauritius, Kenya, Vanuatu and Mongolia.

TYPES OF GREEN GOVERNMENTAL PARTICIPATION

Structure

The first Greens to enter a government were not the relatively strong West European veteran parties, but Greens in Central and Eastern Europe who after the collapse of the Soviet bloc were offered the portfolio of environment. Even though these parties enjoyed a short period of relative strength in 1989–90, they were not large enough to be needed to form parliamentary majorities. Instead, a Green personality – perhaps a professor of biology, agriculture or forestry – was *individually co-opted* to participate in the government. This type of governmental participation has also occurred outside Europe, for example in Kenya, where the Nobel Prize laureate Wangari Maathai (1940–2011) was Green Minister of Environment from 2003 to 2006, and Senegal, where the leader of the Green Party (FEDES), Haïdar El Ali, was appointed Minister of Environment in 2012.

Only in 1995 was a Green party able to join a government thanks to its political strength, when the Finnish Greens secured one ministerial post in a multi-party government. However, even then, the support of the Greens was not needed to ensure the government a parliamentary majority. Rather, the Greens were included in order to enable a multi-party government to survive the exit of any of the coalition partners. Such *resilience-creating participation* in government later followed in several countries, including France in 1997. However, when in 1998 Die Grünen formed a Red-Green government with the Social Democrats (SPD) their participation was needed to achieve a parliamentary majority; this could be described as a *necessity-based participation in majority government*. A further type could be called a *legitimacy-creating participation in a minority government*, which implies that the government, despite including the Greens, doesn't command a parliamentary majority; the inclusion of the Greens is thus due to a wish to secure widened support from environmentally and socially sensitive voters. One example is the Danish Socialistisk Folkeparti's participation in a centre-left three-party government from 2011 to 2014, another the Swedish Greens' coalition with the Social Democrats from October 2014. In both cases support from at least one more party was needed to secure a parliamentary majority.[2]

Political constellation

An important aspect of Green participation in government is the political constellation involved: Greens have joined *Red-Green* governments (Germany, France, Sweden, Italy and Ukraine), *centre-left* governments (Belgium, Denmark, Luxemburg), a *centre-right* government (Latvia), a broad coalition with *both right-wing and left-wing* parties (Finland), and finally a coalition with only *right-wing* parties (Czech Republic and Ireland).

Relative strengths

A relevant question is whether Greens join a government after an electoral victory or following a defeat. This aspect has no relevance in the cases of individual co-optation. In the other twelve cases, nine Green parties joined a government after an electoral success, in two cases the electoral setback was marginal (Sweden and Italy), and only in one case was the previous election a clear defeat (Denmark).

Categories

Of the Green periods in government in former communist countries, eight must be characterised as having involved *individual co-optation* (Bulgaria, Estonia,

Georgia, Lithuania, Poland, Romania, Slovakia and Slovenia). The remaining 12 parties can be divided into a number of categories (+ indicates victory, - defeat, (-) marginal defeat in previous election):

Structure:	Resilience	Necessity	Legitimacy
Constellation:			
Red-Green	1. France + Italy (-) Ukraine +	2. Germany +	3. Sweden (-)
Centre-Left		4. Luxemburg (-) Belgium +	5. Denmark -
Broad	6. Finland +		
Centre-Right		7. Latvia +	
Right	8. Czech rep +	9. Ireland +	

GREEN EXPERIENCE OF PARTICIPATION IN GOVERNMENT – BY COUNTRY
(For facts about the parties beside their participation in government, see the Appendix)

Cases of individual co-optation

Bulgaria
Several Green ministers in the 1990s had a background in the NGO Ecoglasnost. In the period 2005–2009 the Green Party was part of the ruling coalition. The vice chairman, Dimitar Bongalov, was appointed Deputy Minister of Justice, but lost the confidence of the party in 2007 and was replaced by Ilonka Ivancheva-Raychinova. However, the Greens left the government prematurely because of political disagreements.

Estonia
In April 1989, the Estonian Greens had 12% support in opinion polls and a year later their leader, Toomas Frey, was appointed Minister of Environment. After independence, interest in the environment faded and the Greens shrank to insignificance. However, in 2007, a reorganised Green party secured six seats in parliament, which were subsequently lost in 2011.[3]

Georgia
In the early 1990s Georgia had a strong Green representation in parliament. Due to the chaotic conditions, however, most of the leading Greens chose

to join Shevardnadze's Citizens' Union. Although the Green Party had no parliamentary representation, a party member, Nino Chkhobadze, was appointed Minister of Environment, a position she held for five years.[4]

Lithuania

One of the Green movement leaders, Zigmas Vaisvila, was elected to parliament in 1990 and signed the Lithuanian Declaration of Independence. Before independence was internationally recognised, he was Deputy Prime Minister.[5]

Poland

The Greens in Poland existed in the 1990s as a group within Solidarity, the Ecological Forum. The EF leader Radoslaw Gawlik was Minister of Environment from 1997 to 2000. Thereafter, the Polish Greens played a marginal role in Polish politics.

Romania

In 1991 the environmental expert Marcian Bleahu, a member of the Green party MER, was appointed Minister of Environment. Bleahu lost his post in connection with a shipment of hazardous waste for which he was alleged to be responsible. The Greens were nevertheless able to retain a small parliamentary

Figure 10 Marcian Bleahu, speleologist and veteran Romanian Green, with his wife and the author, 1997. Bleahu was minister of environment in the early 1990s. He was an example of 'individual co-optation', a model of Green participation in government, which was common in Eastern Europe after the fall of communism, but has also been observed later in other parts of the world. Photo: Ulrika Åkesson.

representation during the 1990s. In 2012 Partidul Verde (The Green Party) won two seats in the framework of a coalition.

Slovakia

Slovakian Greens participated in the broad coalition that defeated the authoritarian Vladimir Meciar in 1998 and as a party in a ten-party coalition received a vice minister post, after having gained 2.5% of the vote and four seats in the parliament. In 2002, however, the vote dropped to 1% and zero seats. The party has not recovered and won no seat in the elections of 2014.

Slovenia

The Slovenian Green Party was part of the broad anti-communist coalition that gained power after the regime change, and several Green ministers were appointed in May 1990. However the support for Green politics faded and the Green Party disappeared. It has in the 2000s been replaced by the Youth Party.

Limited influence by individual co-optation

The above-mentioned eight cases of individual co-optation are rather similar. The Green Ministers of Environment paved the way for new environmental legislation in countries which had no or only fragile environmental rules. But when the economic and social costs of the switch from a state-controlled to a liberal market economy hit the populations in the 1990s, the Greens lost support. While in 2015 there are Green parties which are members of the EGP in all these countries, they remain weak and marginalised, with a few exceptions: In Bulgaria the Greens participated in a government in the 2000s. The Estonian Greens seemed to make a comeback with parliamentary representation, but lost it. In Romania a restored Green party has gained two MPs, and in Georgia there is one Green MP. Individual co-optation may be useful in the short term, but has a limited and temporary impact and cannot replace the building of a strong Green party.

Red-Green/Resilience

France

In 1997 Les Verts, through cooperation with the Socialist Party (PS), obtained six seats in the National Assembly. Dominique Voynet became Minister for Environment and Territorial Planning, as part of a multi-party left-wing government supported by 319 out of 577 MPs; it thus held a majority even without the support of the Greens.

In France 75% of electricity comes from nuclear power. Thus it was a victory when Les Verts were able to put through a freeze on new nuclear reactors. When a conflict erupted between the EU Birds Directive and French hunting traditions, Dominique Voynet is credited with having found a workable compromise. On the other hand, she was accused of mismanaging the problem of oil spills after the sinking of the tanker Erika off the French Atlantic coast. Overall, however, her ministerial period is considered successful.[6] She resigned in 2001 to become the party's general secretary and was succeeded by Yves Cochet until the defeat of the 'plural left' in the 2002 election, when Les Verts got only 4.6%. In contrast, the 2009 European election was a success, with 16.2% and 13 seats in the European Parliament.

In the autumn of 2011 Écologie-Europe/Les Verts (EELV) made an agreement with the Socialist Party for a common government, which included a promise to reduce the dependence of France on nuclear energy from 75% to 50% and to shut down 24 nuclear reactors, introduce carbon taxation, and raise income taxes for the richest. The agreement was approved by 74% of the 150 delegates at a congress in November 2011. In the election of 2012 EELV got 5.4%, 17 MPs and two ministers, Cécile Duflot (housing and territorial equality) and Pascal Canfin (international development). However, once again, the Green MPs were not needed to create a left-wing majority (PS plus some smaller left-wing parties had 314 out of 577 seats without the 17 Green MPs). Later, an expert on the history of the Greens in France wrote: 'The first year of the five-year period of Hollande is deceptive for all ecologists.'[7] Thus, it was not surprising that in April 2014 the two ministers, Cécile Duflot and Pascal Canfin, resigned, partly because of the appointment of former Minister of Internal Affairs, Manuel Valls, who had made humiliating comments about Roma people, as Prime Minister. But the Greens' resignation was also a result of their disappointment with President Hollande, which Duflot developed in a book published in September 2014: 'I thought that I would be able to convert François Hollande to ecology and that he would abandon the austerity policy. When I realised that the presidential period would continue along the wrong way, I resigned.'[8] Duflot maintains that Hollande 'has never been an environmentalist; environment, biological multiplicity, the climate crisis, etc., are alien territories to him, as a genuine productivist he believes that growth is the only answer'. In the EU elections held a short time after the resignation of the Green ministers, EELV lost considerable support, their vote down to 8.9% and 6 MEPs.

Summary: There was strong internal support among French Greens for participation in governments, which contributed to the Green victories in 1997 and 2012. But after participation in government the French Greens suffered losses, in 2002 and 2007, as well as at the EU elections of 2014. Cécile Duflot's description of the Socialist president as uninterested in ecological issues is worth considering.

Italy

Federazione dei Verdi participated in the Italian government during two periods: 1996–2001, with two ministers consecutively (Edo Ronchi,

Minister for Environment 1996–2000, Alfonso Pecaro Scanio, Minister for Agriculture 2000–2001), and 2006–2008 (Alfonso Pecaro Scanio, Minister for Environment). According to Rüdig the two Green ministers in 1996–2001 had influence through a series of new environmental protection laws.[9] The Minister for Agriculture achieved a high profile in 2000–2001, particularly by taking tough measures against mad-cow disease and a radical line against GM foods.[10]

In correspondence with the author in the autumn of 2014, Alfonso Pecaro Scanio gives his image of the experience of Verdi in government:

I was minister of agriculture 2000–2001. Then I managed to block GMOs in Italy and implemented reforms of agriculture, forestry and fishing. We also adopted laws on alternative cultivation and protection of land. Then we were again part of a ruling coalition from 2006 ... I was the president of I Verdi ... and from the autumn of 2004 we started work on a common programme ... Our non-negotiable demands were: no to all ideas about the rebirth of nuclear energy, an end to subsidies for fossil energy and waste incineration, an emphasis on energy efficiency and renewable energy, first of all solar energy ... We demanded increased support for the protected areas, implementation of Natura 2000, an end to pointless megaprojects, such as a bridge across the straits of Messina and a tunnel for high speed trains, instead we wanted investment in smaller and public projects scattered over the whole country ... Concerning social issues we demanded a kind of basic income for jobless people (redditto di cittadinanza per i cittadini disoccupati). I managed to have a flag of peace inserted into the symbol of Verdi ... We also worked hard to achieve an opening about rules for de-facto couples, especially homosexual couples ... we managed to stop the bridge across the straits of Messina, delay a decision about the rapid train tunnel; we achieved a break-through in solar energy ... we created 100,000 jobs in the renewable energy sector, including wind and geothermic energy. We got the Italian troops out of Iraq, but not from Afghanistan. We didn't manage to legislate about de-facto couples and homosexuals ... The party congress in July 2004 had chosen a president, national council and executive with a mandate to participate in a centre-left coalition ... Among the Greens the result was considered excellent ... Already in the spring of 2005 we were rewarded in the regional elections ... We gained in the local elections of 2007. In 2008, however, the situation had totally changed, because the Prodi government was toppled by a collapse of the coalition. PD [Partito Democratico, established in 2007 by a merger of several centre-left parties; since 2013 its leader has been Matteo Renzi, Prime Minister since February 2014] pursued a campaign against all left-wing groups and the Greens and demanded a vote that was useful for PD against Berlusconi ... The Greens were obliged to make an alliance with the Left only, and that alliance didn't manage to pass the hurdle. However, PD without the Left and the Greens, lost the election, Berlusconi and his centre-right won. Today Stelle (of Beppo Grillo) pursues several Green themes and has attracted many Green activists.

Summary: Verdi prepared for participation in government through extensive internal democracy. This was, however, not enough to prevent devastating splits and defections. It is impossible to know if the electoral losses and the eradication of the Greens as an independent force in Italian politics is related to their participation in government, or rather an effect of the chaotic political landscape in the country. Pescaro Scanio's mentioning of Beppo Grillo's movement 'Five Stars' (which won 25.6% of the vote in the 2013 elections) as possibly attracting Greens is interesting. However, even if Five Stars takes some Green positions, its structure, with one man in control, is at odds with Green grassroots democracy. (In January 2015 a Senator of Five Stars switched to the Greens).

Ukraine

Ukraine's Green Party (PZU) was founded in 1991, partly in the aftermath of the Chernobyl disaster of 1986. A well-known environmental activist, Yuri Shcherbak, became party leader and was appointed Environment Minister. However, he resigned in 1992. Nevertheless, in 1998 the party managed to make a comeback with 5.5% and 26 seats in the parliament. In 2001 one of the leading figures in the party, Sergei Kurykin, was appointed Minister of Environment in the government led by Anatoliy Kinakh (in office 29 May 2001 to 16 November 2002), who had been an MP during the communist era and later become leader of a party which supported the pro-Russian Party of Regions. By 2002 support for PZU fell to 1.3% and no MP. The party failed to make political profit from its ministerial post and was torn apart by internal division. In the 2012 election PZU got only 0.35% of the vote.

Red-Green/Necessity for majority

Germany

Die Grünen joined its first regional government (Hessen) in 1985 and had participated in almost a dozen regional governments before becoming part of a Federal Red-Green coalition (SPD-Die Grünen, 1998–2005), in which it took three Ministerial posts: Joschka Fischer (Vice Chancellor and Foreign Minister), Jürgen Trittin (Environment) and Andrea Fischer (Health), who in 2001 was replaced by Renate Künast (Consumer Affairs and Agriculture).[11] One of the party's successes was to secure a decision on the decommissioning of nuclear power within about 20 years. The Greens also had some success in terms of pushing through environmental taxes and minority policies, in particular the liberalisation of citizenship rules. NATOs military action against Serbia in 1999 became a serious stumbling block, when Fischer's support for German participation caused violent internal protests culminating in Fischer having a bucket of red paint thrown in his face during a party congress. Faced with Fischer's resignation threat, however, a majority of the congress gave the go-ahead.

After the 2002 election the Red-Green coalition remained in power, but support for the government later faded. After defeat in state elections in North Rhine-Westphalia in spring 2005, Prime Minister Schröder decided to call fresh elections, without consulting Die Grünen. The result was a defeat which, however, led to the SPD remaining in power, in a grand coalition with the CDU, while Die Grünen were relegated to the opposition. This also seems to have been the end of Joschka Fischer's political career, which many feared would be a major setback for the party.[12] However, in 2009, Die Grünen's first election in opposition following their government involvement resulted in a victory, with 10.7% of the vote. The result in 2013, however, was significantly weaker, at 8.4%, while the EU election of 2014 saw the party return to 10.7%.

In correspondence with the author, Ludger Volmer, former Secretary of State in the Red-Green government and author of several books about Die Grünen,[13] gave his impressions of the experience of Die Grünen as a governmental party:

Concerning foreign policy a number of meetings took place in 1997/98 … This work was successful and we knew that the coalition wouldn't collapse because of the foreign policy [earlier it was considered among media commentators that Die Grünen were impossible partners in a coalition because of the foreign policy]. For some years there had been regular meetings between Greens and left-wing SPD parliamentarians … But there were no formally settled agreements.

Already on the night of the elections the executives of both parties made statements in favour of a coalition and negotiations started the next day. The negotiators for the Greens were: the co-presidents of the party and the parliamentary group, the party secretaries and six persons representing certain issues (with a balance of women/men and realo/fundi) … The party congress (Bundesdelegiertenkonferenz, BDK) as a matter of fact had no direct influence over the results of the negotiations … However, there was almost no hesitation in the BDK … The Red-Greens realised a lot of reforms and mastered extremely complicated situations (Kosovo, the 9/11 terror attacks in New York and Washington, the Iraq War). However, meetings of the parliamentary group of the Greens only served the purpose of affirmation of the compromises in the government. The party and the parliamentary group became a chorus of applause for Joschka Fischer … the media appointed him as the only leader and the Greens didn't want to destroy that image. On this basis Fischer and Trittin could divide the whole party between them ... and after the dissolution of the coalition they weren't capable of efficient opposition activity ... During the coalition period many members left both Die Grünen and SPD, because of Agenda 2010/Harz [a series of welfare and labour reforms which critics found too neoliberal], the military activities, etc. Many of these defectors joined Die Linke (The Left). So far Die Grünen haven't recovered from the collateral damage of the coalition ...

Summary: Die Grünen prepared the way for participation in government with a wide and deep internal process. There was no formally agreed common programme before the election, but there had been several informal preparations made through personal contacts in parliament and elsewhere. According to Volmer, however, the internal democracy during the period in government was merely superficial; Fischer was allowed to play the role of sole leader, which has caused Die Grünen 'collateral damage', and which may have been a contributing reason for the decreasing share of the vote in the election of 2013. But it is not clear if the party has been caught in a falling trend. According to seven opinion polls conducted in December 2014, sympathy for Die Grünen is between 0.6 and 3.6% higher than their election result of 2013 (8.4%).[14]

Red-Green/Legitimacy for minority

Sweden
During the period 1998–2006, the Swedish Green Party (Miljöpartiet de Gröna) was almost a government party through its close cooperation with the Social Democrat government. The cooperation (in which the Left Party was also included) was escalated step-wise until there were Green political experts employed in several ministries. But the Prime Minister, Göran Persson, who wouldn't have had a majority without the support of the Greens, refused to accept the entry into the government of Green ministers. The Red-Greens lost the election of 2006 to a right-wing four-party coalition. Göran Persson resigned and the Social Democrats got a new female leader, Mona Sahlin. The Greens decided to demand full membership of a Red-Green government; otherwise the party would act as an opposition party. After some time an agreement was reached with Sahlin to go for a Red-Green two-party government. However, left-wing groups in the Social Democratic Party, as well as trade unionists, demanded the inclusion of the Left Party. This was rooted mainly in the suspicions among trade unionists about Green policies. In 2009 negotiations led to the adoption of a comprehensive Red-Green governmental programme. But the election in September 2010 was won by the right-wing coalition. Many commentators blamed the defeat of the Red-Green alliance on the inclusion of the Left Party (however, the Greens got their best result ever, at 7.3%).

The election of September 2014 was a disappointment for Miljöpartiet. The party had done very well in the EU election in June, with 15.4% and four MEPs. However in the parliamentary election Miljöpartiet received only 6.9%, a loss of 0.4%. One reason given was that a feminist party (Feministiskt Initiativ) had a very good election (unfortunately winning just under 4%, thus getting no MPs). Together the Red-Greens got more votes than the right-wing alliance, but the xenophobic Sweden Democrats doubled their vote (to 12.9%). None of the two major blocks achieved a majority in the parliament. Nevertheless, the new Social Democratic leader, Stefan Löfven, was elected Prime Minister. He formed a Red-Green government with Social Democrats and Greens. Miljöpartiet got six portfolios (out of 24): Deputy Prime Minister and Minister for Climate and the Environment (Åsa Romson), Minister for Education (Gustav Fridolin), Minister for Financial Markets and Consumer Affairs, Deputy Minister for Finance (Per Bolund), Minister for Housing and Urban Development (Mehmet Kaplan), Minister for International Development (Isabella Lövin) and Minister for Culture and Democracy (Alice Bah-Kunke). The right-wing parties stayed together and proposed an alternative state budget, which the xenophobic Sweden Democrats supported. After this Löfven declared that he would call another election. But between Christmas and New Year 2014, an agreement was reached between the Red-Green government (supported by the Left Party) and the right-wing alliance to abstain from a further election; instead it was agreed (with a 'gentlemen's agreement', rather than by changing procedural rules) that the largest party 'constellation' would be allowed to get its state budget adopted by the parliament, which meant that the democratic opposition would abstain from voting for its own budget proposal. A main aim of this construction was to keep the Sweden Democrats from having political influence. Some critics objected that this led to parliament having a diminished influence.

One interesting aspect of this 'political circus' was that Stefan Löfven chose continued cooperation with the Greens, despite appeals from anti-Green trade unionists to form a one-party Social Democratic government, which would then have been able to get support from right-wing parties on nuclear energy, arms exports and similar issues.

Centre-Left/Necessity for majority

Belgium
The late 1990s saw a number of national scandals, from dioxin in chicken to the Dutroux case (involving the murder of young women).[15] A distrust of the old political parties contributed to Green success in the 1999 elections: Ecolo won 7.4% and 11 MPs, Agalev 7.0% and nine seats. This paved the way for the Greens' entry into a centre-left coalition. Numerically, only one of either Ecolo or Agalev was needed to form a majority, but since both parties made it clear

that they would either act together in the government or not at all, there was a need to involve both of them and each were given two portfolios: Isabelle Durant (Mobility and Transport) and Olivier Deleuze (Energy and Sustainable Development) from Ecolo, and Magda Alvoet (Public Health and Environment) and Eddy Boutsmans (Development Cooperation) from Agalev.

The Greens managed to convince the government to make a decision to opt out of nuclear power; marriage for homosexuals was made possible, an anti-discrimination law was adopted, and several thousand illegal immigrants were legalised. However, in August 2002 Magda Alvoet had to resign, which she explained in an email to the author in 2014: 'I can be very clear, I gave my resignation because of the weapons export to Nepal ... I was part of a decision that was bad for Nepal and bad for my party.'

Despite the initial support of the party membership, complications ensued. During the government years of 1999–2003 the leadership of Ecolo changed four times. Finally the Ecolo ministers resigned two weeks before the 2003 elections because of a dispute about night flights over Brussels. This is believed to have contributed to the subsequent electoral catastrophe – Ecolo's votes fell by more than half to 3.1%, only sufficient for four parliamentary seats.[16] Agalev, which had changed its name to Groen! (Green!), got only 2.5% in 2003, losing all their parliamentary seats.[17] However, the parties have since recovered. In 2014 they were back at their pre-government level.[18]

In an email to the author in August 2014, Magda Aelvoet described the governmental experience as follows:

> There were no negotiations with other parties before the elections ... We indicated what we called breaking points: things that we would never support, because they are unacceptable for a Green party ... We also discussed before the elections which parties we would agree to start negotiations with. A xenophobic party was excluded, and ... it would be very risky for us to build a government without the socialists on our side. So inside the party we made our negotiation platform (the priorities and breaking points), we indicated the people who would lead the negotiations: the party steering group, the broadest party level, right under the party congress, elected the negotiators, and chose a group of ten party members to whom the negotiators had to report ... at the end of the process the negotiation results were presented to the party congress ... Things to be taken in consideration: will you be part of a coalition of 2 or 3 parties ... in our case 3 parties were needed (Liberals and Socialists and Greens, French and Dutch speaking) ... the Greens were the smallest party of the three, and we felt very regularly that the two biggest made their agreements behind our backs ... The communication about what you do inside government is of the greatest importance: we did not sell well enough what we did; we created a strongly performing Food Agency, we

voted for an end to nuclear power in the parliament and elaborated an exit plan, we fought and won the struggle of the gay marriage, in the agricultural field we secured an enormous reduction of the use of pesticides, we managed to stay out of the war in Iraq…

Summary: No negotiations took place before the election. The Belgian Greens carefully anchored the negotiations in the party organisation and allowed a party congress to make the final decision about the governmental agreement with other parties. The Belgian experience indicates the possible problems that can arise if more than two parties are members of a coalition. It also demonstrates the importance of informing the electorate about Green achievements in government.[19]

Luxemburg

For the first time in its history the Green Party of Luxemburg entered a government following the election of October 2013. The Socialist Workers' Party decided not to prolong the coalition with the Christian Social Union of Jean-Claude Juncker (since 2014 President of the Commission of the EU), which lost several seats in the election, after having been the leading government party since 1979. Instead a coalition was created between the socialists (13 seats), the liberal Democratic Party (13 seats) and Dei Greng (6 seats), altogether 32 out of the 60 seats of the Luxemburg parliament. Dei Greng got three ministerial portfolios (out of 15) in a government led by the liberal Xavier Bettel: Sustainable Development and Infrastructure (Francois Bausch), Justice (Felix Braz), Environment (Carole Dieschbourg).

Centre-left/Legitimacy for minority

Denmark

After the election of September 2011, despite having lost heavily (down from 23 to 16 MPs), Socialistisk Folkeparti (Socialist People's Party, SF) joined a three-party centre-left coalition (SF, Radicals and Social Democrats) led by Helle Thorning-Schmidt (Social Democrat). SF got six portfolios: Foreign Affairs (Villy Søvndal, party leader), Taxes (Thor Møger Pedersen), Environment (Ida Auken), Health (Astrid Krag), Commerce and Investments (Pia Olsen Dyhr) and Business and Growth (Ole Sohn). Despite consisting of three parties the government did not have a majority in the parliament (77 out of 175 seats). The support from the 12 MPs of the Left-Green Enhedslisten (Unity list) was in principle enough, but the Social Liberal Radicals often obliged the government to get support from the right-wing opposition before proposing a bill, which made many left-wing proposals impossible. SF was seriously weakened when internal strife forced Villy Søvndal to resign as party president in September 2012. He was replaced by Annette Wilhelmsen, who won an internal plebiscite with 66% of the members' votes, against 34% for Astrid Krag. In the fall of 2013 Søvndal was hospitalised because of heart problems and resigned as Minister of Foreign Affairs to be replaced by former party leader Holger K. Nielsen; also Jonas Dahl (taxes) and Annette Vilhelmsen (social affairs) became new ministers for short periods. At the local elections in November 2013 SF lost almost two thirds of its support in 2009 (down from 14.5% to 5.6%). Criticism of the bleak results of SF's participation in government increased, and when in January 2014 the government decided to sell a state-owned energy company to the private sector, there was a revolt inside SF, Vilhelmsen resigned, and the party soon afterwards left the government. Pia Olsen Dyhr was elected new party leader. A flagrant sign of SF's fragility was that immediately two of the former ministers switched to other parties, Ida Auken to the Radicals and Astrid Krag to the Social Democrats. In January 2015, SF had low support according to opinion polls, 6–8%, which was less than the Left Socialist Enhedslisten (Unity List).

Broad/Resilience

Finland
The Finnish Greens (Vihreät) were invited to participate in a coalition government in 1995 by the Social Democrat Paavo Lipponen, with one portfolio, Environment (Pekka Haavisto, who was succeeded by Satu Hassi). The Greens were not needed to create a parliamentary majority but wanted for balance in a broad coalition, from communists to a right-wing party. After success in the 1999 elections the party secured another government post (Health and Social Affairs, Osmo Soininvaaraa). In 2002 a decision on a fifth nuclear reactor forced Vihreät to leave the government.[20] Nevertheless, in the election of 2003, the Greens increased their vote to 8% and 14 seats, while the result in 2007 was a further increase to 8.5% and 15 seats, after which the party was able to form part of a new left-centre-right six-party government with two ministerial posts: Tuija Brax (Justice) and Tarja Cronborg (Labour), succeeded by Anni Sinnemäki. In the spring of 2010 a major investment in renewable energy was driven through. In 2011 the number of votes decreased a little, to 7.3%, but a third of the seats were lost. Despite this Vihreät retained two portfolios: Ville Niinistö (Environment) and Heidi Hautala (International Development and 'ownership steering'), succeeded by Pekka Haavisto. Hautala chose to leave after having been accused of siding with Greenpeace against a state-owned petrol company for which she was responsible; by the time she was formally acquitted she had already resigned.[21] In September 2014 another

decision to build a nuclear reactor made it once more impossible for the Greens
to remain in the government. According to political scientists Jan Sundberg
and Niklas Wilhelmsson, 'government experience has changed the party. It has
come a long way from a movement that was reluctant to become a party of
importance and coalition potential ... This means that the party will not lose its
importance in the near future.'[22]

Laura Nordström, a political assistant to Heidi Hautala (MEP, former MP and
minister), told the author in an email about some aspects of the governmental
negotiations:

> In 2011, just after the election, Green priorities for participation in
> government were established, by the MPs and the members of the 40-person
> party council (puoluevaltuuskunta). Of course preparations had been
> done earlier and our party programme also was the election platform ...
> The government was, however, negotiated after the election. The MPs
> and the party council together are entitled to decide if the party is to join
> or leave a government. The party council and party board also establish a
> framework for the politics, but the daily political decision-making is made
> by the ministers and MPs. The last time we decided to join a government
> it was based on our estimation that the most important of our demands
> were fulfilled.

Summary: Vihreät had informal contacts with possible coalition partners before
the election, but approved a governmental agreement only after the election.
The party has been very careful about internal democracy. The reaction of
voters has been divided.

Centre-right/Necessity for majority

Latvia

Latvia's Green Party was given a ministerial post in the early 1990s without
significant voter support. However, in 2002 the party gained four MPs and
one minster. For a short period a Green even held the position of Prime
Minister (Indulis Emsis in 2004). Since 2006 the Greens have been included
in a centre-right coalition government. Since 2014 they have had six MPs and
two ministers, Raimonds Vejonis (Minister of Defence) and Guntis Belevics
(Health), in the framework of the Union of Greens and Farmers, which in
October 2014 got 19.5% and 21 seats. The 21 seats of the Union of Greens
and Farmers are needed to create a parliamentary majority together with
the centre-right Unity Party (23 MPs) and the right-wing National Alliance
(17 MPs). However, the six Green seats would not have been needed to form
a majority.

Right/Resilience

Czech Republic
In 2006, the Czech Greens, Stranka Zeleni (SZ), gained 6.3% of the vote and six seats in the parliament. SZ joined a coalition in 2007 with the right-wing Civic Democratic Party (ODS) and the Christian Democrats (CDU). ODS and CDU together had 104 of the 200 seats in parliament, thus the six Green MPs were not needed to create a majority. The Greens got four ministerial posts: party leader Martin Bursik, Vice Premier, Environment; Karl Schwarzenberg, Foreign Affairs; Dana Kuchtova, replaced by Ondrej Liska, Education/Youth/Sport; Dzamila Stehlikova, replaced by Michael Kocab, Human Rights, Minorities. At first there was gender balance among the SZ ministers, but later all four were men. Bursik and Schwarzenberg supported plans for a US rocket base in the Czech Republic. Prime Minister Mirek Topolánek made awkward right-wing statements and became embroiled in scandals, such as being photographed naked at one of Italian Prime Minister Silvio Berlusconi's swimming-pools. These and other issues created internal strife. In 2009 the government lost a vote of confidence because four MPs from the government bloc (no Greens) voted for no-confidence. In the following elections SZ lost all its MPs. In the EU elections of 2014 there was some sign of recovery, with 3.8% of the vote, but no MEP.

Right/Necessity for majority

Ireland
In 2007 the Irish Greens secured 4.7% of the vote, six seats and two ministerial posts in a coalition with the right-wing Fianna Fáil (77 MPs) and the right-liberal Progressive Democrats (2 MPs); the six Green MPs were needed to form a parliamentary majority. An agreement was reached and confirmed by 86% of the Green members on 13 June 2007. At first two Greens became senior ministers, John Gormley (Environment, Heritage and Local Government) and Eamon Ryan (Communications, Energy and Natural resources), plus one junior minister, Trevor Sargent (Food and Horticulture) – three men, no woman. However in March 2010 the Greens got two more junior ministers, Ciaran Cuffe (Horticulture, Sustainable Travel, Planning and Heritage) and Mary White (Equality, Human Rights and Integration) – four male, one female Green minister. In government the Greens had to accept projects they had earlier opposed, such as the M3 motorway and the use by US military of Shannon airport. The 2008 budget included energy efficiency tax credits, a ban on incandescent bulbs, financial subsidies for bicycles, and a vehicle registration tax based on carbon emissions; the 2010 budget included a carbon levy. The Greens also managed to pass new legislation granting rights to same-sex couples.

Already in September 2009 the political editor of the *Irish Independent*, Fionnan Sheahan, reported that 'Gormley threatens to pull out': John Gormley sent a letter to his members clarifying his party's position: 'If two-thirds of them don't back the new deal, the party will pull out of government.'[23] The same year a writer in the London-based *Mirror* summarised the achievements of the Greens in government in a devastating way: 'John Gormley and his party have gone back on almost every promise they made at the last election … Before they entered Government John Gormley promised there would be no incineration and that the Tara landscape would be saved. For their loyal support Mr Gormley has rewarded his constituents with one of the biggest waste burners in Western Europe and Tara has a brand-new motorway.'[24]

In 2009 the veteran Patricia McKenna left the party in protest at the 'shift to the right'. The 2009 European parliamentary election also saw a setback, with vote share down to 1.9% and no MEP. Local elections in 2009 saw a decline by 1% to 2.3% and the loss of many members of local councils. Comhaontas Glas quit the government in January 2011, after having forced the Prime Minister to call an early election, which led to a defeat for the Greens. With only 1.8% of the vote all MPs were lost.

The Greens did register some successes during their period in government, such as legislation on same-sex partnership ensuring almost, but not fully, the same rights as married couples (a referendum to introduce full marriage rights for same-sex couples was held in 2015, which was won by the supporters), introduction of planning reform, an increase in renewable energy, and a programme for better insulation of houses. In a book published late in 2011, it is alleged that the Green Party struck a 'deal with the devil' by entering into coalition with Fianna Fáil. The author admitted that the Greens had irritated its coalition partners with their pursuit of a ban on stag hunting, the introduction of civil partnerships for same-sex couples, and restrictions on planning. However, this had not been enough to satisfy Green voters; at the same time Green issues were pushed aside because of the financial crisis. 'Their three-and-a-half-year period in Government cost them dearly at the polls.'[25] That is true. However, signs have appeared that the party is recovering. At the EU election in 2014 the party doubled its votes, to 4.9%, just narrowly missing out on a seat.

POLITICAL SCIENCE ON GREENS IN GOVERNMENT

Conditions for Green involvement in government

What is it that determines whether a Green party will have the opportunity to participate in a government? Rihoux and Rüdig think it is important that the parties are deemed capable of government, not least in economic affairs and foreign policy. The 'Green rise to power may not be so much a reflection of change of Green parties themselves, but of changed perception of the Green parties by established parties'.[26] Dumont and Bäck have analysed European countries with Green parties as potential government partners. They found that there is a high probability that, after an election where a coalition has to be formed, a Green party will join the government if the political-ideological distance between the Greens and the government-forming party is relatively small, if the Greens have suffered an electoral defeat before in their history, and if they had a different election result in recent elections than the largest Left party.[27] This seems to fit with some of the cases described above.

One example is Sweden. The political-ideological distance between the Social Democrats and Miljöpartiet has been reduced through cooperation on the state budget from 1998 to 2006 and the comprehensive common Red-Green governmental programme elaborated by the Social Democrats, Greens and the Left Party in 2009 for the 2010 election. Miljöpartiet suffered a crushing defeat in opposition, in 1991, when the party lost all its MPs. That experience led to a series of internal reforms. The EU election of May 2014 showed a decline in support for the Social Democrats and an advance for the Greens. However, this trend was reversed in the parliamentary election of September 2014 (even if marginally).

Possibilities of new parties having an impact

According to one analysis, influence can be exercised in two main ways: through blackmail potential, or through government potential.[28] To some extent it may be said of the Greens that the 'fundis' are in favour of blackmail, while the 'realos' prefer to rely on government potential. According to a model of their life-cycles,[29] parties evolve in several stages: declaration – authorisation – representation – blackmail or government. This model is affected by different countries' legal systems, but on the whole it may be true that new parties are first formed/launched, then registered/authorised to participate in elections, then possibly win parliamentary representation and, finally, can lay claim to political influence, either through 'blackmail' or by participating in a government. The general risks associated with government involvement for all political parties are: a) being punished by voters for the government's (real or perceived) mistakes, and/or b) being punished by their own fundamentalist supporters for (real or perceived) betrayal. The risk of loss of votes is particularly severe for a small party polling around the minimum threshold for entry into parliament. The situation can be exacerbated by the risk of being neglected during the mundane everyday practice of government.

Deschouwer argues that government involvement leads to an 'identity change', in any case for pure protest parties; he attempts to find a common pattern for all new parties in government, but fails, not least due to the fact that Green parties differ markedly from protest parties. The conclusion must be that the kind of 'identity change' that can be demonstrated in the case of protest parties does not necessarily have to be made by Green parties. This does not mean that Green parties are not affected by the exercise of power, but they are probably more resilient than traditional protest parties. Deschouwer observes that new parties have a greater chance of surviving government involvement if they have been in existence for several years. A Green example could be the Czech Republic, where Stranka Zeleni came into the government almost immediately after gaining representation in parliament. The lack of experience gained from a reasonable period of time as a parliamentary party could have contributed to the party's setback in the 2010 election. According to Deschouwer, however, there is nothing to suggest that government involvement would lead to 'strong or radical change' in the party's basic ideology, because ideology represents a party's' *raison d'être* 'and therefore cannot be changed in an instant'. This is of course stronger in ideological parties, such as the Greens, than in protest parties, where the ideology is more diffuse. Regarding organisation, Deschouwer shows that there are changes for parties in government compared to their infancy, but that the changes have often been effected before entering government, not as a result of it. This is true for several Green parties, such as the German and Swedish, where the loss of all MPs in the early 1990s led to wide-ranging reforms of the party organisation.

What influence do Greens exercise on government policy?

In parliamentary systems it is very rare for a bill to be submitted and processed without going through the government, although it is formally possible. The government's central role in law-making is one reason why parties aspire to government involvement. There is also direct government power through, inter alia, regulations and appointments, and not least, initiatives in foreign policy. Generally speaking, an ideological 'centre party' has a greater opportunity for influence because it potentially might support a different coalition. The same goes for an electoral majority-creating party because it determines whether the coalition government gets a majority or not. Since new parties in general are often neither ideologically in the centre nor tactically in the position of majority-creators, they often have little influence.[30] Green parties, however, often claim to be 'neither left nor right'. In both Sweden and Germany there is Green cooperation with centre-right parties at regional and local levels, despite the organised Red-Green co-operation at the national level. Die Grünen and

Miljöpartiet are thus trying to avoid being 'locked up' in a left block, which would reduce the opportunities for influence.

The participation of Greens in governments does not appear to have influenced the ways in which governmental powers are exercised. This is an interesting finding, because it might have been expected that parties with an alternative organisation (grassroots democracy, etc.) as a hallmark could to some extent influence forms of government. The Belgian Ecolo, facing a possible renewed participation in a government in 2009, formulated some ideas about environmental requirements Greens should make if given positions in government: Choose a building for the ministerial office that is as ecological as possible, taking transport, energy use, etc., into consideration. Choose eco-labelled equipment. Establish tough environmental standards for parking and internal communication, valid also for ministers. Promote the use of public transport, as well as cycling and walking, even for ministers. Compensate for climate damage when unavoidable flights are made. Introduce ecological, social and ethical criteria for all deliveries of commodities.[31]

A not uncommon apprehension about Green involvement in government is that the government's stability could be threatened, particularly as the Green parties are assumed to be more likely to anchor their policies continuously in party organisational structures and the parliamentary wing of the party, which could lead to a party breaking off its involvement in government prematurely. In cases where the Greens have left a government early, conspicuously Finland, Belgium, Denmark, Ireland and France, it has been due to substantive political disagreement between the Greens and the government majority. Rihoux and Rüdig have not found any cases in which the internal divisions of a Green party have caused the fall of a government.

Rihoux and Rüdig tone down the impact of Green government involvement. 'The political options for radical change through Green politics are very limited, the Greens in government experience is not a Green Revolution.'[32] Maybe one governmental period doesn't achieve a Green Revolution. But it seems likely that future research will find that the emergence of Greens from the middle of the 1990s as partners in government has changed the political scene considerably by putting new issues on the agenda, by changing the logic of traditional right-wing confrontation, and also by affecting the way politics is conducted. One example is the system of gender-balanced co-presidents adopted by several Green parties. This gives their political activity a new face. In Sweden the Greens have managed to get it accepted that when party leaders make major public appearances together, the Greens are represented by both their speakers, which has of course made some other parties think about introducing a similar system.

A risk for Green parties that make excessive demands in exchange for their government involvement continues to be that they will not be allowed to join the ruling coalition. This is obvious when it comes to individual co-optation, resilience or minority models, as the blackmail potential is small. Even if the Greens do have a majority-creating position, however, there are other options for other parties, more so if the party system is less fixed in a right-left dichotomy. One conclusion of this, of course, is that the only sure way to guarantee strong Green political influence in government is that Green parties are so strong that they themselves become the government-forming party. Rüdig (2006) drew the following broad conclusions: government involvement is not 'necessarily a bad thing' for Greens, they may benefit from the increased attention and the display of competence. The renewed Green parties have the opportunity not only to survive, 'but to increase public support'. Just as it was for the new socialist parties around a hundred years ago, it takes some time from the first participation in a government as a minor party to becoming the major and dominant ruling party.

How are Green parties affected by government involvement?

After an analysis of 14 Green government periods in the East and seven in the West, Rüdig drew the following conclusion: 'Overall it would clearly be misleading to suggest that Green parties entering government are bound to suffer losses at subsequent elections.'[33] According to Rüdig there are two contradictory approaches that Green parties in government can take to minimise the risk of punishment by the voters: a) to govern with some distance from the government mandate so as not to appear to share the blame for unpopular government measures; b) to very visibly take full responsibility for the government mandate so as to demonstrate competence and efficiency. Certainly, parties often point out that government policy is a compromise and make clear what is their real position. For a government party to go one step further and suggest that it does not feel jointly responsible for a certain part of government policy could be risky. On the one hand, it would be a radical way to mark your own profile; on the other, it would create the impression of fragmentation and encourage speculation about the government's early collapse. Soon after the start of the Swedish Red-Green government in 2014, the Green Vice Premier and Minister of Environment, Åsa Romson, drew some attention by publicly distancing herself from a decision by the Social Democrat Minister of Agriculture (in charge of hunting regulations) to allow the hunting of a predetermined number of wolves; her declaration was welcomed by organisations for the protection of nature and wildlife, while constitutional experts remarked that such dissociation on the part of a minister from a governmental policy was unheard of in Swedish political history.

In any case, the overall impression is that Green parties have usually accepted responsibility for government policy, although demonstrating their own profile. At times when they were not able to do so, they have chosen to leave the government, with very different voter reactions. The Finnish case involved a question which everyone knew was a core issue for Vihreät, nuclear power. In other cases, the reason for resignation, although over Green issues (like nightly over-flights, the sale of a state energy company, etc), may have been considered less important. One conclusion may be that Green reasons for premature resignation from a government must be extremely obvious in order to be accepted by the voters.

How are Green policies affected by government involvement?

Three main types of adjustment may be envisaged:

1. Strategic alignment, i.e. a political and ideological change of views before a government is formed in order to get the party to present itself as 'ready for government'. An example that some analysts have given is the Swedish Green Party's decision to remove the demand for Sweden's exit from the EU from its party platform in 2008. Representatives of the Green Party have explained that the change of position was a response to a changing reality and took place after a membership vote and therefore cannot be perceived as a strategic alignment.
2. Ideological adaptation, i.e. a change of views during the course of government. A striking example is the acceptance by Die Grünen of Germany's NATO membership at the very beginning of government in 1998. The new Foreign Minister, Joschka Fischer, actually promised, while visiting the USA, that Die Grünen had abandoned the requirement even before it had done so through a regular party decision.
3. Compromise adjustment, i.e. a political/ideological compromise with coalition partners in order to allow the formation of a government and/or the conduct of government – without involving a change of the party's own opinion. This is by far the most common form of adaptation. While strategic and ideological alignment means a permanent shift in Green politics, compromise adjustment does not in principle need to have a long-term impact. However, political scientist Thomas Poguntke has observed that after government involvement there is no going back to 'pure protest and criticism', because the party must now take responsibility for some of the things it might really want to criticise.[34] Thus, a compromise adjustment may turn out to be irreversible.

How does a party become ready for government?

According to political scientist Nicole Bolleyer, the answer is that it depends on three variables: the party's relative strength, its 'ideological compatibility' (willingness to compromise), and 'organisational trust' (a partner must be confident that the commitments made will be kept, the government must be able to rely on support from the party's MPs in strategic votes). Bolleyer believes that several adjustments are needed: 1) anticipatory substantial adaptation: the anti-establishment rhetoric is toned down, along with certain ideological requirements, and 2) anticipatory organisational adaptation: the organisation is adapted to a more centralised leadership, which is 'clearly more demanding' than ideological or rhetorical adjustment. According to Bolleyer, government involvement puts a number of demands on the party organisation: 1) for better coordination of the party's various bodies and agencies, which also carries a risk of central control, 2) for more careful selection of party representatives in government-related bodies, which carries a risk of discontent among people who are not selected, 3) for increased knowledge and expertise at different levels in the party, which creates a risk of professionalisation, and a marginalisation of the grassroots supporters and 'amateurs', i.e. the risk of a gulf opening up between the party apparatus and party members. In sum, all this leads to increased power for the party's central management body and a change of the party from a people's movement into a power apparatus.[35]

Joschka Fischer is once said to have remarked that 'the march through the institutions has tended to change the marchers far more than the institutions'. There is no doubt that government involvement imposes demands on party organisation which the original 'grassroots democracy' does not in all respects satisfy.

RESULTS OF GOVERNMENT PARTICIPATION FOR 12 EUROPEAN PARTIES

In three cases – Germany, Finland and Latvia – the reactions by voters have been mainly positive, although this trend is not without ups-and-downs. Three Green parties have been hit by severe losses in elections or opinion polls and still show no sign of recovery, in Denmark, Ukraine and Italy. Three others have also been hit by considerable election setbacks after their periods in government, but show, to some extent, signs of recovery, in Belgium, the Czech Republic and Ireland. The Belgian Greens have retaken their positions from before the governmental experience. Neither the Czech nor the Irish Greens have so far managed to regain seats in parliaments, but show signs in elections that they have a considerable electoral support.[36] For three parties it is too early to judge: France (although there the meagre result in the EU election just after the exit from the government was a warning), Luxemburg and Sweden, these last two having been in government for too short time; however, the result in the EU election of Dei Greng and opinion polls in Sweden imply that so far the voters are satisfied.

Why have voters reacted so differently? One reason may be the variable success the Greens have had in imposing their policies. However, from the accounts above of the Green periods in government it appears that almost all Green parties have had some influence, especially upon environmental legislation, including energy policy (in favour of renewables, against nuclear and fossil energy), but also upon rights for immigrants and sexual minorities, and to some extent peace policy. The bleakest record appears to be the Danish case, while Green government participation in Sweden and Luxemburg, as just mentioned, is too recent to evaluate. There is no obvious discernible general correlation between political impact and voter reaction, except possibly in the Danish case, which is also the only one where the Green party (SF) joined a government after a considerable election defeat.

Another reason may be the structure of the government. Here it seems clear that for a party to be needed in order to secure a majority is positive, although both the Belgian and the Irish Greens lost heavily before recovering a little. In both cases another negatively counteracting factor may have been that both parties quit the government prematurely. The same behaviour may have contributed to the SF loss in Denmark as well as to the meagre result in the 2014 EU election of the French EELV. Probably the only party that has been able to quit without being punished by voters is Vihreät. To participate in government only to give resilience or legitimacy is risky: out of seven Green parties which have done this, four lost heavily – Italy, Ukraine, the Czech Republic and Denmark – and only Finland has managed it without damage, while in Sweden and France is too early to say.

A third factor may be the political constellation of the government. Here the only hint of a pattern is that joining a government with only right-wing parties, as Stranka Zeleni and Comhaontas Glas did, is hazardous. But with centre and/or left parties in the coalition the outcome for the Greens may be very varied.

The conclusion – though based upon rather vague and diffuse facts – could be that it is better for Greens to join a government

- after an *electoral success* (rather than after a setback)
- when they are *needed to create a majority* (not only to contribute by giving resilience and/or legitimacy)
- when there are *not only right-wing coalition partners* (but also centre and/or left-wing partners)
- in addition: it is advisable to *remain in the government* rather than quit prematurely.

There have been exceptions to all these prerequisites, but the more numerous the exceptions, the greater risk governmental participation seems to be for the future of the party.

RECOMMENDATIONS FOR A GREEN PARTY ENTERING GOVERNMENT

By following the recommendations below, Green parties entering a government would increase their influence, as well as the prospect of being rewarded by voters in future elections, while decreasing the risk of betrayal of basic Green values and beliefs:

1. Join a government primarily *after an election victory*. A marginal setback may be acceptable, but think twice!
2. Don't join a coalition where all the other partners are right-wingers, only join the *Greenest possible centre-left, centre-right or Red-Green* coalition governments! It must be clear to members, sympathisers and voters that the coalition 1) is in a credible way the Greenest possible according to the parliamentary situation, 2) will pursue a policy that is Green enough to be perceived as making real Green progress.
3. If possible, join a government where the *Green votes are needed to create a parliamentary majority*. Otherwise, be sure that the government programme is Green enough and the partners credible.
4. Undertake measures to guarantee that *government business is conducted in an ecological way!*
5. *Don't join a government with only one Green minister!* Green ministers need to approach a 'critical mass' to be able to retain their moral strength.
6. *Take the environment portfolio!* The post as Minister of Environment is a necessity for Green parties.
7. *Demand a portfolio with power over economic policy!* Without influence on economic policy the Green impact is limited.
8. *Implement a double strategy*, including *compromises* as well as active external *manifestations of basic Green thinking*; compromises should be called compromises and not be presented as if they are what the Greens really want.
9. *Keep some basic aspects of the Green alternative grassroots structure*, like rotation, gender balance, collective leadership and non-cumulation of positions. A distinct alternative profile – such as two co-speakers (a woman and a man) instead of one male party leader – has in many countries become an attractive symbol of the Greens.

10. *Remain in government until its term ends!* A party which quits a government before the end of an electoral period may be considered irresponsible, if the reason is not crystal clear to everybody. As a rule Greens must remain in the government until the following election even if that means living with some nasty aspects.

At the beginning of the third millennium the political scientist Wolfgang Rüdig came to the following conclusion about the effect of Green participation in governments so far:

> Generally, Greens in government have not posed radical challenges to the status quo, and thus there is little reason to believe that the major political parties of the left – and perhaps increasingly the right – will not regard the Greens as potential coalition partners. What will be far more difficult for the Greens, particularly after their first period in office, is to enthuse voters who may be disillusioned with what the Greens have achieved (or not achieved) in government.[37]

The last sentence is of special interest. That Green parties should try participation in government if given the opportunity and if the conditions are reasonable is obvious. At the same time there are limits to what can be done by a government in a democratic state. The necessary transformation into an ecological society can only be achieved through struggles on several levels: personal, local, regional, national and international. Greens in governments are an indispensable part of a Green future, but not the only one.

6

GREEN GLOBAL GOVERNANCE
FOR THE TWENTY-FIRST
CENTURY

According to the 2014 yearbook of the Stockholm International Peace Research Institute (SIPRI), in recent years 'there has been an upward trend in fatalities caused by state-based conflicts ... There has also been a rise in internationalised intrastate conflicts.' At the same time 'there has been a notable decline in the number of peace agreements'. The main recommendation by SIPRI is that the UN should 'take on increased responsibilities as a conflict prevention and resolution mechanism'.

Large parts of the world, not least Europe, have been struck by a social and economic crisis that has mobilised huge protest movements and led to the creation of new left-wing parties, like Syriza in Greece[1] and Podemos in Spain. However, the democratic ambitions of the movements which began in the Arab Spring have in most cases been thwarted; the strong momentum towards democracy and social justice has deteriorated into civil war (Syria), chaos (Libya, Yemen) or the establishment of authoritarian rule (Egypt). Only Tunisia still gives some hope for a more democratic development.

Violent Islamism is creating havoc in large parts of the Middle East (Syria, Iraq), sometimes reaching the heart of Europe (the terror attacks in Paris and Copenhagen, January/February 2015). Some commentators claim that the 'clash of civilisations', predicted by Samuel Huntington in the beginning of the 1990s, has become a reality.[2] Xenophobic populist parties, claiming that an Islamic takeover is imminent, are gaining strength in several European countries.

Is there a place for Green politics in this world of seemingly growing conflicts of the traditional type, which have plagued humanity for all of its known history – conflicts over material goods, political and economic power, territorial control and ideological dominance?

GOOD NEWS

A January 2015 press release from Diakonia, a think-tank close to the Church of Sweden, calls attention to the fact that despite the bleak and chaotic appearance of the world, there is also 'good news'. Some examples: According to the medical journal *The Lancet* the number of children dying because of infections and illness has decreased from 9.9 million in 2000 to 6.6 million in 2013, thanks to improved healthcare. Sri Lanka is making a comeback towards democracy, ten years after the devastating tsunami. The EU has decided to introduce a register of owners in order to combat money laundering. A new UN agreement to limit the spread of arms has come into effect.[3] Perhaps then the basic motivations behind the emergence of the Green movement and the creation of Green political parties are being taken care of? Sadly, this is not the case.

WE ARE TRANSGRESSING PLANETARY BOUNDARIES

There is no end to scientific reports on the human-made dangers to the environment and health. Some examples from the end of 2014 and beginning of 2015: A Swedish scientific magazine reports on 'microplastic – the concealed threat in the sea', which is assembled in enormous quantities, often in nano-sized pieces, and does not biodegrade for hundreds or thousands of years.[4] *Le Monde* claims that lead, bisphenol A, and other chemical molecules change the development of the brain and diminish the cognitive capacities of new generations.[5] A German magazine asserts that the destruction of the Amazon rainforests continues as always.[6] A French study establishes that sperm quality has degraded by a third, thanks to the effects of bisphenol A, phthalates, PCB, etc.[7] The WHO reports that 38 million people are dying every year because of noncommunicable diseaces, i.e. heart and lung diseases, stroke, cancer and diabetes, 16 million of which are premature and would be preventable if action were taken.[8] As an example of relevant action the report mentions Hungary's introduction of a tax on food and drink components with a high health risk, such as sugar, salt and caffeine, which had the effect that the risky consumption levels dropped by 27%. In fact, as noted by a major Swedish newspaper, these diseases are 'welfare' diseases, partly caused by the conspicuous consumption levels of an unecological growth economy.[9]

These are only a few examples of the continuous pollution and destruction of all parts of the Earth by human activities. Altogether, we are crossing the *planetary boundaries* of what the earth can manage without the main carrying system collapsing. The concept of planetary boundaries was first presented in 2009 by a group of scientists led by Johan Rockström of the Stockholm Resilience Institute and Willy Steffen from the Australian National University. Their report suggests that if human activity passes certain thresholds there is a risk of 'irreversible and abrupt environmental change'. According to their estimation, already three of nine planetary boundaries have been transgressed: climate change, biodiversity, and nitrogen in the biosphere. Most of the other six are now in a risk zone: stratospheric ozone, land-use change, freshwater use, ocean acidification, aerosol loading and chemical pollution.[10]

The basic facts are known and for the most part acknowledged. Already in 2005 the Millennium Ecosystem Assessment of the UN, compiled by 1,300 scientists from 95 countries, asserted that the earth's ecosystem had deteriorated over the previous 50 years and that 60% of the ecosystem services were being destroyed. Despite this, political decision-makers seem incapable of grasping the situation and taking the necessary action. The Copenhagen summit on climate change in 2009 was a failure. 'After Copenhagen: Europe is Weeping, OPEC is Laughing', reported Le Monde on Christmas Eve 2009. Also after the +20 summit in Rio de Janeiro in 2012 the media reported failure. The Swedish newspaper Dagens Nyheter summarised: 'If the 49 pages of the final document are checked carefully, with its 283 points, it appears that there are no concrete commitments.'[11]

FAILURES EMBEDDED ALREADY IN RIO 92

Maybe the failures have been unavoidable. In section #7 of the Rio +20 draft document, with the visionary title 'The future we want', the political leaders were supposed to confirm their 'commitment to advance progress in implementation of the Rio Declaration on Environment and Development and Agenda 21'. The Rio Declaration and Agenda 21 were agreed in 1992 – and in 2012 they still needed implementation! And the commitments of Rio 92 were not revolutionary.

On 30 May 1992, 200 Greens, present in Rio for the First Planetary Meeting of Greens, made a 'last minute appeal' to UNCED (United Nations Conference on Environment and Development) where they expressed their feeling that 'all signs point to failure, with dramatic consequences for the environment and peoples of the earth'.[12] In the appeal the Greens urged the OECD countries to introduce energy taxes and phase out nuclear energy. It was also suggested that a new UN Commission, directly elected by the General Assembly, should be established, with a mandate to oversee the implementation of Agenda 21, and given the necessary financial means. The appeal estimated that a cut in military expenditure of 10% would make it possible to establish a Green Fund of $125 billion per year to meet the goals of the UNCED.

The European Greens could boast before the UNCED that the European Parliament had adopted 20 out of 21 Green amendments, which gave the EP resolution 'a decidedly green tinge'. This, however, did not prevent the EU Commission from missing an opportunity to take on a leading Green role in Rio. The Environment Commissioner, Carlo Ripa di Meana (who later became leader of the Italian Greens and a Green MEP), wanted to go to Rio with a proposal for a CO_2 tax. But after 'an unprecedented lobbying effort by energy-intensive industries paid off', the CO_2 tax proposal disappeared. The Greens in the EP stated that they 'deplore Europe's abysmal failure of leadership in Rio'.

There are two major conclusions to be drawn from Rio 92: 1) There is still a profound contradiction between quality of life and the ruling economic system. 2) There is a lack of efficient governance on the global level. An article in *Science*, presented as 'a key contribution of the science community to the 2012 UN Conference on Sustainable Development (Rio+20)', proposes a 'fundamental overhaul of global environmental governance', including the establishment of a UN Sustainable Development Council.[13]

LATE LESSONS FROM EARLY WARNINGS

In December 2014, five years after the Copenhagen climate failure, Oxfam, Climate Action Network and Friends of the Earth unanimously agreed that at the preparatory climate meeting in Lima, COOP 20, 'nothing has been done to prevent the catastrophic effects of the climate change'.[14] The political systems are obviously not able to react in a responsible way, and not for the first time.

Already more than a century ago the Swedish winner of the Nobel Prize for Chemistry in 1903, Svante Arrhenius (1859–1927), predicted, based upon his 'greenhouse law', that emissions of carbon dioxide from fossil fuels would eventually lead to a human-made global warming, a scientific insight that political decision-makers took almost a century to accept as fact, but which even today has not been met by appropriate counter-measures.[15]

A couple of seminal reports from the Environmental Agency (EEA) of the European Union should have shaken the decision-makers, but they passed by without significant attention. At the beginning of the third millennium a report with the title *Late Lessons From Early Warnings* was published in which 14 cases of serious environmental hazard were analysed in terms of the time-lag between the first well-founded warning and the initiation of reasonably adequate counter-measures. Only in a few, well-publicised cases, like the presence of growth hormones in meat and mad-cow disease, was the non-activity period 'only' a couple of decades. In the majority of the investigated cases the period of inactivity was between 30 and 100 years, one example being asbestos, the harmfulness of which was established in 1898, although it took the EU until 1999 to agree on a ban.[16]

In 2013 the EEA published a follow-up report, in which another ten examples were presented.[17] One of the most notorious cases of course is lead, about which the Emperor Nero's military doctor had already sounded the alarm. This millennia-old knowledge didn't prevent the car industry from starting to blend lead into petrol in the 1920s, with the result that by the 1970s about 200,000 tons of lead was emitted into the air in Europe and the USA and then into the blood of human beings. Despite overwhelming evidence, the major car producers pretended that a ban would destroy the car industry. Today, when lead in petrol has been banned for more than a decade in most countries, nobody regrets it. Other similar cases treated in the report are tetrachloroethylene, mercury, vinyl chloride, biphenol and DDT, which became world famous through one of the classics of modern environmentalism, *Silent Spring* by Rachel Carson.[18] It would be a gross exaggeration to pretend that these revelatory EEA reports had any impact. One reason may be that the analysers were not content with reminding the public of cases where almost everybody today agrees that action should have been taken much earlier (like asbestos and lead), but also pointed out the potential harmfulness of nuclear energy, genetic engineering and nanotechnology, all three technologies which according to mainstream decisions-makers are the keys to a brighter future.

The utterly insufficient action against climate change, and the EEA reports on the massive delays between the scientific discovery of a hazard against life, humans and the environment, and adequate counteractions by governments, show that the problem is not one of a lack of knowledge. A dramatic example is that despite an increasing number of alarm bells – e.g. 'Australia urged to prepare for influx of people displaced by climate change'[19] – the political elite of Australia abolished the carbon tax from 1 July 2014. The only reasonable conclusion is that knowledge of the facts is not enough. Political struggle is unavoidable.

POLITICAL HYPOCRISY

Every year in December the Right Livelihood Award (the alternative Nobel Prize) is given out at a ceremony in the Swedish Parliament.[20] The laureates are usually highly critical of the existing world order. The ceremony is inaugurated with a speech by the founder of the Prize, the former Green MEP, Swedish/German/British Jakob von Uexküll. The laureates are introduced by parliamentarians from the Greens, the Social Democrats, the Left Party, the Liberal Party, the Centre Party and the Christian Democratic Party; only the right-wing Conservatives usually choose to stay away and the xenophobic Sweden Democrats are not invited. A considerable section of the power elite is present, including representatives of trade unions and business organisations. The same people or their predecessors wouldn't have dreamt of participating in such an event in 1980, when the Right Livelihood Award was created. In one of his many inaugural speeches, Jakob von Uexküll emphasised that 'continued GDP growth may worsen the situation for most people'. One of the laureates, David Suzuki, said: 'The present economic system is basically flawed and unavoidably destructive.' These statements were met with wild applause. When the present author asked Margot Wallström, then EU commissioner, and since October 2014 the Swedish Minister of Foreign Affairs, what she thought about this, the reply was a Mona Lisa smile.[21] Why do these representatives of political parties which give the highest priority to GDP growth in their practical policies participate in such an event? Why do they applaud statements demanding de-growth? Isn't that a demonstration of elite hypocrisy over environmental issues? Almost everybody pays lip-service to radical action to save our common earth. But very few, except the Greens, are prepared to change the economic, social and political system that is the cause of the environmental destruction. But will the Greens succeed?

HOW TO AVOID THE IRON LAW OF OLIGARCHY

In order to achieve a Green transformation the Green parties must resist the 'temptations of careerism'. The *iron law of oligarchy*, developed by the German sociologist Robert Michels in the early twentieth century, states that the larger and older a radical movement gets, the more it will adapt to the surrounding social and political system; the voluntary activists will turn into salaried functionaries; the goals will change from what was originally demanded to what is perceived as possible. Greens have been more aware of the hazards of the iron law of oligarchy than most other 'revolutionary' movements.[22] However, it is not only personal inadequacy or lack of moral strength that can be blamed for the adaptive transformations of old radicals. Another important aspect is the enemy. How to struggle with volunteers against a professional enemy? How to maintain wide internal democratic deliberations if the enemy is a hierarchy headed by a Leader with a capacity for immediate decision-making and implementation? Most radical movements have been caught in this dilemma.

According to the Norwegian sociologist Thomas Mathiesen, a radical movement when adapting is 'defined in': it may gain some 'power' to participate in the administration, but it loses the possibility of affecting basic changes; it becomes a *competing non-alternative*. But if a movement holds to its original positions then it is 'defined out': excluded from participation in the governance of society, and risking deterioration into a powerless sect, it becomes a *non-competing alternative*. The goal of a radical movement is thus to avoid both dead ends and become a *competing alternative*. The trick to achieving this is to refuse a definitive choice, to hold both doors open, in a position that Mathiesen has called the *unfinished* status.[23] This implies an eternal balancing act, between contributing to government bills and taking part in street demonstrations; between keeping representatives in office to exploit their experience and replacing them regularly in order to avoid the emergence of a leadership caste, and so on. The system with two spokespersons (male/female) could be seen as an 'unfinished' balance between one Leader and a collective leadership. To keep an 'unfinished' system going requires continual and repeated adaptions in order not to lose the balance. The enemy should never know for sure where the Greens are!

DE-GROWTH AND THE RETURN TO THE RURAL?

Greens oppose GDP as a measure for progress and are generally sceptical of economic growth. Many Greens claim that, on the contrary, what is needed is *de-growth*. The Green goal is no less than to change the paradigm of the society. However, what has been called *industrial fatalism* is so strong that not even all Greens dare to stand up to it, but try to find a way out with 'technological fixes'.[24] This cannot be explained away as cowardice; there are real, respectable reasons to be careful. One is that large parts of the world population need and have the right to a considerably higher level of consumption. That is why Greens or alternative thinking groups outside the well-to-do states of Europe, North America and the Pacific often express apprehensions about ideas of less growth, no growth or de-growth. When the Malaysia-based *Third World Resurgence* analysed the euro crisis it concluded that an exit from the euro would make several radical measures possible, such as the nationalisation of banks and Keynesian reforms. However, the magazine warned: 'A main problem is to prevent an exit from the euro resulting in a return to national autarchy.' Some de-growth supporters would protest and claim that a return to autarchy is one of the aims of the change. The French economist and de-growth theoretician Serge Latouch has even mentioned the Amish people in the USA as a relevant example for Greens in the twenty-first century.[25] He is not the first. The Swedish professor of biochemstry Gösta Ehrensvärd (1910–80) had already in the 1970s forecast that a return to a rural and agricultural form of life would be necessary.[26] In several books the Swedish author Lasse Berg has followed the San people of the Kalahari in South Africa, who still to a large extent live as hunters and gatherers; he argues that this is the original and 'natural' lifestyle of human beings and that the introduction of agriculture was the great sin of human beings.[27] The American writer James Howard Kunstler has written a novel about what would happen if the USA had to roll back 100 years.[28] Even if Kunstler has no intention of scaring people away from the 'hand-made' life, he gives a realistic picture of the many severe conflicts that would be generated by a move from a high level of material consumption to a radically lower, pre-industrial level, especially if the transformation was rapid. So what is the correct Green attitude towards utopias/dystopias of a return to the rural society of the nineteenth century?

GREEN TRANSFORMATION = MODERNISATION

The fact is that the rural society of the nineteenth century was a patriarchal class society characterised by huge inequalities between rich and poor and women and men, and by discrimination against everybody who fell outside the category of 'normal' – disabled people, homosexuals or people of another colour or religion. The same goes for many rural societies today. In principle it is of course possible to create rural communities with a gender balance, religious tolerance and a high ecological consciousness. Undoubtedly many rural societies have a very close relation to nature and there are many examples, often referred to by Greens, of ecologically motivated protests by peoples in, for example, the deep Amazon, against the intrusions of 'modern', industrialised society. Some people consciously choose to live in 'primitive', rural conditions rather than in an urban surrounding. How, then, should Greens act towards existing societies which are ecologically sounder than cities, but do not conform to the basic values of human rights, gender balance and personal freedom? The main reply is probably that the liberation of human beings, such as the liberation of women, must come from within. The military invasion of Afghanistan, for example, didn't liberate the women of that country. The efforts of the teenage Nobel Peace Prize laureate Malala Yousafzai, from nearby Pakistan, were much more important and efficient, not to mention those of the radical feminists in Afghanistan and similar countries who risk their lives in standing up for women's rights.

Greens must of course defend the rights of indigenous and rural peoples, even if they don't fulfil every aspect of the ethics of human rights. At the same time Greens must react against all types of oppression, even if upheld by ecologically right-minded groups. While rejecting its excessive levels of material consumption, the Green vision embraces several aspects of modernity, including freedom of expression and thought, gender balance, sexual freedom, scientific research and technological development. When the Swedish Greens chose as a slogan for a party congress some years ago 'Here modernisation is ongoing', some commentators were confused, but most of the Greens agreed. The Green project is not one of returning to imagined earlier paradises, but one of modernising in a way that is compatible with the resources of Mother Earth.

THE GREEN MISSION – CHANGE BEFORE COLLAPSE

However, despite Green efforts to transform the modern world without retrograding, it may be too late to avoid dramatic setbacks, even collapses. Some believe that humanity so far has proved itself incapable of responding to the ecological demands for change, and that collapse will be the only way to move decision-makers from lip-service to effective action. Jared Diamond's survey of states and societies that failed because of their inability to cope with environmental hazards is both revealing and frightening. However, he offers no example of an ecological collapse leading to insight and the taking of adequate measures.[29] The idea that a collapse would be a step towards a sustainable society is just as far-fetched as the dubious belief of the Baader-Meinhof gang in the 1970s, or the Islamic State terrorists in 2015, that a total breakdown of the old social structures will pave the way for their Utopia. From a Green point of view an ecological collapse is sign of failure. The Green mission is to effect change before the collapse.

ECOLOGISM – NEITHER CAPITALISM NOR SOCIALISM

Already at the end of the 1980s it was alleged that 'Green capitalists' would adapt the capitalist system to the ecologically necessary demands.[30] There have been several refutations of this idea, for example by the Belgian ecosocialist Daniel Tanuro, who has explained why Green capitalism cannot work.[31] A desperate alarm was sounded by the veteran theorist Immanuel Wallerstein a couple of years ago, warning that the alternative to the present, defunct capitalism might be 'a non-capitalist system that retains all the worst features of capitalism (hierarchy, exploitation, and polarisation)'.[32] In a foreword to a book on ecosocialism by the British Green, Derek Wall,[33] the Peruvian revolutionary Hugo Blanco writes: 'The capitulation of many green parties to capitalism has converted them into anti-ecologists.' But is that so? Many Green programmes lack explicit demands to abolish capitalism. But complete implementation of most Green programmes wouldn't be compatible with the continuation of the present capitalist system. Are Greens then watermelons – green outside, red inside? It may be a matter of words. Wall emphasises that there is no blueprint 'constructed by a committee'; in practical terms he proposes a trial-and-error strategy, which is very much the mainstream Green approach.[34] Wall lists ten 'favoured transitional policies':

1. Defending indigenous control of rainforest and other vital ecosystems.
2. Allowing workers to take control of bankrupt businesses.
3. Using government bailouts to mutualise resources.

4. Arms and SUV conversion as an essential element of a Green New Deal.
5. Legislating for open-source patenting.
6. Land reform.
7. Massive funding for libraries and other forms of social sharing.
8. A tax and welfare system to support the commons.
9. Competition reform to reform ownership.
10. Social ownership of pharmaceuticals and medicine.

Only points 6, 9 and 10 are possibly 'ecosocialist', but even these appear in 'mainstream' Green thinking.

WHY THE TAINTED 'SOCIALIST' LABEL FOR THE NEW ECOLOGISM?

Another writer who claims that Green ecologism must be socialist is the editor of *The Monthly Review*, John Bellamy Foster, who claims that Karl Marx was an ecological pioneer. August Bebel, Karl Kautsky, Rosa Luxemburg and Nikolai Bukharin are also presented as early ecologists, even Vladimir Lenin is alleged to have 'incorporated important ecological considerations' into his dialectical materialism. Foster admits that the Soviet Union developed an extreme form of productivism, but that was the fault of Stalin, who was guilty of ecocide. But, he maintains, real socialism is the same as ecologism; 'thus transformation to socialism is the same as transformation to an ecological society'.[35] The point of using the tainted label 'socialism' for the new, untainted ecologism of the Green movement is not clear. Why waste time and energy trying to explain away everything about the old socialism that the new ecosocialism assures it does not stand for – like centralised bureaucracy, extreme productivism, non-democratic politics, infractions of human rights? Why not completely avoid the label 'socialism' and stick to *ecologism*? That there are aspects of socialism, as there are aspects of other ideologies and philosophies, which are essential to contemporary ecologism is indisputable. But to base a strategy for Green ecological transformation upon the writings of Marx or other socialist theoreticians appears to be far-fetched. Most of them made important contributions to the understanding of social systems, but they were also hard materialists and unidimensionally anthropocentric in their outlooks. Green thinking is different.

TOWARDS A POST-MATERIALIST HEGEMONY

In 2014 Erik Damman, a Norwegian ecologist pioneer since the early 1970s, and the founder of The Future in Our Hands, published a new book, in which he claimed that we need values other than free competition and growth.[36] That is correct – at the core of the problem are the dominating values. However, the dominating values are not unchangeable. Already in the early 1970s, the American sociologist Ronald Ingelhart showed that a growing number of people, especially in developed countries, were adopting *post-materialist* values.[37] This was a major incentive for Greens, because it was interpreted as proof that Green ideals were supported by a change of values in a significant part of the population. Advocating values that one believes would make the world a better place is basic to every political movement. Thus, if Greens want to get the support of the majority of the population, they must affect their values. In the end it is about what the Italian thinker Antonio Gramsci called *hegemony*, that which is considered to be normal by the majority. If the majority of the people have short-termist and materialist attitudes it is difficult to secure support for ecological proposals which may entail reducing material consumption. But if a mood of post-materialism becomes hegemonic, Green proposals have a greater probability of being accepted as the wisest.

NON-VIOLENT CARNIVALS INSTEAD OF SABOTAGE AND CONFRONTATIONAL MARCHES

Civil disobedience, such as refusing to pay taxes, enlist for compulsory national service or obey oppressive laws, was a classic tactic of the precursors to Green parties, such as the peace and environmental movements. Greenpeace is probably the most illustrative example of this trend. A very special form of the tactic is what has been called *monkeywrenching*, a kind a green sabotage strategy, mainly used by the US-based group Earth First. The expression has its origin in a novel by Edward Abbey's, *The Monkrey Wrench Gang*, about environmental sabotage in the USA.[38] Another inspiration has been Dave Foremans *Ecodefense*, which includes concrete advice on eco-sabotage.[39]

While non-violent civil obedience is and should be a part of Green strategy, monkeywrenching and eco-sabotage are usually counterproductive. Of course a sabotage action may catch the attention of media – but will it lead to a change in people's thinking in the intended way? All experience shows that the result is most often a debate about political methods, which serves the interests of the enemies of the Greens. One of the most well-known Swedish civil disobedience activists, Per Herngren, who in 1984–85 served a 15 month sentence in a US jail for having destroyed military equipment together with members of Pershing Plowshares, has argued against protest methods which are similar to the activities of the power elite, including mass demonstrations, claiming that huge marches of tens of thousands of people are like military exercises and should be avoided by radical movements; instead the alternative groups should stage carnivals, festivals and alternative markets in order to catch the imagination of people.[40] Greens should try to find a balance between joking about people's anti-ecological behaviour and respect for their deepest emotions.

FROM ANTI-GLOBALISATION TO ALTERNATIVE GLOBALISATION

In a way the Greens are confronted by the same dilemma as the Russian revolutionaries were after 1917: is 'revolution' possible in one country only? Dobson refers to a Dutch study which has shown that the Environmental Plan of 1989 would cost 2.6% of GDP if the Netherlands implemented it alone, 0.6% if other countries followed suit.[41] This is only one hint that a Green transformation may be difficult to realise in one country, far less in one local community alone, while the rest of the world continues to pursue 'business as usual'. In 2015 every corner of the world is linked to every other corner, through economic and information exchange via conventional and social media. Not even the remotest Yanomami of the northern Amazon, Greenlanders close to the North Pole, or the San in the Kalahari are completely cut off from the global stream of goods and information. How then would it be possible to establish a Green Ecotopia that would have a chance of survival? The truth is of course that, from a contemporary Green point of view, Trotsky was right: the revolution must be global to stand a chance of survival. In the short term there may have been an impression that Stalin was right, that it was possible to establish socialism in one country. But the system that was his legacy could not survive the pressure from a different world. From an ecological point of view it is obvious that the Green revolution, even if it starts in local Green islands, must be global to be able to achieve its goal – to save our common Earth and common future. (See also Chapter 1, 'Green islands').

In 1999 the present author, while attending EU meetings,[42] also joined the huge demonstrations during the WTO summit in Seattle. Quite a few of the participants brandished Green symbols. The same was the case in Prague in September 2000, during protests against the summit of the World Bank and the IMF. But by the time I participated in the WTO summit in Doha, Qatar, in November 2001, as member of the EU delegation, the situation had changed. One reason was of course that Qatar didn't allow the same influx of demonstrators as had been the case in Seattle and Prague (and many other places during the previous years); another reason was the terrorist attack of 11 September 2001. But in hindsight it is clear that there also was a further reason: the anti-globalisation movement sometimes created the wrong impression that it disregarded the fact that the world and humanity constitutes a unit, that we are all part of the same Gaia. After some time this was understood and the movement changed its slogan to 'globalisation from below' or 'an alternative globalisation', as powerfully expressed in the World Social Forum conferences, where the presence of Green parties and politicians has always been massive. In 2010, ten years after the first WSF conference in Porto Alegre, Brazil, one of the most visible personalities of the movement, Susan George, made some proposals for the movement to fight for: partial nationalisation and socialisation of any banks that receive public money; job-creating Keynesian Green infrastructure projects; initiating a debate on income limitations; reinstating taxes on wealthy individuals which neoliberalism has abolished, and using the proceeds to finance public services; debt cancellation against reforestation and bio-conservation in the Lowest Developed Countries.[43] This list may seem too reformist for some 'revolutionary' left-wingers and too left-wing for some Greens. But George's proposals are in fact not very socialist, but rather ecologist. Without a profound change of the international financial system the transformations that Green policies could achieve will be very limited.

That some EU countries have decided to introduce, from 1 January 2016, a Tobin tax on financial transactions is a small but important beginning. The actions by the EU against tax havens are also steps in a positive direction. Despite everything, the international system is not made up only of the World Bank, the IMF and Davos conferences and other anti-ecological or hypocritical institutions and events of the power elite. Greens should recognise that there has also been another trend, a kind of *alternative globalisation from above*, led by powerful organisations, from at least the 1972 UN environmental conference in Stockholm which led to the establishment of the United Nations Environmental Programme (UNEP), with headquarters in Nairobi. Then followed the Brundtland Report in 1987, *Our Common Future,* which led to UNCED Rio 92.[44] In Johannesburg 2002 there was the Rio +10 conference. Despite the meagre results of such major summits, some multinational environmental agreements have been achieved: on the protection of wetlands 1971; the Convention on International Trade in Endangered Species of Wild Fauna and Flora (CITES) 1973; the Vienna convention 1985/Montreal protocol 1987, on ozone depletion; the Basel Convention 1989, on hazardous waste; hazardous chemicals, Rotterdam 1998; bio-safety, Cartagena protocol 2000; persistent organic pollutants, Stockholm 2001. In 2009 unfounded accusations made against the IPCC for manipulation of the facts received enormous attention and triggered hilarious reactions from climate-deniers; this revealed that all kinds of criticism of the anti-ecological hegemony, not only from Green parties, environmental NGOs and alternative manifestations, but also when it comes from within the power elite, will be confronted by vicious counter-measures from political and financial groups which have vested interests in 'business as usual'.

For Green political parties, besides being active on the grassroots level and present at WSF and similar international meetings, it is also important to take part in and influence the established policies of *alternative globalisation from above*, pursued by institutions like EEA, UNEP, IPCC and others.

GREEN DEMOCRACY INSTEAD OF CHINESE ECO-AUTHORITARIANSIM

According to the Belgian sociologist Marc de Vos, 'China is king of capitalism 4.0 and has the key to the future.'[45] Is that true? Is authoritarian China the model for the future? There are signs in that direction. 'We are trying to maintain constant growth while at the same time wanting to protect the environment. This is a contradiction', vice minister Li Jinjun told a visitors' group from the European Green Party at the beginning of January 2014 (led by Philippe Lamberts, MEP). Similar views were expressed by Chinese representatives throughout the week-long visit which, in addition to discussions in Beijing with representatives of the central government and city authorities, also included a visit to Hanergy PV Group's massive solar-panel field in Qinghai and to the headquarters of the IT giant Huawei in Shenzhen. When in China, it is impossible to avoid the impression that the country has the biggest environmental problems in the world, while at the same time it is seen as becoming a world leader in environmentally friendly technology. The Environment Ministry has calculated that air pollution has caused GDP to fall by 2.5%. Prime Minister Li Keqiang declared in March 2013 that 'China cannot sacrifice the environment in the interests of growth.' That does not mean that China's leadership believes in zero growth or de-growth. Even if China is a world leader in environmental pollution, it will still be a long time before the country reaches the same level of consumption as the EU or the USA. To take just one example: in 2000 1.8 million cars were sold in China and 17.4 million in the USA; in 2013 the figure in China had risen to 21 million, and in 2020 it is expected to reach 34.7 million, which is twice as many as are sold in the USA. But in spite of this rapid growth in car sales, in 2020 there will still only be 16 cars per 100 inhabitants (aged 15–79) in China, as against 99 in the USA and 69 in Germany. It is facts like these which lead Chinese representatives to insist on calling China a 'developing country'.

According to an opinion poll conducted in September 2013, the Chinese people's concern about the environment is growing rapidly. From 2008 to 2013 the proportion of people who were concerned about air quality increased from

31% to 47%; in relation to food safety the figure rose from 12% to 38%; and on water quality from 28% to 40%.[46] This raises the question as to whether the centrally determined objectives are actually implemented. Some observers have doubted the existence of a central state in China that is capable of taking decisions. 'There is no Single Market in China', claimed an official of the EU Delegation in Beijing. A similar picture has been given by Jonathan Waters, who maintains that China embodies the worst features both of dictatorship and democracy. 'Power lies neither at the top nor the bottom but within the middle class of developers, polluters and local officials who are difficult to regulate, monitor and challenge.'[47] If he is right then there is a risk that the Chinese central government's environmental objectives will remain a dead letter. A somewhat brighter picture is given by Joy Zhang and Michael Barr in their book *Green Politics in China*. They emphasise that 'even authoritarian states require the mobilisation of social actors'. Green activism in China has been ridiculed for being peripheral: tree-planting, bird-watching, garbage-collecting. But the authors defend these activities as means of increasing the awareness of nature and the environment. Although environmental organisations in China are not confrontational, they establish a 'critical supervision of political accountability' of the state institutions.[48]

At the Party Congress of 2012, President Hu Jintao pleaded for another way than the Western: 'China is resolved to abandon the same old path that goes from environmental degradation to rehabilitation, and now advocates ecological progress to save energy, protect the environment and develop its economy at the same time.' It is still too early to know if China will seriously be able to follow another track in relation to the ecological constraints than the flawed path followed by the West. However, even if it may seem like China is meeting the ecological challenge in a more adequate way than the Western democracies, there are still quite a few arguments in favour of democracy, apart from basic considerations for human rights: democratic decisions are more legitimate, because participative, and thus tenable; authoritarian policies may instigate repulsion; democracy admits uncertainty, which is a basis for the important precautionary principle; open discussion produces more appropriate decisions, avoiding mistakes and cover-ups. However, conventional democracy does not take into account certain groups like future generations, the non-human world, etc. That is why a Green democracy is needed.

The Green political movement has moved beyond its infancy and is in many countries across the world an integral part of the political system. Green parties grow and become stronger and more relevant, despite absurd and anti-democratic obstacles in countries otherwise regarded as democracies, such as prohibitive demands for financial deposits or other 'technical' requirements for official electoral registration. In quite a number of countries Green parties would without doubt be much more influential and visible had they not been the victims of unfair barriers in the electoral regulations.

THE 'UNFINISHED' GREENS: BEARERS OF THE COMPETING ALTERNATIVE

Green political parties undoubtedly have a chance to push the world in a Green direction. To achieve this they must resist the iron law of oligarchy by retaining the basics of alternative organisation. They must also stick to their basic deep convictions, while at the same time being able to make necessary compromises to achieve some direct leverage in the short run. Greens must never forget their links to the grassroots and always be prepared to take part in peaceful demonstrations and even to pursue actions of non-violent civil disobedience. Greens must take seriously the fact that they are expected to live as they teach. As politicians they must be amateurs in spirit but professionals in their execution of their work in councils, parliaments and governments. They must be activists in the streets, as well as bureaucrats in their offices. They must be perceived as reliable individuals, but they should never let their enemies be quite sure of where they stand as political creatures. A real Green is someone whose ecological conviction is deep and clear, but whose position in the political struggle is always 'unfinished', always the carrier of a competing alternative.

TOWARDS A GREEN GLOBAL GOVERNANCE

The world in 2015 may seem far from mature enough for the Green message; pessimists may allege that we are once again embroiled in the kind of primitive conflicts that 100 years ago deteriorated into the Great War. But a lot has changed. There were no Greens in 1914. The consciousness of our belonging to one human kind, sharing One World, was rare. Today that feeling of being part of a common world can be found in the remotest areas. That is the paradigm shift that Greens must build upon. While xenophobic populists and unimaginative traditional politicians try to exploit the fading remnants of the nationalist and isolationist emotions of the bad old times, the Greens must be the carriers of the true global mission to establish a democratic and ecological Green global governance in order to secure Mother Earth and create a life system in which quality, not quantity, is the guiding star.

APPENDIX: GREEN PARTIES IN 100 COUNTRIES

A. AFRICA
www.africangreens.org/news

MEMBERS OF THE AFRICAN GREEN FEDERATION, AGF, IN 'GOOD STANDING', NOVEMBER 2014 (FOR A DEFINITION OF 'GOOD STANDING', SEE CHAPTER 3, AFRICA)

As no new information is available about the new associate members of AGF, Burundi, Gabon and Zimbabwe, the original set up has been retained. More information will appear at the site of AGF.

Burkina Faso: Rassemblement Des Ecologistes du Burkina Faso

Le Rassemblement des Ecologistes du Burkina Faso, RDEBF (The Rally of Ecologists in Burkina Faso), was founded in 2003 by the former Minister of State (1999–2002), Ram Ouédraogo, who is still the president of the party.[1] He had also founded an earlier Green party in 1991, Union des Verts pour le Developpement du Burkina. In an interview in January 2014 Ouédraogo demanded the resignation of President Blaise Compaoré (in office since 1987).[2] He also emphasised that protection of the environment and economic development are complementary aspects. In June 2014 Ouédraogo declared that his goal was still to become president. At the same time he affirmed that if the Greens were invited to join the government they would accept, 'but I don't reveal why I would do it.'[3] In October 2014, a short time before a planned parliamentary decision to prolong the mandate of the president, a popular uprising forced him to resign. Power was taken by Lieutenant-General Yacouba Isaac Zida, but after international interventions a civilian president installed for a transition period of one year, Michel Kandando, took over on November 21, with Zida as Prime Minister. RDEBF deplored the violence, but supported the change of power. The general secretary of RDEBF, Adama Sere, is a member of the Conseil National de Transition, which serves as the legislating institution until the elections in 2015, in which RDEBF is planning to participate. At a rally in February 2015, marking the start of the RDBEF's election campaign, Ouédraogo warned that the absence of former president Compaoré from the country constitutes a danger; 'his presidency had both a positive and a negative aspect'. Nevertheless Ouédraogo emphasised that his party totally supports the transition.[4]

Chad: Union des Ecologistes Tchadiens

Union des Ecologistes Tchadiens/Les Verts, UET (The Union of Chadian Ecologists/The Greens) was founded in 2006, as an opposition party. In a letter from the secretary general of the Chadian Greens, Badono Daigou, to the Greens in the Ivory Coast, it is emphasised that 'in this moment when our planet is ill, the political ecology is one of the projects of society which is capable of harmonising the socioeconomic and environmental needs'.[5] Among the basic principles of the UET are to ensure food self-sufficiency and the security of property and persons; to stimulate and manage the economic operators; to educate the youth; to make the army serve the people; to achieve peace and social cohesion; to organise scientific research; to support childhood and family welfare; to protect the environment in Chad and the World; to promote health; to promote sustainable development; to promote women; to promote Chadian art; and to improve the level of the political debate.

In the election of February 2011 UET gained one MP.

Congo: Parti Ecologiste Congolais, PECO (DRC)

Parti Ecologiste Congolais, PECO (The Ecologist Congolese Party), was founded in October 2008. Its main goals are: the relaunch of tourism by rehabilitating national parks and zoological and botanical gardens; promotion of quality of life; establishing of a new health policy; and the elimination of corruption. A core issue is to protect the fauna and flora of Congo (DRC). The president of the party is Didace Pembe Bokianga, former MP and Minister of Environment from 2007 to 2008 (as a member of the Christian Democratic Party).

http://peco.over-blog.com

Egypt: Egyptian Green Party

The Egyptian Green Party (Hizb al-Kudr), was founded in the late 1980s by the founder of the Papyrus institute in Cairo, Hassan Ragab. It never managed to play a role during the Mubarak regime. In January 2010 the daily *Al-Masry al-Youm* asked: 'Does Egypt have a Green Party?' Yes, certainly, was the reply of the president of the party since 1999, General Abd al-Moneim al-Aasar. He claimed that even if the party so far hadn't been able to influence the political process with MPs, it had had influence in other ways, among other things the removal of hundreds of thousands of mines from Sinai. At the same time the article announced that 'if you look for the party online, you'll be directed to a site run by someone who was asked to leave the party'.[6] Al-Aasar resigned some months after the 2011 revolution, and was replaced by vice president Hisham

Zayed, who asserted that the party had 18,000 members in eight governorates.[7] In an interview some days later, Hisham Zayed stated that the Greens base their policy on scientific facts, but admitted that the basic spirituality and religiosity of Egyptians must be respected, which is expressed in the Green Party slogan: 'God – human beings – environment'.[8] In October 2011, *Al-Masry al-Youm* reported: 'After 25 January, environmental activists began talking of forming a new party, but it now seems that most Egyptians who support green initiatives have become politically involved in two ways: forming alliances with liberal parties and trying to revive the Egyptian Green Party, a party which was only nominally allowed under Mubarak. The problem with the party, some activists say, is that it is crippled by the culture of corrupt politics that flourished under Mubarak.'[9] On 1 January 2012, the electronic newspaper *The Green Prophet* published a presentation of the Egyptian Green Party, including an interview with Hisham Zayed. He mentioned, as an incitement of Greens protests, the Toshka megaproject in 1998, which aimed at creating a new river delta by diverting large amounts of water from the Nile. A comment to this article, on 2 January, was: 'Simply, you met with wrong person. The name you said, Hisham Zayed, is not the Egyptian Green Party representative, even for the time being, he is not a member. He was one of the followers of the old regime. Regards, Mohamed Awad, Chief of executive & admin. Committee of Egyptian Green Party.'[10] The following was then added to the homepage of *The Green Prophet*: 'Rectification: At the time of the interview the leadership of Egypt's Green Party was the subject of a juridical dispute between Mohamed Awad and Hisham Zayed. After a long juridical battle, the Civil Court made their final ruling in favour of Mohamed Awad on 12 February 2012.'

In December 2012 Mohamed Awad was appointed member of the Egyptian parliament (by Muslim Brotherhood President Mursi; Egypt's president has the right to appoint a number of MPs). Awad is also member of the executive committee of African Greens and president of the North African Greens. On 15 December 2014 the Arabic version of *Egypt Today* published a report from a congress of the Egyptian Green Party[11] (also on the website eg-greens. org) which, according to an email to this author from Mohamed Awad, was about the 'old guard' party, which is active despite its loss of the law suit. The situation in Egypt, after the Tahrir revolution, and the short period of Islamic rule followed by a military takeover, is complicated, without much room for genuine Green politics.

http://www.egyptiangreens.com/docs/firstpage/index.php (homepage of
    Awad)
http://egyptgreenparty.blogspot.se/2013/08/the-legacy-of-egyptian-greens.
    html (homepage of a group claiming to represent a Green Progressive party)
http://eg-greens.org (homepage of the 'old guard')

Guinea: Parti des Ecologistes Guineens

Le Parti des Ecologistes Guinéens – Les Verts, PEGV (The Party of Guinean Ecologists – The Greens) was created in 1992 by the environmentalist Dixit Oumar Sylla, who served as secretary general for several years. In an interview in 2001 he underlines that 'to struggle against the destruction of the environment is not enough, the protection of the environment is achieved by the struggle against precarity and poverty'. He talks about the vast reforestation campaigns by the party activists, but rejects any suggestion of joining the government. 'I don't want to help those in power who are responsible for the destruction and environmental degradation.'[12] In September 2009 the PEGV opposed the violent suppression of protests by the authorities.[13]

The PEGV has a male president, Mohamed Tounkara. It identifies as neither left nor right, as environmentalist and social ecologist, and both bio- and anthropocentric. It has an ambition to achieve gender balance and has some no-cumulation and rotation rules, as well as a requirement that MPs donate some of their salary to the party.

Kenya: Mazingira Green Party of Kenya

The Mazingira Green Party (Environmental Green Party) was founded in 2003 by Wangari Maathai. The basis for the Mazingira Party (= environment in Swahili) was the Green Belt Movement, founded by Maathai in 1977, which has been very active in tree-planting. In 2002 Maathai was elected to the parliament; from 2003 to 2005 she served as Minister of Environment. In 2004 she received the Nobel Peace Prize. In 2007 another member of the Mazingira Party was elected MP. Maathai died of an illness in 2011.

http://www.greenbeltmovement.org/wangari-maathai

Madagascar: Le Parti Vert Hasin'i Madagasikara

Le Parti Vert Hasin'i Madagasikara (Antoko Maitso Hasin'i Madagasikara/ The Green Party of Madagascar) was created in 2009 and hosted the congress of the African Green Federation in July 2014. The most important themes in its political programme are ecological wisdom, social justice, participatory democracy, non-violence, sustainable development, gender equality and a secular state. The party claims to have some tens of thousands of members; it has pursued campaigns on environmental issues, such as to protect the zebu; also the international women's day on 8 March has been celebrated with large Green demonstrations. Furthermore the Greens have struggled for a rebirth of genuine democracy in the country.[14]

The party is led by a woman, Saraha Georget Rabeharisoa, a professor of philosophy, who won 4.52% of the vote in the presidential election of 25 October 2013. Facing the second round she gave her support to the winner of the first round, Jean-Louis Robinson, who, according to Rabeharisoa, had almost the same outlook as the Greens on the fight against corruption and the restoration of a state of justice and democracy. However Robinson lost to Hery Rajaonari-mampianina on 20 December 2013. The Greens then expressed their hope that the new president would make the correct decisions.[15] However, in April 2014 the Greens described as 'horrible' some statements about justice and human rights made by the president in Brussels.[16] In the election of 20 December 2013, the Greens became the fifth-largest party with 3.8% and two seats (out of 151). Three independents later joined the Green Group in the parliament.

https://fr-fr.facebook.com/pages/Parti-Vert-Hasini-Madagasikara/12640940
    4344

Mali: Parti Ecologiste du Mali

Parti Ecologiste du Mali (The Ecologist Party of Mali) was founded at the beginning of the 1990s. In the local elections of 2009 the party won nine seats out of 11 in the little town Tienfala. According to the female president of the party, Diallo Fadimata Bintou Touré, the significance of this was great, because Tienfala is a microcosm of environmental hazards facing Mali. In a common statement with the French Greens and the Global Greens on 2 April 2012, Fadimata Bintou Touré condemned the recent military coup. In a radio interview she emphasised that ecologism is a 'new vision' which may be difficult for many people to understand. She also gave examples of popular actions to protect the environment and underlined that the Greens are in favour of industrialisation, provided it is done in a clean, non-polluting way.[17] At the parliamentary election of November 2013 the Greens won no seats.

Mauritius: Les Verts Fraternels

Les Verts Fraternels (The Brotherhood Greens) is an activist party, which in previous years has staged hunger strikes and other demonstrations to push their political demands. It has campaigned in favour of compensation for the descendants of slaves. A hunger strike in 2012 had to be terminated after three weeks when the president of the party, Sylvio Michel, was hospitalised.[18] The party has also been active on environmental and social issues and protested against injustices in the election system. Before the election of 10 December 2014, Michel announced that the Greens could only field 42 candidates instead of the planned 60, because the deposit demanded for every candidate had been increased six-fold, from 125 to 1,500 Mauritian Rupees (6.5€ to 39€). In the elections, the Greens got 0.5% of the votes and no MP.

Morocco: Parti des Verts Pour le Développement du Maroc

Parti des Verts Pour le Développement du Maroc (The Green Party for the Development of Morocco) was founded in June 1992 by Fatima Alaoui, who is still its secretary general. She is a very charismatic woman, with several sites on the web. Important issues for the party are women's rights and keeping Morocco free from GMOs. The African Green University, held in 2009, was a breakthrough in public life for the Moroccan Greens. In 2002 and again in 2006 the Greens submitted their party statutes and other required registration documents to become an official national party, but the Interior Ministry refused to grant them official recognition, except for some localities.

http://lesvertsmaroc-lesvertsmaroc.blogspot.se

Niger: Rassemblement pour un Sahel Vert/Parti Vert du Niger

Le Parti de Rassemblement pour un Sahel Vert, RSV-Ni'Im (The Association for a Green Sahel) was founded at the beginning of the 1990s. The theme of its extra-ordinary congress in 2012 was 'preserving the environment for a sustainable development'. The president of the party, Adamou Garba, expressed satisfaction that Niger was still a democracy, albeit surrounded by wars and conflict. He praised the president of Niger for having launched a programme of renaissance, which would also strengthen sustainable development.[19] In 2013 the party organised a tree-planting campaign to make the surroundings of the capital Niamey greener.[20] In the elections of 2011 the party won no seats in parliament.

Rwanda: Democratic Green Party of Rwanda

The Democratic Green Party of Rwanda (DGPR) was officially registered on 9 August 2013, after a four-year struggle with the authorities since its foundation on 14 August 2009. The party faced great problems facing the presidential election of August 2010. Three days prior to the founding congress of the African Green Federation three senior members defected, and in July the first vice president of the party, Andre Kagwa Rwisereka, went missing and a day later was found decapitated. This awful act of violence caused a lot of uneasiness. In its political platform for the 2013 elections DGPR called for non-violence and peaceful means of conflict resolution, social justice and equal opportunity, participatory democracy, unity and reconciliation of Rwandans, balancing the interests of a regulated market economy and community-based economics, special care to protect and defend the rights of the innocent and defenceless members of society, fiscal responsibility, limits to taxation and control of spending, and the protection of the unalienable rights of the people, including the right to life, liberty, peaceful assembly, expression, worship and the pursuit of happiness. DGPR was officially accepted as the eleventh member in the National Political Parties Forum on 3 April 2014. The president of DGPR, Frank Habineza, is also the president of the AGF. According to an end of year message by Habineza, 2014 was the year when DGPR established itself at the grassroots level, by setting up party structures in six districts and arranging women's training conferences at provincial level. The DGPR considers itself to be environmentalist and socialist, and anthropocentric rather than biocentric; it accepts the Global Greens Charter. DGPR has the goal of achieving gender balance in its organisation; it has no anti-cumulation rule, but does have rules for the rotation for party posts (maximum two terms), and requires elected representatives to donate 10% of their income from political positions to the party.[21]

http://www.rwandagreendemocrats.org/about-rwandagreens

Senegal: Fédération Démocratique des Ecologistes du Sénégal

Fédération Démocratique des Ecologistes du Sénégal, FEDES (Democratic Federation of the Ecologistes of Senegal) was founded in 2004, and was an efficient organising host of the Third Global Greens Congress in Dakar in 2012. Its president Haïdar El Ali is a veteran environmentalist, director of the Oceanium of Dakar. In 2012 he was appointed Minister of Environment and in 2013 moved portfolio to take charge of Fisheries. In the 2009 local elections the Greens won some hundred seats in local assemblies. El Ali was elected second vice president of the Dakar regional council. Before the local elections of 29 June 2014, where the Greens fielded a lot of candidates, El Ali declared that he wished the ecologists to be the third force in Senegalese politics.[22] After the elections El Ali said that 'even if we didn't get an ecologist mayor, we have got many councillors'.[23] In July 2014 he was dropped from the government when there was a reshuffle. He later said in an interview: 'I am not against president Macky Sall, but I think that concerning ecology he has missed the opportunity'.[24]

http://fedesenegaal.com

Togo: Afrique Togo Ecologie (ATE)

Afrique Togo Ecologie, ATE (Ecological Africa Togo), was founded in October 2011 by Irénée Nissao Napo, who claimed that none of the hundred or so parties already in existence had any interest in protection of the environment; he mentioned as an example the enormous number of plastic bags submerging the territory.[25] In a press conference about a year later Irénée Nissao Napo reported on the achievements of the party so far, claiming that it had identified areas in need of reforestation and drawn public attention to environmental threats from iron and phosphate mines. The party also had two members elected to positions in the African Green Federation.[26] In February 2014 it was recorded that ATE congratulated the customs authorities on a large confiscation of illegal ivory.[27]

Tunisia: Tunisie Verte/Tounis al-Khadra

Tunisie verte/Tounis al-Khadra (Green Tunisia) was founded in 2004 but officially registered only after the revolution, in January 2011. Its president is Abdelkader Zitouni. The party joined the Popular Front, consisting of Arab national and left-wing parties, in 2012. However, it left the Front in May 2014 accusing the spokesperson of the Front, Hamma Hammami, of abuse of power.[28] In an article in the newspaper *Quotidien Tunisien* in February 2011 Tunisie Verte is praised for its tough refusal to cooperate with the previous Ben Ali regime. The regime showed no interest in environmental issues and refused to accept the existence of an independent Green party. In 2006 it instead created its own 'Greens'. One reason for the negative attitude of the regime was that Tunisie Verte acted not only on environmental issues but also in favour of more democracy and transparency. Zitouni claims that he was constantly harassed by the police under the dictator's regime.[29] Since the revolution, however, the Tunisian Greens have not managed to play a major role. In the elections of December 2014 they won no seats in the parliament.

https://ar-ar.facebook.com/Parti.Tunisie.Verte

Uganda: Ecological Party of Uganda

The Ecological Party of Uganda (EPU) is led by a woman, Robinah Nanyunja. It works according to the motto 'Peaceful co-existence for sustainable development' and the basic Green principles of ecological wisdom, social justice, participatory democracy, non-violence, sustainability, respect for diversity as well as gender mainstreaming and transparency. Out of 15 members elected to the National Technical Committee (the party executive) in January 2015, five are women. Nanyunja, a veteran environmentalist, has said that the party plans to field several dozen candidates in its first election, 2016, also stating: 'My target is to have half of the contestants as women.' Robinah Nanyunja is president of Pilot International, a foundation which has organised

World Clean Technology summits. In November 2013 she was elected Secretary General for the Eastern African Green Federation.

http://www.ecologicalpartyofuganda.org/ecopartyug

Zambia: Green Party of Zambia

The Green Party of Zambia was founded in May 2013 by an environmentalist veteran, Peter Sinkamba, who is also the president of the party. The news was presented on the website of Virgin Airlines with the grossly incorrect headline: 'Africa's First Green Party Enters Zambian Politics'. In an interview Sinkamba expressed his ambition to pursue Green politics and explained why he had now turned from non-parliamentary to parliamentary activity: 'My 15 years of environmental advocacy has taught me a lesson: for one to better achieve sustainable development, green values or green economy, he or she needs to be in the driver's seat'. Sinkamba founded Citizens for a Better Environment (CBE) in 1998. In 2004 he was chosen to become a Fellow of Ashoka, which is an international organisation for social entrepreneurs (www.ashoka.org).[30]

According to bylaw no. 6 of the party, gender equality should be implemented. Some internal bodies are managed by co-presidents, but not the presidency of the party.

In April 2014 the Green Party of Zambia hit the headlines by demanding the legalisation of the cultivation of marijuana for the export market.[31] The call to legalise marijuana for export was a key issue for Sinkamba in his campaign for the presidential by-election (due to the sudden death the incumbent) of 20 January 2015. His arguments were more about the economic benefits for Zambia than about 'personal freedom'.[32] The Zambian voters obviously were not convinced; Sinkamba received 1,410 votes, 0.08%.

www.zambiagreens.org

MEMBERS OF THE AGF, NOT IN 'GOOD STANDING', NOVEMBER 2014
(for a definition of 'good standing' see Chapter 3, Africa)

Angola: Partido Nacional Ecológico de Angola

Partido Nacional Ecológico de Angola (The National Ecological Party of Angola) has entered into an agreement for extensive cooperation with Partido da Terra, 10 November 2011, signed by the president of the Ecological Party, Gregorio Nsumbu Mbala and the president of Partido da Terra, Joam Evans Pim.

Benin: Parti Vert du Benin/Benin Green Party

Les Verts du Benin (The Greens of Benin) was part of a four-party alliance at the 2003 parliamentary election, which won three seats (out of 83); however no Green became MP. In an interview of 8 May 2011, the president of the party, Toussaint Hinvi, accused the government of neglecting important environmental issues, such as the quality of drinking water, the hazards of uranium transports from Niger to the harbour of Cotonou (Benin), and the pollution from 'motos-taxis' (motorcycle taxis).[33]

Burkina Faso: Parti Ecologiste pour le Développement du Burkina Faso

Parti Ecologiste was part of the ruling coalition of the toppled president Compaore; as of January 2015 it has not paid its dues to the AGF.

Burundi: Burundi Green Movement

According to the AGF this is not yet a party, but is in process of becoming one.

Central African Republic: Mouvement des Verts de Centrafrique

Le Mouvement des Verts de Centrafrique, MVC (The Green Movement of Central Africa), was founded in 1999. Its founder and president, Laurent Avit Bokonas, died in March 2013. He had been an MP from 1993 to 1999. The fact-finding mission of the AGF in 2009 found a functioning party, but more pro-government than oppositional. MVC had supported the president of the republic, but complained that they felt excluded from influence.

Ivory Coast: Parti Écologique Ivoirien

Le Parti Écologique Ivoirien (The Ecological Party of Ivory Coast) was founded in 2001 after bloody conflict in the country. On its homepage it is emphasised that the mission of the party is to promote ecology and 'especially political ecology'. The party also has adopted a governmental programme 'which makes it possible for us to manage the affairs of the country if we would accede to power'. As 'founding members' a list of ten men is presented. The party president is N'Gouan Kouamé Edouard, who is also the founder.

http://parti-ecologique-ivoirien.org

Nigeria: Nigerian Green Movement

Green Movement Nigeria, GMN, published the following presentation in 2010: 'The Green Movement Nigeria (GMN) was birthed by professionals of environment and development in Nigeria and abroad to articulate a progressive agenda for sustainable development and sound environmental management for Nigeria.'[34] GMN called for the election of President Goodluck Jonathan in the presidential election of 2011.

In May 2013 a Nigerian newspaper published an article proposing the founding of a Green party. The writer, Thlal Gasmis, of the Department of Mass Communication, University of Maiduguri, wrote that 'it will be a good thing for friends of the environment in the country to come and put ideas and resources together, draft a constitution and form a "Green Party" which should be headed by notable environmental activists ... In view of the many environmental problems besetting the country, there is no better time to solve the problem than now.'[35]

Somalia: Democratic Green Party of Somalia

The Democratic Green Party of Somalia (DGPS) was created in 2009. Among its main objectives are to protect, analyse and monitor the environment to protect against its misuse or degradation, to rescue the Somali people from the unnecessary violence and wars, and to build grassroots democracy. Fifty per cent of the members of the executive committee are supposed to be women.

In Somalia there is also the Somalia Green Party (SGP), which is said to be a member of the Horn of Africa Greens together with the Green parties of Djibouti, Eritrea and Ethiopia.

http://www.gpsomalia.org

South Africa: Ecological Movement of South Africa

The Green Party of South Africa (GPSA) was founded in 1999 by Judy Sole. It was preceded by the Ecology Party, founded in 1989 and soon disbanded, and the Green Party in 1992, disbanded after an election failure in 1994. The GPSA has contested all elections since the 2000 local elections, but has never won more than 0.5% of the vote. However, in 2014 the GPSA abstained from participation due to a funding shortfall. In an interview in March 2014 Sole stated that the country couldn't wait another five years to get an eco-friendly government.[36]

GREEN PARTIES – NON-MEMBERS OF THE AGF

There are several parties in Africa outside the AGF which claim to be Green. Some of them are parties-in-the-making which may become AGF members, such as the Ghana Green Movement. The Parti Vert Gabonais (The Green Gabon Party) is a new party, whose leader is Hamissou Yaro. It is finalising its registration process and was present at the Central African Greens Congress in Kinshasa in November 2014. The Ecological Party-Movement of Earth in Mozambique is a party, but has not paid up its dues to AGF. In Sierra Leone the Green Movement/Green Watch, is under construction. There have also been reports about a Green party in Mauritania, Parti mauritanien pour la défense de l'environnement (The Mauritanian Party for the Protection of the Environment), founded in 2001. However, in 2014 the AGF reported having no news about or contact with it; it is doubtful if the party still exists. According to an interview in 2001 with the founder of the party, Ould Dellahi, he had understood the importance of the protection of the environment when working as secretary general of the Association of Fresh Food Exporters.[37]

B. THE AMERICAS
http://www.fpva.org

GREEN PARTIES, MEMBERS OF THE FPVA (AUTUMN 2014)

Bolivia: Partido Verde de Bolivia/Verde Ecologista

Partido Verde de Bolivia (Green Party of Bolivia) was founded in 2007. It demands the defence of a participative pluralist democracy and a socio-political ecology and is critical of the negative effects of globalisation on the environment and social security. In its governmental programme it also calls for respect for indigenous cultures and pacifism.[38] Facing the elections of 2014 it sealed an alliance with the National Council of Ayllus and Markas of Qullasuyu (CONAMAQ). The leader of CONAMAQ declared that the main goal was to work for a Plurinational State 'and in the 2019 election we would arrive in power to transform the Colonial State into a Plurinational State'. In the presidential election of October 2014 Partido Verde fielded Fernando Vargas as candidate for the presidency and its leader Margot Soria Saravia for the vice presidency. In the simultaneous parliamentary election 50% of the Green candidates were women; the Green Party got 2.65% of the vote, which it considers a victory; it claims that it won one seat which was taken away illegally by the authorities. On 20 October 2014, the party changed its name to Verde Ecologista, which necessitates a re-registration with the election authority.

https://es-es.facebook.com/PartidoVerdeBolivia

Brazil: Partido Verde

Partido Verde (Green Party) was founded in 1986, but a starting point for Green activity in Brazil was the creation of the Associacão Gaúcha de protecão ao Ambiente Natural (gaucho = cowboy or inhabitant of Rio Grande do Sul), AGAPAN, in 1971 by José Lutzenberger, who wrote *Manifesto Ecológico Brasileiro*. Around 1985 discussions about forming a Green party were initiated, especially by former political refugees like Fernando Gabeira, Alfredo Sirkis, Herbert Daniel and Carlos Minc. A decision to establish a party was made in January 1986. In November 1986 Partido Verde entered into a coalition with PT (Partido dos Trabalheros/Workers' Party) for the local elections in Rio; Gabeira got 7.8% of the vote in the election for governor, but PV was attacked for its demand for the liberalisation of marijuana. Minc was elected as state deputy. Provisional registration was made in March 1988. In the same year Sirkis was elected local councillor (verdeador) in Rio. For the presidential elections of 1989, PV at first nominated Hebert Danil, a homosexual with aids. Following protests, however, Danil withdrew and was replaced by Gabeira, who got less than 1% of the vote. In 1990 the PV got its first federal deputy, Sidney Miguel. In 1992 Sirkis was chosen as party president. On 30 September 1993 the PV got its final registration. In the election of October 1992, 54 Green verdeadores and 3 prefeitos were elected. For the presidential elections of 1994 PV supported Lula (Luiz Inácio Lula da Silva), the leader of the Workers' Party. Gabeira became the only federal deputy. In 1996 PV got 189 verdeadores and 13 prefeitos. The progress continued from 1998 to 2002. In 2002 the PV helped Lula to win the presidential elections. However, rather soon PV found that Lula's policies relative to the Amazon rainforest, nuclear power and GMOs were a disaster, as was his economic policy of supporting industry whatever the environmental consequences. As a result, the Green Party broke with Lula.

According to a Brazilian observer there are some differences between European and Brazilian Green thinking. A document by the Green Group in the European Parliament in which 'the love to bear and take care of children is reduced to "non-remunerated work of reproduction"' represents an 'ideology which is hardly adapted to the relations of Brazilian women and men to children'. About drugs PV believes that tobacco and alcohol are no less evil than narcotics. The issue of abortion has been difficult for PV, because of the contradiction between the sacredness of life and personal autonomy. After long philosophical discussion it was finally concluded that 'the right to freely decide over one's own body is politically indisputable'.[39]

These issues caused some problems when in 2010 PV nominated the former Minister of Environment in President Lula's administration, Marina Silva, as its candidate for the presidential elections. Silva is conservative on religious and moral issues and forced the party to put demands for free abortion, homosexual rights, etc. on hold. Already in 2004 the PV showed an interest in Silva by alleging that she was 'an outcast in the government, the Minister of Environment has become a kind of NGO whereby the minister is heard but unconsidered by the government'.[40] Marina Silva won 19.3% of the votes. However, facing the elections of 2014 she left the Greens, becoming the candidate for another party, but didn't make it to the second round. At the simultaneous parliamentary elections PV gained only 2.07% of the vote and eight deputies (down from 15); however they regained a seat in the Senate. The fact that a new Ecological Party contested the election cannot wholly explain the PV setback, as the new party got only 0.7%. Perhaps the interlude with Marina Silva was punished by voters. In January 2013, at a meeting celebrating the 27th anniversary of the party, its president José Luiz Penna emphasised that PV had always stood for the rights of Afro-Brazilians, women, and homosexuals.

http://pv.org.br

Canada: The Green Party of Canada/Parti Vert du Canada

The Green Party of Canada/Parti Vert du Canada was founded at a national convention in Ottawa in November 1983. However, according to a founding member, this meeting 'failed to achieve the results hoped for by the organizers' because 'nothing short of a cultural revolution will satisfy many Greens'.[41] In 2004 the party got 4.3% of the vote, which made it entitled to federal funding. In 2006 it gained a little, up to 4.5%, but still not enough to secure a seat because of the majority election system. In 2008 it achieved a record result, 6.8% (but still no MP), partly because, after long deliberations, it was allowed to participate in some televised debates. In 2011, despite a loss of votes (down to 4%), the breakthrough came with the election of its first MP, Elizabeth May (chair of the party since 2006). In 2013 an MP from another party switched to the Greens, thus doubling the number of Green MPs.

The Canadian Greens have adopted the six principles of the Global Greens as their ideological foundation. Furthermore, the party demands increased taxes on polluters, cutting subsidies for industries that pollute, subsidies for public transport and environmentally friendly technology, transfers to municipalities for infrastructure, mandatory labelling of genetically engineered food and food ingredients, federal animal welfare reform, a significant shift to investment in renewable energy, scaling back military spending to 2005 levels, and a reorientation towards peacekeeping. The party also demands the introduction of proportional representation. Like some other Greens it wants to legalise, regulate and tax cannabis.

At the end of the 1990s, the then president of the party refused to support a local candidate in Newfoundland because he had expressed an understanding for seal hunting and mining, both of which had wide support among the local population, but were hardly inside the framework of Green politics. A proposal in 2004 to reduce income and corporate taxes, in exchange for increased taxes on energy and pollution, led to a debate about the ideological status of the party: Was it moving from its usual centre-left position to a more neoliberal, 'eco-capitalist' strategy? Its cooperation for a period with the Liberal Party provoked similar reactions. However, the trend for the Canadian Greens is clearly upwards.

An important asset for the party is the strong position of its leader, Elizabeth May, who is, according to polls, Canada's most popular politician. She has even been voted 'Parliamentarian of the Year', 'Hardest Working MP' and 'Best Orator' by her parliamentary colleagues, almost all from competing parties. She does not hesitate to use tough language, such as warning that 'the next elected dictator could be Trudeau or Mulcair' (leaders of larger parties). The Canadian Greens claim that Canada is slipping away from good democracy, and as well as demanding proportional representation also dare to challenge the 'holy cow' of most democracies – the media. The Greens demand an independent review of media ownership. They also try to block hyperbole surrounding the 'fight against terrorism', which is abused to curb civil liberties.

According to polls in early 2015 the Greens stand at 8.5% nationally and 16% in British Columbia. The Greens' best chance in the election in the fall of 2015 thus lie in BC, and that is precisely where it is concentrating its resources. Commentators consider it possible that the Green presence in the Federal parliament could increase from two to six MPs.[42]

http://www.greenparty.ca

Chile: Partido Ecologista Verde de Chile

Partido Ecologista Verde de Chile, ECOV (Green Ecologist Party of Chile) was founded in 2002 and officially registered in 2008. However, in 2014 the registration was annulled by the election authorities with the argument that the party didn't achieve 5% of the votes in the elections of 2013. Since then efforts are being made to merge with a similar party, Partido Ecologista Verde del Norte.

Already in the late 1980s the Coordination of European Greens received a 'petition to help the Greens in Chile'. A Green party, Los Verdes, was created in 1987 and survived until 2001, but without any electoral success. The Chilean Greens were also infiltrated by the Humanistas.[43] In 2006 the Greens supported Michele Bachelet, the Socialist candidate for president, with whom they reached a programmatic agreement that included a temporary moratorium on nuclear power, 10% of energy to be renewables, GMO labelling and the creation of a Ministry of Environment. In 2013 ECOV won 2.35% of the votes with a Green candidate in the presidential elections, but only 0.75% in the simultaneous parliamentary elections. It is ECOV's ambition to promote participant democracy and give the people an option that is different from traditional left and right. On its homepage ECOV tries to illustrate its ideological positioning by showing a figure with three dimensions: green-grey, left-right, libertarian-authoritarian, where the Green position is the first item of every pair. Apart from basic Green points, ECOV demands: a reduction of military expenditure by 50%, the removal of mines at the borders with Bolivia, Argentina and Peru, an unemployment allowance of 75% of the salary and a minimum salary of 300,000 pesos (408€). The party also demands a law to guarantee women 50% of all posts in the state administration; however in its own structure the party is overwhelmingly male: out of six members of the central executive, only one is a woman, and out of three members of the central 'tribunal', none is a woman. The president of the party 2014–17 is a man, Felix Gonzales Gatica. There are two Green local councillors.

http://www.partidoecologista.cl

Colombia: Alianza Verde

La Alianza Verde (The Green Alliance) was formally established in 2013, but has a long pre-history. In 1998 Partido Verde Oxigeno was founded by Ingrid Betancourt, who had been elected to the parliament in 1994. In 1998 she became a senator with a record number of votes. However, she became unpopular among some parts of the population for demanding negotiations with the guerrilla, FARC. In 2002 she was Green candidate for the presidential election. However, before the elections, on 23 February 2002, she was abducted by FARC and then held in captivity for more than six years, being released on 2 July 2008, after an action by the Colombian army.[44] By then her party had been already dissolved and replaced by Partido Verde Opcion Centro, in 2005.

During the first week after her release Betancourt expressed gratitude to President Uribe and went to France and embraced President Sarkozy. These and other early statements by her caused uproar among some sympathisers, who accused her of being a political traitor. Others retorted that it was natural that just after her release she was able to embrace just about anybody who had contributed to her rescue. In any case, she left Colombia for France, wrote books, made speeches, and has so far not returned to politics, neither in Colombia nor in France.

The civil war in Colombia continued for years; only in 2013 were negotiations started and in mid December 2014 FARC declared a unilateral truce.

The new Green party in 2009 dropped the second part of its name and became Partido Verde. It had some success in elections, winning some MPs and local councillors. In 2010 the Green candidate Antanas Mockus came second in the first round of the presidential election with 21.5% of the vote, but in the second round he lost, with 27.5%. In 2013 the party merged with the Movimiento Progressista and formed Alianza Verde. The Greens are established as a part of the Colombian political spectrum and in the parliamentary elections of March 2014 the party won 3.9% for the Senate and five senators (out of 102) and 3.4% for the Chamber and six MPs (out of 166).

The party has a comprehensive programme, including demands for better education, protection of the environment and biodiversity, equal civil rights, sustainable development, and the elimination of all types of sexual or gender discrimination. This last point has not prevented the fact that the executive council presented on the homepage consists of seven men and no women.

http://www.alianzaverde.org.co/Inicio.aspx

Dominican Republic: Partido Socialista Verde

El Partido Socialista Verde, PASOVE (Socialist Green Party), founded in October 2009, was formally registered in February 2010. The president of the party, Antolin Polcano, has stated that the party does not plan to remain forever like traditional parties, and that it should have a horizontal rather than a traditional vertical structure. Polcano appears frequently in Colombian media with statements on most political issues, for example in a speech in February 2015 when he protested against a violent attack on a former president of the republic as well as making environmental demands.[45]

Another Green party, PVUD, has disappeared. The PASOVE is the successor to El Partido Verde de la Republica Domincana, which was a founding member of the FPVA. The party was first given status as observer, later as a member; however problems with a split are unresolved and the situation not quite clear.

http://pasoverd.org

Mexico: Partido Verde Ecologista de Mexico

Partido Verde Ecologista de Mexico, PVEM (Green Ecologist Party of Mexico), was founded in 1986 and is one of the strongest Green parties in America, having had elected representatives for many years. Having been earlier in alliance with parties to the right of centre, it is currently in an alliance with the centre-left PRI (Institutional Revolutionary Party). The first president of the party was its founder, Jorge González Torres, who was replaced by his son, Jorge Emilio González Martinez, from 2001 to 2011, who, however (as emphasised by PVEM representatives), was not appointed but formally elected. Since September 2011 the position of president has been removed from the statutes and replaced by a group of three 'leaders', the national spokesperson (Arturo Escobar y Vega), the executive secretary (Jorge Legorreta Ordorica) and the technical secretary (Diego Guerrero Rubio) – three men.

In 1997 the PVEM became the fourth largest party in Mexico. In 2000 it took part in an alliance that backed the conservative Vincente Fox, who was elected president of the republic. However, rather soon the Greens distanced themselves from Fox because of his non-ecological policy. In the local elections of 2003, PVEM ran mostly independent candidates and won 17 deputies and five senators.

The PVEM caused consternation among other Greens when in 2008 it supported the death penalty for certain serious violent crimes. A source in the PVEM has given the author the following explanation: 'There is a high amount of violence, kidnappings and deaths in Mexico. In 2008 the local deputies of Mexico City made an inquiry asking the population about their views about this problem. 96% of them demanded the death penalty. So the Greens decided to follow the orders of their constituency and put it in an initiative. However, to correct the situation, the National Committee of the PVEM issued new documents in 2009 taking out this initiative and replaced it with a demand for more years of penalty for the perpetrators of such violent crimes. That was the end of it in Mexico.'

Some European Greens have worried about a seemingly anti-left bias in the PVEM. The source in the PVEM comments: 'Things are different in the Americas, and parties don't want to be in alliances with the radical left or the right. They are trying to move beyond that classification of the nineteenth century ... Left parties in Mexico and other Latin American countries don't care at all for the environment; the same thing goes for the neoliberal right.' In its first federal election in 1993 the party got a little over 1% of the vote. From 2003 the result has been 6–7%. In the elections of 1 July 2012, the PVEM got 6.4%, 29 MPs (12 women) out of 500, and nine senators (three women) out of 128. In 2014 a law prohibiting the use of animals in circuses was adopted on a proposal by PVEM. The party has played an important role in the establishment and functioning of the Federation of American Greens.

According to preliminary results of the June 7, 2015, parliamentary elections the PVEM won a clear victory, getting 7.15–7.55% and 41–48 MPs.

http://www.partidoverde.org.mx/pvem

Peru: Partido Ecologista Alternativa Verde del Peru

Partido Ecologista Alternativa Verde del Peru (Green Alternative Ecologist Party of Peru) was founded in 1995. It participated in elections in 2000 and 2006. Its female secretary general is Flor de Maria Hurtado, one of the founders of the Alternative Ecological movement of Peru.

The origins of the Peruvian Greens lie in the environmental movements of the late 1990s and the opposition to the dictatorship of former Peruvian president Alberto Fujimori. The Greens opposed a toxic waste plant in the Pantanal Region. In 2001, they joined a centre-left coalition to support Alejandro Toledo, who became the first president of indigenous origin. However, the Greens soon became disappointed with the corruption of the Toledo regime. In 2003 they managed to get some representatives elected to regional councils and gathered 7,000 petition signatures to register the party.

In 2005 Hurtado was threatened by a gunman because of her defence of the Amazon jungle and the rights of indigenous people. This caused a wave of support from Greens all over the world, until the Peruvian Ministry of the Interior granted her protection. In the elections of 2011 the Greens won no seats. There is also a Partido Verde, which is not a member of the FPVA.

https://es-es.facebook.com/vozverdeflor

USA: Green Party

The Green Party of the USA was founded in 1991, but already in 1984 a Committee of Correspondence for the state Green parties was established. It is one of the most radical Green parties, especially concerning foreign policy where it regularly criticises the military interventions by the USA, as well as the US support for the Israeli occupation of Palestine. With a proportional representation system, the US Greens, with about a quarter of a million members, would undoubtedly be a major political factor in the USA, but due to the majoritarian system the Greens have only about 100 elected representatives on the lower levels of the political hierarchy, including one state representative in Arkansas. Quite a number of thinkers and writers on ecological politics and Green thinking have been from the USA, for example Murray Bookchin, Fritjof Capra, Ernest Callenbach, Carolyne Merchant, Stephanie Mills, Charlene Spretnak, Kirkpatrick Sale, etc. The US Green Party is based upon ten key values: grassroots democracy, social justice and equal opportunity, ecological wisdom, non-violence, decentralisation, community-based economics, gender equality, respect for diversity, personal and global responsibility, future focus and sustainability.

From the beginning the US Greens have contested the presidential elections with Green candidates. When in 1996 the veteran ecologist and citizens advocacy activist Ralph Nader was Green presidential candidate for the first time, a newspaper commented: 'Why does Nader Candidacy worry White House? The Green party nominee may be the spoiler of a close race.'[46] Nader did not campaign on classical environmental issues, but on fighting corporations, big money and similar. He got 0.71%, 685,000 votes. Nader was also the Green candidate in 2000 and reached an all-time high for the Greens, with 2.9

million votes, 2.7%. However, this result brought him, and the Greens, a lot of accusations of having prevented a victory for Al Gore, vice president to Bill Clinton and considered almost Green in his outlook because of a number of statements and books.[47] In the following presidential races the Green results plummeted: 2004, 0.1%; 2008, 0.1%; 2012, 0.4%. In 2008 and 2012 the Green tickets had two female names, in 2008 Cynthia McKinney and Rosa Clemente, and in 2012 Jill Stein and Cheri Honkala. In a foreword to a book by Derek Wall, McKinney states that the Green Party was 'providing a voice for those who suffer from the lack of a living wage, from erosion of civil liberties, from the refusal to provide universal healthcare, from the insistence on waging interminable war and from reckless pursuit of profit at all costs even at the expense of the earth'.[48] The results in elections to the Congress have been about on the same level as in the presidential elections, for the House of Representatives 0.3–0.5%, for the Senate 0.2–0.9%.

http://www.gp.org/index.php

Venezuela: Movimiento ecológico de Venezuela

Movimiento ecológico de Venezuela, MOVEV (The Ecological Movement of Venezuela), was founded in 2005 and officially registered in 2008. In 2011 it joined the anti-Chávez coalition Mesa de la unidad democratica, MUD (Democratic Unity Roundtable). The Greens claim to be an organisation of environmentalists who want to show respect for all forms of life, work for the protection of the environment and the containment of the ecological destruction, and create a sustainable society which allows the population of Venezuela to live in social justice and harmony with the Nature. In the local elections of 2013 the Greens got a dozen local and regional councillors. Its slogan is 'The logic is ecologic'.

http://www.movimientoecologico.net.ve

GREEN OBSERVER PARTIES OF THE FVPA (AUTUMN 2014)

Argentina: El Partido Iniciativa Verde

El Partido Iniciativa Verde (Green Initiative Party) was founded in 2006 by Juan Manuel Velasco, a former MP and responsible for environment in Buenos Aires. The party struggles for basic Green aims such as eco-taxes, renewable energy, dismantling of nuclear reactors, promotion of collective transport and sustainable eco-social economy, extended support for unemployed people, prevention instead of repression in the judicial system, and the legalisation of 'soft' drugs, and is against all forms of 'machismo' and sexism. It also supports non-violence and proposes that the military should be used to protect nature. The party also espouses spirituality: 'The transformation of the interior of persons to improve the planet.' PIV received 0.45% of the vote in Buenos Aires in 2009.

http://www.partidoverde.org.ar (under construction February 2015)

Costa Rica: El Partido Verde Ecologista de Costa Rica

El Partido Verde Ecologista de Costa Rica (The Green Ecologist Party of Costa Rica) was founded on 11 September 2004. Its mission is to respect all forms of life, protect the environment and stop the ecological deterioration, establish a sustainable development and social justice and a life in harmony with nature. Other basic principles are tolerance and respect for diversity and that Costa Rica should be free of GMOs. The party argues that the Bible recommends an ecological lifestyle: 'Our conscience and action are inspired by our belief in God – sustainability and survival.' The leadership is all male, with Carlos R. Arrieta Jimenez as secretary general. In 2012 another green party, Partido Verde, was established, but didn't manage to get registered and was accused by the PVE of stealing its name.

http://partidoverdeecologistacr.yolasite.com

Guatemala: Los Verdes

Los Verdes (The Greens) has been a member of the FPVA. In 2012 a section of the party merged with others into Todos (Everybody). However, Todos didn't want to take on a Green identity; the Greens were supposed to be just a section inside Todos. This made some of the Greens decide to restore Los Verdes, which was given observer status to the FPVA. The party will regain its full membership when it has managed to re-register officially.

http://www.robertoalejoscambara.com/noticias/todos-vamos-por-guate
    (homepage of the leader of Todos)

Guyana: Les Verts-Guyane

Les Verts-Guyane (The Greens of Guyana) is considered to be a branch of the French Greens, EELV, and therefore has been accepted by the FPVA only as an observer, since 2008. The party is regularly invited to FPVA meetings, but according to the FPVA, hasn't shown up for several years. In the EU elections of

2014 the Guyana Greens had a big victory, winning 41% of the votes; however only about 10% of the eligible voters participated in the election.[49]

GREEN PARTIES, NEITHER MEMBERS NOR OBSERVERS OF THE FPVA

Nicaragua: Partido Verde Ecologista de Nicaragua/Verdes en Alianza

Partido Verde Ecologista de Nicaragua, PVEN (The Ecologist Green Party of Nicaragua), was founded in 2003. Its president is Edward Martín Salazar Cruz. In a programme adopted in 2007 (called Hacia 2017) the PVEN defines its aims for 2017 in order to achieve a shift away from the inhuman and dangerous conditions of the current system. In 2000 the PVEN was invited to attend a meeting of the FPVA in Peru and became a member of the FPVA in 2003. In 2003 PVEN joined an alliance with Herty Lewites, who had broken with the FSLN (Frente Sandinista de Liberación/Sandinista National Liberation Front). The alliance caused surprise among other Greens as it included a movement that had been supported by the CIA during the civil war. The PVEN motivation was that it sought a third way. A key value for PVEN is gender equality, because 'the Nicaraguan society is based upon anatomical differences between sexes, which are converted into social and economic differences'. According to information from FPVA, in November 2013 the Greens of Nicaragua lost their status as observer, after not being able to fulfil the requirements.

C. ASIA-PACIFIC REGION
https://www.asiapacificgreens.org/asia-pacific-greens

GREEN PARTIES, MEMBERS OF THE APGF

Australia: Green Party

The Australian Green Party was founded in 1992, but has a much older origin, furthermost in the United Tasmanian Group, created in 1972 to prevent the damming of Lake Pedder; this led to the establishment of the Tasmania Green Party, with veteran Australian Green Bob Brown as initiator. The first Green Senator was Jo Vallentine, who was elected in 1984 to represent the Nuclear Disarmament Party, but switched to West Australia Greens in 1990. The first parliamentarian to be elected on an Australian Green ticket was Bob Brown in 1996. The party is much more than an environmental party and speaks on behalf of those who wouldn't otherwise get much of a say inside parliament: children, refugees, students, individuals and families living in poverty and, of course, the natural environment. Its four core values are ecological sustainability, social justice, grassroots democracy, and peace and non-violence.

At the celebration of the 40 year anniversary of the United Tasmanian Group in 2012, the Green Party leader Christine Milne made a toast to recent Green political victories, such as a carbon tax and the removal of the federal veto over territory legislation, which she said might 'presage new moves on Brown's pet projects: voluntary euthanasia and gay marriage'. In 2012 the Australian Greens were in a better position than ever before, with 10,000 members, ten federal MPs, and 24 state and territory MPs, including two cabinet posts and partnership in a coalition government in Tasmania, and more than 100 local councillors around the country. The parliamentary elections of 7 September 2013 were a victory, the number of senators (elected at different times by proportional representation) increased by one, to 10 (from 1 July 2014), while the only seat in the House of Representatives (single member constituencies) was retained. The Greens got 8.7% of the vote. The victory of 7 September 2013 was celebrated as a major breakthrough. The party was considered by Australian media to be a genuine third force in Australian politics.

According to the political scientist David Hetherington, the rise of the Greens 'was propelled by three factors, two external and one internal. The first was the emergence of global climate politics in the mid-2000s, best symbolised in public consciousness by Al Gore's *An Inconvenient Truth* and in policy circles by Nicholas Stern's landmark 2006 report. The second factor was broad disillusionment with the mainstream political parties around the same time.'

The Greens also tried to target special socioeconomic groups in a way uncommon to the Green parties: a) the so-called 'doctors' wives', affluent liberal voters who historically voted conservative but swung on the twin social issues of climate change and refugees; b) more traditional left-wing voters who felt that Labour had drifted too far to the centre in its embrace of economic liberalisation. Finally, most commentators agree on the importance of the leadership of Bob Brown, who retired in 2012 as a winner. Despite the celebrations, the 2013 election when scrutinised carefully was no clear victory. The number of Green votes fell, for the House of Representatives from 11.8 to 8.7%.

What had happened? Commentators agreed that a vital factor was that the Greens had achieved their coveted position as an established party, in a situation when voter's confidence in established parties was low and several fresh populist protest parties entered the scene. Some add that the fact that the Greens voted down what they considered to be an inadequate proposal for an emission trading scheme might also have hurt them. Some also believe that the new leader, Christine Milne, hasn't had enough time to fill the gap left by Bob Brown.

David Hetherington believes that the Greens can make a political comeback by renewed combined activity on climate change and refugees and by occupying the traditional social democrat space vacated by Labour as it has moved to the political centre.[50] A positive sign for the Australian Greens was the result of the state elections of New South Wales in March 2015, which saw a clear victory, with an increase in seats from one to three.

http://greens.org.au

India: Uttarakhand Parivartan Party

Uttarakhand Parivartan Party, UKPP (The Uttarakhand Transformation Party), was founded in January 2009 in the northern Indian state of Uttarakhand, which was separated from Uttar Pradesh in 2000. The party has its origin in anti-dam and ecological struggles in the Central Himalayan Region. It has fielded candidates in several elections, but never received more than below 1% of the votes. The party is multiethnic and multi-religious. The co-founder and Convener of UKPP, Suresh Nautiyal, admits to the author that the participation of women is only 10%, which is 'not adequate', as the party adheres to the principle of gender balance. After a climate action Nautiyal wrote: 'I believe it is the duty of the developed world to realise the damage caused by them, recognising that they are consuming most of the manufactured products no matter where they are made, and recognising the power they have to make the changes needed.'[51] There have been several attempts to establish a nationwide Green party in India. An attempt by Nautiyal together with the activist Anandi Sharan of Bangalore failed because most environmental NGOs didn't want to be part of a Green political process. In an article in 2009 titled 'A Green Party' in India? It's About Time!' it was stated: 'The possible introduction of an Indian Green Party gives us hope. Some of us have heard about the recent coup d'état by the environmentalists in Kolkata who managed to remove all old and polluting vehicles in the city.'[52] The 'coup d'état' was initiated by an environmentalist 'maverick', Subhas Dutta, who according to reports had been planning to start a Green party.[53]

On the web a National Green Party of India can be found; it has tried to launch 'A business plan for developing an active and recognised Green Party in India – The first 10 years of the party'.[54] In May 2014, on the homepage of Global Greens, Suresh Nautiyal praised the Aam Aadami Party, AAP, which was 'able to inspire the youth to be interested in politics and seek greater political participation'. Nautiyal, however, observed that 'the AAP manifesto does not offer any specific prescription for environmental governance'.

The Indian newspaper *The Hindu*, on 27 March 2013, recalled that it was exactly 40 years since the *Chipko Movement* started, initially a group of Himalayan peasants resisting tree-felling by forest contractors. The Chipko people were dismissed as agents of Western imperialism and enemies of 'development'. The economic liberalisation from the 1990s onwards didn't improve India's ecological mess. The article ends with the hope that 'A new Chipko movement is waiting to be born.' Just before the elections of May 2014, the *Hindustani Times* affirmed: 'Green politics absent, parties give environment a miss'; and this despite the extremely pessimistic picture given in the article of the environmental degradation in the country.[55]

It might be believed that the country of Mahatma Ghandi would be at the forefront of ecological politics. However, in a book written some years ago by Mukul Sharma, *Green and Saffron*, it is alleged that environmentalism has been hijacked by Hindu conservatives, who pay lip-service to the environment, but earn money from destructive mega-projects.[56] The internationally most well-known Indian ecologist is probabaly Vandana Shiva, who, however, is not active in party politics.[57]

The parliamentary election of May 2014 was a disappointment for Aam Aadami, which won only four seats (out of 543). However in the election for the Dehli legislative assembly in February 2015 it won a major victory with 54% of the vote and 67 (out of 70) seats and now is ruling the Indian capital.

http://www.aamaadmiparty.org

Indonesia: Sarekat Hijau Indonesia

Sarekat Hijau Indonesia, SHI (Indonesian Green Union), was founded on 6 July 2007, at a congress in Jakarta. The SHI has declared that its goal is to 'build a united front of a progressive mass movement to strengthen the struggle of the Indonesian people'. SHI says that 'Indonesia faces crises in many dimensions which increase the dangers of ecological disasters to perpetuate poverty. This situation is due to the workings of the corrupt political and economic elite or the political oligarchy.' SHI criticises the 'greed-driven motives as the underlying logic of capitalism system' and the 'economic exploitation'. An analysis by political scientists claims that degradation of the environment, global warming and illegal logging are very sensitive issues in Indonesia where many farmers have failed with their farms, lots of fishermen lost their fish, and many people vanished from their forest; this gives the Greens a chance to gain lots of voters.[58] The SHI is led by Koesnadi Wirasapoetra. The party did not get any seats in parliament in the election of 9 April 2014.

http://sarekathijauindonesia.org

Japan: Greens Japan

Midorino-to (Greens Japan) was founded on 28 July 2012 (16 months after the Fukushima nuclear disaster). It is led by four gender-balanced *co-repre-sentatives*: Ms Uiko Hasegawa (former candidate for Upper House election),

Figure 11   A demonstration in Japan, after the Fukushima nuclear disaster, 2011, with activists from Japan Greens Reiko Kondo (sitting at right) and Koji Sugihara (standing in the middle). Photo: courtesy of Global Greens.

Mr Hitoshi Nakayama (Councillor of Niigata City), Ms Namiho Matsumoto (former candidate for Upper House election), and Mr Heiwa Hasegawa. Some of the core objectives of the party are to substantially increase the use of renewable energy sources, to end Japan's dependence on nuclear power and to greatly reduce carbon dioxide emissions.

One origin of the new party was a political organisation called Midori no Mirai (Green Future), comprising about 70 lawmakers in local assemblies. The organisation was disbanded to form the Greens Japan.

A leading Japanese newspaper, *Asahi Shimbun*, saw the establishment of the Green party as a step to 'nudge Japan to abandoning nuclear power by fielding candidates in upcoming national elections'.[59]

According to one research paper presented at the IPSA (International Association of Political Science) conference in Fukuoka 2009, there were at the beginning of the 2000s several organisations at the prefectural level and hundreds at the municipal level in Japan that focused on Green issues, such as environment, social welfare, women's rights, local autonomy, peace, as well as promoting a more healthy lifestyle and doubting the benefits of eternal economic growth.[60] But the constraints on the establishment of a national Green party that could enter parliament were (and still are) numerous: the mixed electoral system is a major problem. Three hundred seats are elected according to the majority system. The remaining 180 seats are elected proportionally, but only inside every constituency, which makes it difficult for small parties in constituencies with few seats.

In the Upper House election of 2007 the Greens decided to run an independent young person, Ryuhei Kawada, who was infected with HIV as a result of a blood transfusion when he was 10 years old. He had made a moving speech to the Global Young Greens Conference in Nairobi in January 2007, with the title 'I Do Not Give up Hope': 'My experience as a victim of the medical and industrial crime made me realise that people can live happily when, and only when, our society cares for the values of peace, life and human rights ... We have to appeal the importance of Green politics which values not only peace, but also the global environment and biodiversity, aiming at a truly sustainable society.' Ryuhei Kawada was elected. But he has since, to the disappointment of the Greens, joined the right-wing.

On the 22 November 2010 Kazumi Inamura became the first popularly elected Green Mayor of Japan, in the city of Amagasaki, as well as the first female mayor of the city, with 54% of the vote. The Japan Greens did not participate in the Lower House elections of 2014 because of lack of financial resources. To participate in an election a deposit of 3–6 million yen must be paid (22,500–45,000 euro) for every candidate. According to information from Rikiya Adachi, Secretary of International Relations of Greens Japan, the minimum cost for deposits for an election campaign would be 24 million yen (180,000 euro), with campaign expenditures on top of that. The party has 38 local councillors (15 women).

http://greens.gr.jp/world/english

Korea: Green Party Plus

The Green Party Plus, GPP (Noksaekdang), was initiated on 20 October 2011 and formally inaugurated on 4 March 2012. However, there was a predecessor, Korean Greens, which participated in the founding of the Asia-Pacific Green Federation in 2005.

GPP claims to be a party in which grassroots members take leading roles, chosen by direct democracy and lottery, and reflecting minorities' opinions including those of women, the disabled, immigrants and youth. It presents itself as an alliance of regional parties, where every entity is independent, but shares its goals and values with Green Party Korea, including ecological wisdom, social justice, grassroots democracy, non-violence, peace, continuity and respecting diversity. The president of the party is Mr Seungsoo Ha.

The election campaign in 2012 focused on non-nuclear energy, especially in regional districts where nuclear power stations are placed. The party won

APPENDIX: GREEN PARTIES IN 100 COUNTRIES   151

about 100,000 votes, 0.48%, which was too little to keep the official registration. However it managed to re-register in October the same year, by adding 'plus' to its name. In the local elections of 2014 the Greens fielded 23 candidates, but no Green was elected to any municipal office.

www.kgreens.org

Mongolia: Mongolian Green Party

Mongolia has two Green parties that are members of the APGF. The Mongolian Green Party (Mongolyn Nogoon Nam) was founded in 1990, the first Green party on the Asian continent. From 1996 to 2000 it was part of a coalition government with three other parties. Its basic aims are to improve human rights and democracy and to protect the environment. It had one seat in the parliament from 2008 to 2012.

Civil Will Green Party (Irgenii Zorig-Nogoon Nam), which is a member of the Liberal International, was created in 2012 through a merger of the Civil Will and the Green parties. It won two seats in the 2012 elections and is part of a coalition government. However, the merger was opposed by parts of the Green Party, as reported in media in February 2011: 'The recently concluded alliance between the Green Party and the Civil Will Party has run into rough weather as the former cancelled the membership of its former Chairman, Mr. D. Enkhbat, who was chosen to head the alliance. Long-time CWP leader and former Foreign Minister S. Oyun distanced herself and her party from the development, saying this was an internal matter of the Green Party. She added, however, that it would be "shameful" if two parties that have only one seat each in Parliament cannot come together to act as a strong opposition force.'[61] However, the merger was carried out on 28 January 2012, at a meeting with 500 participants, who unanimously decided to create the new Civil Will Green Party (CWGP).[62]

Nevertheless the Mongolian Green Party still exists. Its leader is Olzod Boum-Yalagch. It claims to have 2,100 members and 65,000 supporters, but due to the internal changes and Mongolian rules it must re-register. According to MGP it was damaged by fraud in the 2012 election. It also explains that the leader of the Civil Will Green Party, Ms Ouyn, joined the MGP in 2000 and was elected MP first as candidate of the MGP, then of the CWGP. The MGP does not accept the CWGP as Green and alleges that the CWGP is in favour of uranium mining and has close relations with certain big business. Obviously the split and exit of some of the MGP leadership and members to the CWGP has caused problems.

After an investigation the APGF has accepted both parties as members.

Nepal: Green Civil Society

Green Civil Society (Nepali Greens) is dedicated to raising a strong voice to ensure Nepal's physical security, social security, environmental security, economic security, health security, food security, energy security and national security, putting the environmental agenda centre stage. In August 2014 the Nepali Greens launched a 'youth self-employment campaign' on the occasion of International Youth Day. The party adheres to basic Green values, such as environment conservation, sustainable development and peace. As stated on its homepage, it is committed to conserving natural and cultural resources and to the development of a sustainable and peaceful society by respecting and protecting the rights of Mother Nature and living beings including human beings. The party didn't get any MPs in the elections of November 2013. The president is Ballav Timalsina (male).

www.greencivilsociety.org

Hariyali Nepal Party (Green Nepal Party) is another party which was founded in 2007. It has been a member of the APGF. Kuber Sharma, the party's founding president, briefly held the post of Nepal's Minister for Culture and Civil Aviation for a period at the beginning of the 2000s. The party didn't win any seats in the elections of November 2013.

New Zealand: The Green Party of Aotearoa New Zealand

The Green Party of Aotearoa New Zealand (in Māori: Rōpū Kākāriki o Aotearoa) is the oldest national Green party in the world, originating in the Values Party, founded in 1972. The party had lots of initial difficulties, not least due to the first-past-the-post electoral system. However in 1996 New Zealand introduced a mixed election system, and in the 1999 election the Greens gained 5.16% of the vote and seven seats in parliament. Since then the Greens have advanced to become the third largest political party in New Zealand. Its basic principles are: ecological economics, social justice, participatory democracy and non-violence. The party protested against the military invasions of Iraq and Afghanistan, and in a parliamentary speech on 6 November 2014, Green MP Kennedy Graham called for non-violent methods to be adopted in the struggle against the Islamic State movement.

The party gives high priority to gender equality and in June 2014 launched a fierce attack on the outdated abortion legislation of the country. A press release stated: 'The Green Party will decriminalise abortion and assert the right of women to make decisions regarding their own health and the wellbeing of their family or whanau.'[63] The party also defends the rights of the Maori population, adopting some Maori traditions as parts of its basic values (Te Tiriti o Waitangi) and an official status for the Maori language.

The party is led by co-leaders, female and male, Metiria Turei and Russel Norman. The 20 September 2014 election saw a small setback, with the vote share reduced to 10.7%, down from 11.1 in 2011 (which had been up from 6.7% in 2008). However the party kept its 14 MPs.

https://www.greens.org.nz

Pakistan: Green Party

The Pakistan Green Party was founded in 2002. Its leader is Liaquat Ali Shaikh. According to its statutes its main objectives are: grassroots democracy, social justice and equal opportunity, ecological wisdom, non-violence and peace, community-based economics and economic justice, gender equality and respect for diversity. In an email to the author Liaquat Ali affirms that the party in reality has no chairperson, but that Pakistani law obliges it to have one. Its application for registration was rejected twice because there was no traditional leadership; because of this the party in 2008 formally created a position as chair, and was duly registered.

In May 2009 it was reported: 'Pakistani Green Party Leader in the News'. Liaquat Ali Shaikh, during a visit to the USA, was quoted as having said: 'The world at large have said that war against terror is a global war. So these displaced one million people and anyone who is affected and displaced due to combat against terrorism, is a refugee affected by a global war and deserves attention and assistance as a "refugee" not as an IDP.'[64] At the same time the US Greens and the Pakistan Greens called in a joint statement for the termination of drone attacks inside Pakistan. In 2010 it was reported by media that 'the Green Party of Pakistan is growing, and using social networks as one tool to encourage that growth'.[65] During the election campaign of 2012 a Green activist was murdered. The same year, in September, the leader of the party was detained while overseeing the distribution of relief materials for flood-affected people. In June 2013 the party leader, his wife and his driver were robbed in the Sind province. These acts of violence caused a flood of protests, not least from other Green parties. In the elections in 2012 (Senate) and in 2013 (Representatives) the Greens won no seats.

https://www.facebook.com/pages/Pakistan-Green-Party/168311941055

Philippines: Partido Kalikasan

Partido Kalikasan (Philippine Green Party) was founded on 6 December 2003. However, two of the founders, Delfin Ganapin and Dr Angelina 'Nina' Galang, as well as the first chairperson, Reverend Jose Pepito Cunanan, left the fledgling party after a short time. For several years the activists couldn't agree to continue to form a real political party. A special aspect of the PK was its close relation to the Christian Church. Some wanted to insert 'Almighty God' in the preamble of the political programme. After discussion this was replaced by 'Creator'. Still PK emphasises creation and spirituality. Otherwise it adheres to common Green aims, such as agrarian reform, implementation of environmental laws, energy self-sufficiency through renewable non-nuclear power, and the promotion of small and medium enterprises. The PK blames the ecological, social and economic problems on colonialism. Precolonial times are depicted as a golden age when communities were ruled sustainably by benevolent chieftains; gender balance is not treated as a matter of concern. Some claim that the problem is solved, as the Philippines is ranked number 9 on the Global Gender Gap Report 2014, just behind the Nordic countries.[66]

PK has contested some elections, getting one councillor. The party has tried to extend its membership and local branches, but in 2012 reported only 500 members nationwide and a 'presence' in 49 of the 80 provinces. It did not contest the May 2013 national and local elections but has vowed to contest the elections of 2016. The PK is active in the field, as shown by its Village Disaster Risk and Reduction Management (VDRRM) process in the autumn of 2014. According to the APGF homepage, the national chairperson, Kiko C. Labro, concluded 'that the national government's inability to provide the necessary logistics and support system during natural calamities worsens the effects of the climate change on the Philippines'. On its Facebook site a number of activities are reported, such as: 'Greens PH will support the call of the most Holiness Bishop Tagle in the celebration of the Mass and Walk against Climate Change.'

https://www.facebook.com/partidokalikasan

Taiwan: Green Party/Lü Dang

The Green Party of Taiwan, GPT (Táiwān Lü Dǎng), was founded in 1996. It developed out of NGOs that formed an 'Alliance of Social Movements for Legislation Inspection' which advocated proportional representation in the National Assembly with the slogan 'Waste Assembly, Recycle the Resources'. However, the Ministry of the Interior banned any naming of a political party after only a colour; thus the first Green Party was named 'Green, Local and Fresh Party', but soon managed to change to the Green Party. In 2005 the party was reorganised and more issues, apart from environment protection, were added to the agenda: gender identity, youth and employment, cultural preservation, human rights, agriculture and animal rights. In 2013 the GPT reported having about 400 members and getting around 3% of the vote from metropolitan middle-class communities, and up to 35.8% in areas affected by environmental issues. The party slogan is 'Political renewal for a Green livelihood'. Some issues prioritised are: 1) Green economy and a nuclear free homeland; 2) carbon reduction and cutting taxation for Green social justice; and 3) enhancing health through food education, Green agriculture and a good environment. The struggle against nuclear power, an issue that received much attention in Taiwan after the Fukushima disaster, has become a particular trademark of the GPT.

In 2006, the GPT got nearly 1% of the votes for the Taipei City Council. In 2008 the party joined a Red-Green alliance, garnering 58,473 votes (0.58%) in the parliamentary election. In 2010, GPT ran four candidates for Taipei City Council, winning an average of 2% of the vote. In the 2012 parliamentary election the GPT got 230,000 votes (1.74%) and became the fifth most popular party. In Taiwan's local elections held on 29 November 2014, the party won two seats. The GPT is led by two gender-balanced co-chairs: Robin Winkler and Yang Chang-ling

http://www.greenparty.org.tw/en

D. EUROPE

WEST EUROPEAN GREENS: THE FOURTEEN VETERANS

Here follows the profiles of 14 veteran Green parties (members of the European Green Party, EGP) in 12 countries in Western Europe, which all have – or until recently had – representation in their national parliaments. Several are or have been partners in coalition governments. All the parties were founding members of the European Federation of Green Parties in 1993 (EFGP), and all have a background as members of the Coordination of European Greens (CoGP) in the 1980s. They are treated in the order of their year of foundation.

(For further information about the activities and achievements of some of these parties as partners in coalition governments, see Chapter 5.)

United Kingdom (1973)

The Green Party of England and Wales (GPEW) (in Welsh: Plaid Werdd Cymru a Lloegr)
Party leadership: one woman – Natalie Bennett.
National elections 2015: 3.8%, 1 MP (Caroline Lucas).
European elections 2014: 7.87%, 3 MEPs.

www.greenparty.org.uk

Figure 12   Some founders of the UK Green Party. From the left: Michael Benfield, David Taylor, Freda Sanders, Elisabeth Whitebread, Clive Lord, Lesley and Tony Whittaker. Photo: courtesy of Global Greens.

The GPEW is one of the oldest Green parties in the world, originating in a party called People, founded in 1973 to challenge the UK political establishment. In 1975 it changed its name to the Ecology Party; in 1985 to the Green Party. In 1990 the Scottish and Northern Irish Greens split off and formed separate parties, while the Welsh Greens remained as an autonomous party within the GPEW.

The first political platform of the Ecology Party (EP), was based upon the four main principles of the 'Blueprint for Survival', published by the Green magazine *The Ecologist* in 1972: 'Minimum disruption of ecological processes; maximum conservation of materials and energy; a population in which recruitment equals loss; a social system in which the individual can enjoy rather than feel restricted.'[67] In 1979, with 560 members, EP contested 53 seats at the general election, gaining under 2% of the vote, but the membership shot up to 6,000. In the 1981 County Council elections EP contested 332 out of 4,600 seats. One Green was elected in Cornwall, with 52%. In 2015 the party has two seats on the Greater London Assembly, numerous local councillors across the country, and won control of Brighton & Hove unitary authority in 2011.

The GPEW always has been critical of many aspects of the European Union, but never campaigned for a unilateral British exit. After the EU elections of 2014, the think-tank Civitas summarised the position of the GPEW in the following way: 'The Green Party (3 MEPs) is critical of many aspects of the way the EU is run, believing that government should be as close to the people as possible. The party also fears that the EU is not adequately concerned about ecological priorities. The party opposed the EU Constitution and the Lisbon Treaty. It also opposes UK membership of the Euro.'

In January 2013 the Green MP Caroline Lucas called for a referendum sooner rather than later.[68] She emphasised that she was doing so because 'I am pro-democracy, not because I'm anti-EU'. She has observed that 'the EU has the potential to spread peace and make our economies more sustainable, and to promote democracy and human rights, at home and throughout the world. But it must urgently change direction, away from an obsessive focus on competition and free trade and towards placing genuine co-operation and environmental sustainability at its heart'.

The leadership of the Ecology Party in 1983 consisted of three chairpersons: Jonathon Porrit, Paul Ekins and Jean Lambert, all later well-known Green figures. In its 1983 election manifesto 'Politics for Life', the Ecology Party declared that while other parties have in common a 'commitment to a form of progress which destroys the world and degrades the person', EP is opposed to a nuclear state, the economics of more and more, the rape of the earth, and a society that leaves no room for the spirit. In a nutshell: peace, sustainable economics of self-reliance, recycling, rehabilitation and repair, reverence for the earth 'and all its creatures', decentralised communities, balance between feminine and masculine values, one world, 'the spirit – responding to people's hunger for meaning, placing less emphasis on material values and more on personal growth and spiritual development'. In 1984 the EP campaigned for proportional elections, against nukes, and for food health. GPEW has been active around the construction of an alternative Green economy, supported by the activities of the independent Green Economics Foundation. GPEW is critical of the neoliberal economics of the EU.

An electoral peak was reached in the EU election of 1989, when the UK Greens won 15% of the votes (with Sara Parkin as the leading personality), but no seats. The UK Greens were given an honorary seat as a full member of the Green Group in the European Parliament. There was a debate about the election system, which was later changed for EU elections. However the system for the British Parliament remained unchanged and the Greens lost some of their momentum, despite from 1999 having representation in the European Parliament (starting with Jean Lambert and Caroline Lucas) and several local council seats. The next breakthrough was the election to the British parliament of Caroline Lucas in 2010. In 2013 the party reported progress in county elections.

In 2015 it is reporting a rapid increase of members, reaching a total of some 50,000. It fielded candidates in 75% of the constituencies in the May 2015 parliamentary elections. Election opinion polls were consistently placing Green support in a range between 4% and 11%. In a message to the public, the chairperson of the party tried to summarise what the election was about from a Green point of view: 'Imagine a political system that puts the public first. Imagine an economy that gives everyone their fair share. Imagine a society capable of supporting everyone's needs. Imagine a planet protected from the threat of climate change now and for the generations to come. That's the future we want to create and we have the means to do it.'

The result of the May 7 election – 1,157,613 votes, 3.8% – was a huge victory and would have resulted in a large group of Green MPs in any other EU country. However, the Greens had only Caroline Lucas reelected. At the same time, the Scottish National Party with 4.7% of the vote got 56 MPs. In the UK it is not only the Greens who believe that an election system that can produce such an imbalanced result is democratically flawed.

Figure 13   Caroline Lucas, the first Green to be elected to the British Parliament, 2010, speaking at the launch of the Brighton and Hove Living Wage Commission. She served as an MEP for two five-year terms from 1999 and was the leader of the Greens of England and Wales 2008–12. Lucas was reelected in May 2015. Photo: courtesy of Global Greens.

In the autumn of 2014 the New British Election Study (BES) tried to establish a profile of the Green voter: she is more likely to be female (57%); younger (average age 41, with 31% under 25); and non-religious (48%); all to a greater extent than the supporters of other parties. She is also more likely to be a graduate (47%), and a *Guardian* reader (28%). According to BES, on a left-right scale running from 0 (far left) to 10 (far right), Greens place themselves at 2.76 on average. While Greens share with UKIP voters some populist disillusion-ment, they have considerably different views on most political issues, including immigration, Europe, British identity, austerity, welfare benefits, crime, gay marriage and the environment; Greens are essentially cosmopolitan leftist social liberals rather than nationalist, right-wing, social conservatives. But they are also more optimistic about the potential for positive outcomes from political participation.[69]

The Scottish Green Party, SGP (Pàrtaidh Uaine na h-Alba)
Party leadership: one man – Patrick Harvie
Elections: in 1999 Robin Harper was elected member of the Scottish Parliament (MSP), thereby becoming the first Green parliamentarian in the UK. At the elections of 2011 the SGP got two MSPs. Since 2012 the party has 14 local councillors (an increase by 6).

The SGP works for independence for Scotland and supported the yes-option in the referendum in September 2014 (which lost), with the support of GPEW and the EGP. The SGP even campaigned in favour of dropping the British pound and introducing a Scottish currency.

www.scottishgreens.org.uk

Belgium (Groen 1979, Ecolo 1980)

Dutch-speaking Groen and French-speaking Ecolo have usually had a common group in the Belgian parliament.

Agalev: Anders gaan leven (To live in another way)
Founded as movement in the early 1970s; transformed into a political party in 1979. Changed name to *Groen! (Green!)* in 2003.
Party leadership: one woman – Merem Almaci
National elections 2014: 5.3% (8.6% in the Flemish region), 6 MPs
European elections 2014: 10.6%, 1 MEP

www.groen.be

Ecolo: Ecologistes Confédérés pour l'organisation de luttes originales (Confederated Ecologists for the Organisation of Original Struggles).[70]
Founded 1980
Party leadership: co-presidents, one woman – Emily Hoyos, one man – Olivier Deleuze
National elections 2014: 3.3% (8.7% in Wallonia), 6 MPs
European elections 2014: 11.7%, 1 MEP

www.ecolo.be

The breakthrough for the Belgian Greens came with the election of 1981 when Agalev and Ecolo both got two MPs each. In the 1980s their support increased and in 1985 they together won nine seats after a campaign against US nuclear missiles. Green MPs illegally entered a US base in Wallonia, were arrested and released only after a special decision by the parliament. In 1993 the Belgian Greens gave their support to the transformation of Belgium into a fully federal system in exchange for the introduction of an eco-tax on bottles.

In a 1985 report on the first four years in parliament, Ecolo listed actions inside and outside parliament: arrival of the new MPs to parliament on bicycles, fighting xenophobia, supporting more power to municipalities and regions, measures to ameliorate linguistic antagonism, support for contentious objectors, proposals for better environment and less pollution, rejecting nuclear energy, and support for international solidarity.[71] Ecolo undertook many non-parliamentary actions, such as the occupation of the office of the regional water company to protest against water pollution. In 1984 Ecolo banned the accumulation of political positions: no more than one elected post was allowed, and no more than one internal post on the same level.[72]

In a report on its activities in parliament in 1987, Agalev listed: initiatives to phase out nuclear energy, environmental legislation, liberalisation of abortion, help for political refugees, campaigns against TGV (high speed trains) and for a basic income and reduction of working hours. At a general assembly in December 1988 Ecolo adopted a programme for the upcoming European elections of 1989 which contained criticism of the anti-environmental effects of the EC Single Market project because of the liberalisation of trade rules.[73]

The elections of 1999 brought Green success. Agalev's representation increased from five to nine MPs, Ecolo's from six to 11. The Green parties were invited to take part in a 'rainbow' government (see Chapter 5). The elections of May 2003 by contrast were a disaster. Agalev lost all its MPs, Ecolo more than half. However, a comeback was already underway at the elections of 2007 and in 2014 the parties were back at their strength before the victory of 1999, Groen a little upwards to 5.3% and six seats, Ecolo a little downwards to 3.3% and six seats. After the 2014 elections Ecolo organised (with Groen participation) a conference on 'Being in a government coalition – what information is needed to prepare the future?' The Belgian Greens were mobilising for a comeback as government parties.

Jack Morael, secretary general of Ecolo during most of the 1980s and '90s, when celebrating his 30 years in Green politics said: 'A tie doesn't matter as long as you don't hide behind it.'[74] This may be a good summary of the efforts of the Belgian Greens to keep their alternative soul despite having become part of the political establishment.

Germany (1980)

Bündnis 90/Die Grünen (Alliance '90/The Greens)[75]
Founded 1980 as Die Grünen in West Germany, merged in 1993 with the East
   German Bündnis 90.
Party leadership: two spokespersons, woman – Simone Peters, man – Cem
   Özdemir.
National elections 2013: 8.4%, 63 MPs
European elections 2014: 10.7%, 11 MEPs

www.gruene.de
(For information on the Red-Green government 1998–2005, see Chapter 5).

Figure 14   Die Grünen in the German Parliament, Der Bundestag,
1983. The star of the party, Petra Kelly, is seen in the first row, with
the Social Democratic leader Hans Jochen Vogel sitting on her
right and the Chancellor, Helmut Kohl, on her left, three seats
away. Photo: courtesy of Global Greens.

Green and 'miscellaneous lists' (Bunte Liste) gained seats in local and regional
assemblies in the 1970s. A strong incitement for the Greens was the wide
popular protests against the NATO decision in 1979 to deploy nuclear missiles
in Western Europe. Petra Kelly, one of the first spokespersons of Die Grünen,
was a shining star of this movement. In the European elections of 1979 a Green
list got 3.2%. However, Die Grünen was not founded until January 1980, at a
congress in Karlsruhe. When the West German parliamentary elections of 6
March 1983 approached, some in the circles of power were troubled. The
Washington Post wrote of 'West Germany's Green menace' and expressed
deep irritation: 'While American and West German leaders scramble to find a
consensus on new defensive missiles for NATO, the Green party is escalating its

emotional peace rhetoric for the March 6 election by taking dead aim at Uncle Sam.'[76] *Der Spiegel* quoted a politician from CDU branding an entry of Die Grünen into the parliament as 'Hausbesetzung' (occupation of a house).[77] Die Grüne Raupe (the Green caterpillar) toured the country and urged voters to let Germany go green, pleading for disarmament, no more exploitation of the third world, an end to nuclear power, waste and the throwaway culture, in favour of gender equality and social rights, and a move away from the failed growth economy to a sustainable circular economy. They stood against military blocs, and for neutrality. Among supporters were the journalist Günther Wallraff and the GDR dissident Wolf Biermann. The election was a victory for the CDU, a defeat for the Social Democrats, and saw a Green entry into the Bundestag (Parliament) with 5.6% of the votes and 27 MPs. A Swedish right-wing newspaper alleged that 'the Soviets strongly praise Die Grünen'.[78]

Die Grünen – two parties in one

Many of the founding members were left-wingers who saw Die Grünen as their only option for party politics. The Communist Party had been outlawed in 1956. Thus, there was no room either legally or politically for any reformed communist parties of the kind that attracted the 'New Left' in other countries. At the same time Die Grünen attracted a lot of pacifists, feminists and environmentalists. This created the basis for conflicts between fundis (fundamentalists) and realos (realists), both about political content (the fundis being more left-wing) and methods (the fundis opposed participation in government). Sometimes the two factions acted as two different parties.

The toughest grassroots rules

In the 1980s Die Grünen introduced some severe grassroots rules. No Green MP was allowed to remain for more than half the period, after which she/he should be replaced by a follower/Nachrücker. Nobody could hold a position in the party structure and a public office at the same time. Greens who received salaries from political positions had to donate most of it to the party. This created problems. The ban on accumulation of positions contributed to divisions between the party and the parliamentary group. And the limits on salaries met with difficulties from the tax authorities. Most of these exacting requirements have been gradually slackened, if not entirely abolished. The most visible remnant of the grassroots rules is that Die Grünen still has no single party leader, but two equal co-speakers (Sprecher), one woman, one man.

Petra Kelly – the assassinated peace symbol

Early in 1984, the most odd of the Green MPs, Gert Bastian – the former Second World War general turned pacifist and partner of the globally well-known symbol of Die Grünen, Petra Kelly – left the Green parliamentary group, alleging that 'communists' had too much influence. He was angry that Petra Kelly had been criticised by left-wingers and complained about inefficient working methods.[79] Kelly defended him, complaining that he had 'continually to excuse himself … for having been once a military officer'.[80] Despite a decision by her party organisation in Bavaria that she should rotate in 1985, she remained in parliament for the full four-year term; this didn't prevent her from being re-nominated and re-elected in 1987 for a second term until 1990. On 1 October 1992 she was shot dead by Bastian, who then shot himself. This tragedy was at first considered to be a joint suicide. But the German feminist writer Alice Schwarzer[81] and the former leader of the UK Greens Sara Parkin[82] accuse Bastian (aged 69) of having assassinated Kelly (aged 44). There are reports that she planned to leave Bastian. It is also alleged that Bastian feared being exposed as having been involved with the Stasi, the GDR security service. By killing himself and Petra he 'spared her' from such negative knowledge. Petra Kelly was a very emotional person. On one occasion, during the final minutes of the dramatic congress of Karlsruhe 1988, she made a vehement appeal in favour of Tibet, and threatened to quit the party if her proposal was not accepted. Some new members of Die Grünen may have been flabbergasted, but most party members admired her despite her whims and approved her demand 161 to 108. Thus, with the passing of Petra Kelly, who never sided with either the fundis or the realos, Die Grünen lost not only a symbol but also an activist who pushed the basic issues of the movement, not least pacifism. It is hardly conceivable that Die Grünen, with 'peace-angel' Petra Kelly still active, would have accepted Joschka Fischer's support for German military intervention in Kosovo 1999 and Afghanistan 2001.

Greens in parliament: 'A giant sensitivity session'
During the first years after the Green entry into the parliament scores of books, including memoirs, about the Green experiment were published.[83] Petra Kelly clarifies: 'With the often misunderstood phrase I have introduced – antiparty party – I have intended a party which always is able to distinguish between power and morality.' She also complains: 'Several of us have become anxious and insecure people because of the regular hostilities from our own ranks and because of the cynicism, malicious pleasure and chilliness encountered from within.' She states that fear of rotation leads to an inability to act. Antje Vollmer, who tried to establish a balance between fundis and realos, concluded that rotation and financial rules create problems because of tax and job security legislation. Joschka Fischer characterises the parliament as 'an unbelievable assembly of alcoholics' and a 'club of men where arrogance and fear of sexuality lead to the notorious male sneers'. What happens in the Green Group is 'a giant sensitivity session'. He became worried when confronted with ideas about exploiting the parliament to create chaos, which he condemned. A kind of

reply to Fischer comes from Thomas Ebermann and Rainer Trampert, former Marxists, who claim that only through steadfast opposition, ruthless revelations of the scandals of the power elite, and optimal mobilisation, could the SPD be obliged to make concessions. But not even the most skilful and sly parliamentary politics could change the basic structure of society, they maintain, which means that the main arena for the Greens is outside the parliament. Fischer replies: 'While the Greens by their ecological criticism define a system issue, they have given a clearly reformist reply by entering the parliament.'

The beginning of the realo-fundi conflict

When Jutta Ditfurth was elected one of three speakers in 1984, the fundi-realo conflict reached new levels. Already after one year demands were made to dismiss Ditfurth because of her accusation that the Greens were accomplices in the 'murder' of a participant in a street manifestation in Frankfurt, who was killed by water-cannon. As the Greens in Frankfurt hadn't voted against the budget post for buying water-cannons, they were, according to Ditfurth's logic, 'accomplices'. Just before the congress Joschka Fischer had been appointed Minister of Environment in Hesse, the first Red-Green coalition on regional level, which the fundis considered to be a treachery. Jutta Ditfurth repeated her accusations in front of the 850 delegates in Offenburg. Despite this, more than two thirds rejected the dismissal demand.[84]

Another example of the hostile feelings between fundis and realos was a statement by another of the speakers, Rainer Trampert: 'I have been presented as a supporter of a Red-Green coalition and of having described Joschka as unfit, but the truth is that I am an opponent of a Red-Green coalition but consider Joschka as fit.'

It was typical of Die Grünen during this period that at one congress someone suddenly announced that everybody must go to the nuclear site in Wackersburg, to support 'our friends' who were struggling with the police. Several dozen buses were ordered, the congress was interrupted and everybody travelled 400 kilometres. It was of a kind of chicken race: which 'real' Green could prefer to talk when action was needed at an anti-nuke demonstration?

The fundis lose the struggle

In its programme for the elections of 1987 Die Grünen reported on its achievements since 1983, including revelations of illegal finances in the old parties (the Flick-scandal), and the foregrounding of women in politics (there were only women in the Green parliamentary group bureau); however it had not been possible to stop deployment of missiles and the introduction of security laws. Die Grünen was presented as a feminist, antisexist and antifascist party. The programme warned against an 'authoritarian security state' and asserted that if the CDU/CSU/FDP regime was re-elected it would 'sharpen the

Figure 15   Jutta Ditfurth, spokesperson of Die Grünen 1984–88, addressing a party congress. Ditfurth was an impressive orator and a fundi hardliner. After some years the rank-and-file Greens became fed up and voted to dismiss her. She left Die Grünen in the early 1990s and has written several books accusing the Greens of political treachery. Photo: the author.

ecological crisis, increase the danger of war and lead to further weakening of democratic and social rights'. The result of the 1987 elections was a success. Die Grünen got 8.3% and 44 MPs; however the right-wing government remained in power.

In March 1988 *Der Spiegel* published accusations of financial irregularities against Die Grünen. Also Daniel Cohn-Bendit, a close friend of Joschka Fischer, made accusations in the Frankfurt Left-Green magazine *Pflasterstrand*. In October the accusations were repudiated by an investigative commission.[85] Nevertheless the Karlsruhe congress of 2–4 December 1988 was dramatic. Some of the Greens began to get fed up with the left-wing troika of speakers, not only the realos (led by Fischer) but also the Aufbruch-group around Antje Vollmer (later vice president of the Bundestag). However, the left-wingers considered both the realos and Aufbruch to be traitors. In an aggressive speech Jutta Ditfurth accused the realos of having leaked false information about the alleged financial scandal to *Der Spiegel*; she was met by loud boos at least ten times and got applause only twice, when she attacked other parties. This author was present and made a note that this was 'a suicidal speech'. A no-confidence motion was passed by 214–186, and the fundi board (Bundesvorstand) resigned. The day after, Petra Kelly told me: 'Jutta acted completely wrongly', and Joschka Fischer admitted privately: 'I am very satisfied, I have lived through similar situations 4–5 times in Hesse; the fundis haven't understood the importance of political responsibility'.

NATO as guardian against German militarism?

In 1988 the party published a booklet called, in a play of words, 'To be or NATO be'. The booklet quotes from the party congress in Oldenburg, September 1987: 'Die Grünen is steadfast on the demand for a unilateral exit by West Germany from NATO.' However, as an attachment to the booklet was a speech by Joschka Fischer against unilateral German exit from NATO.[86] His point was that Germany needed a guardian – NATO – to ensure it did not become dangerous again (like during the first half of the twentieth century). He was not the only German Green to fear a German 'Sonderweg' (separate way) which could lead to renewed militarism, but few agreed that NATO was the best guarantor of non-militarism in Germany. During the first 15 years of the life of Die Grünen, pacifism prevailed. However, after the Green entry into the government in 1998, the fear of a German 'Sonderweg' became stronger – if it was not just a tactical adaptation to being part of a government in a NATO country.

The fall of the Wall and German unification

The reaction of Die Grünen to the fall of the Berlin Wall was swift and, as it appeared, disastrous. In a statement of 17 November 1989, Die Grünen said that 'West-Germany must recognise GDR and the two-state situation of Germany – which is a result of the German initiation of the Second World War.' This was a rejection of reunification. However, only days after the fall of the Wall a first initiative to found a Green party in East Germany was made.[87] The first congress was held in Halle, 9–11 February 1990, with 350 delegates, who elected a board of three women and three men, demanded the dissolution of military blocs, and stated that a unification of Germany could only be realised inside a European framework. A joint conference of the Greens in East and West Germany in Magdeburg in March 1990 demanded 'demilitarisation, dissolution of blocs and a future German confederation in the framework of a European peace order', which may be interpreted as a retreat by the West German Greens. At the first free GDR elections to the Volkskammer (18 March 1990) the GDR Greens got 2%, which according to spokesperson Andreas Schultz was 'not bad';

and he added: 'Now we have to form the process of the unification in ecological and democratic ways.' Germany was reunited on 3 October 1990, and the first all-German elections were held on December 2. The two parts of Germany were treated as two different constituencies, a system that had been promoted by Die Grünen. However, the West German Greens suffered a severe setback, falling from 8.3 to 4.8% and losing all their 44 MPs, while Bündnis 90 (in coalition with the GDR Greens) managed 6.0%, thereby keeping a Green representation of eight MPs in the Bundestag. The irony was that together the West and East Greens got 5% across Germany, and would have had a considerable representation if Germany had been one constituency. In 1993 Die Grünen and Bündnis 90 merged into Bündnis 90/Die Grünen.

Joschka Fischer – the informal leader during two decades
From the mid 1980s until his departure after the fall of the Red-Green government in 2005, Joschka Fischer was the dominating personality of Die Grünen. When he was Minister of Foreign Affairs he was often the most popular politician in Germany. However, when Germans were asked if their admiration for Joschka meant that they planned to vote for the Greens, the reply was often: 'Oh no! The Greens are a bunch a maniacs, but Joschka is something else!' In the first election after Joschka's departure, in 2009, Die Grünen got its best result ever, 10.7%.

Following his departure, Joschka Fischer was sometimes described as corrupted by power, for instance by his former friend Jürgen Schreiber.[88] *Der Spiegel* reported that 'there is nothing the new leaders estimate less than advice from the former patriarch that they haven't asked for'.[89] In the first part of his autobiography Fischer admits that he went too far in ideological effacement when as the new Minister of Foreign Affairs he declared: 'There is no Green foreign policy, just a German one.' Nevertheless he cannot take Green pacifists seriously; he doesn't consider them respectable persons with different points of view, but dreamers or saboteurs or cowards. Reading his autobiography it appears as a mystery why – back in the 1970s when he took the step from left-wing street-fighting to parliamentary politics – he chose the Greens. Was it out of conviction – or because the small and new party seemed the most liable to allow conquest from within? A revealing book has described how Joschka and his pals took over the Frankfurt branch of the Greens in a coup.[90]

One of the first things Joschka did as Minister of Foreign Affairs was to declare in Washington that the Green demand for Germany to leave NATO was 'obsolete'. He became a pioneer in getting Germany to participate in a war, in Kosovo in 1999.[91] If a Green, in principle pacifist, had not given legitimacy to a German entry into a war, would other politicians have dared to do so, risking a backlash of harsh Green attacks? In September 2007 a first major result of Fischer's departure could be seen at the extra party congress in Göttingen, when a majority of delegates (361–264) rejected a proposal to prolong German participation in the ISAF-intervention in Afghanistan.

When in 2011 the present author asked a leading German Green for his opinion on the second part of Fischer's autobiography, the reply was: 'I have promised myself never more to read a single line by that man!' Fischer's reputation had already shrunk significantly, triggered also by a documentary film with the title 'Joschka and Mr Fischer', which tried to catch the transformation of the stone-throwing Joschka of the 1970s into the Mr Fischer of the 1990s, dressed in a three-piece suit. In the second part of his autobiography Mr Fischer repeats over and over again that Germany must always act as a loyal partner to the USA, which is at odds with the Green line of the 1980s. He shows a total disdain for most of his internal Green critics, but he has problems as well with Antje Vollmer who also opposed the Afghanistan war. While not able to credibly discard her as a left-wing maniac he characterises her as 'a Green protestant national pacifist'.[92]

With his tough rejection of all hesitation about the wars in Kosovo and Afghanistan in mind, it may seem odd that Fischer took a very strong position against the US invasion of Iraq in 2003, citing international law and lies of the Bush regime. Why this difference concerning Iraq compared to Kosovo and Afghanistan? Was it due to Green convictions? Or to the fact that his SPD Prime Minister, Gerhard Schröder, took a tough line against the Iraq war? If Schröder had supported the Iraq war, would Joschka have protested and quit or would Mr Fischer have obeyed and remained?[93]

Jutta and Claudia – two different fundis

The antithesis of Joschka Fischer in the history of the German Greens is of course Jutta Ditfurth, who since her dethronement in 1988 has published several libellous pamphlets against her former party. In a 2011 version she devotes a whole chapter to expressing her horror over the abstention of the spokespersons of Die Grünen in 2010 from supporting a so-called Schottern-action – digging out the roadbed of a railway to prevent transports of radioactive waste. She doesn't accept that a parliamentary party cannot participate in violent illegal actions.[94]

While Jutta Ditfurth quit Die Grünen in 1991, quite a few fundis have remained. One is Claudia Roth, co-speaker of the party 2001–2013. In 2012 there were speculations that she might become Minister of Foreign Affairs after a victory in the 2013 elections.[95] But the party preferred the veteran fundi Jürgen Trittin because, according to Der Spiegel, Claudia was considered 'too left-wing, too gaudy, too provocative'. At the same time she was compared with Joschka Fischer, with admiration: 'She doesn't, as Joschka Fischer did, travel to the traditional alliance-partner in Washington to discuss strategic issues at the think tanks. She goes to places where there are clashes and stinks. She visited during the previous years countries such as Afghanistan, Iran, Iraq, Syria, North Korea, and Colombia; or, as only two weeks ago, Libya; always to investigate human rights.' In her political autobiography she tells of the shocking impression made upon her when in 1997 she witnessed an execution in Arizona. She has also struggled at length for equal rights for homosexuals.[96] In 2013 she became vice president of Der Bundestag.

Why the setback in 2013?
The election of 2013 was disappointing. Despite high opinion polls the result was only 8.4% of the vote. What had happened? Analysts gave three main reasons:

1. The *paedophilia scandal*. It was an old story, brought up anew by *Der Spiegel* under the headline 'Shadows of passed times'.[97] For the umpteenth time during his career, Daniel Cohn-Bendit was asked about a problematic passage in a book, published in 1975, where he admitted that while working in a preschool he had let kids open his fly and touch his penis; now, almost 40 years later, he explains that 'we wanted an alternative to the condemning reaction of bourgeois society' against all sexuality in children.[98] Such was the mood during the breakthrough of 'sexual liberalism' in the 1960s and '70s. Mistakes were made, but no normal person seriously supported paedophilia. Nobody seriously believes that Cohn-Bendit has ever been permissive towards the sexual abuse of children, but it is 'gefundenes Fressen' for enemies of Die Grünen, which has been exploited several times and may have scared off some voters.[99]

2. The Greens proposed *an increase of taxes*. One point in Die Grünen's 327-page election programme said: 'Everybody with an income of under 60,000 euro should pay less, the rest higher taxes. The increase in taxes for less than three million people will pay for the reductions of tax for those with low incomes.' Despite these clarifications, the middle class, helped by right-wing media, got the impression that they were in for a tax shock.

3. The Greens proposed a *'veggieday'*, which in the anti-Green propaganda was described as a ban on eating anything not vegetarian. In Die Grünen's election programme it is affirmed that the increasing consumption of meat has negative effects on health and the environment and causes suffering to animals; therefore 'public institutions should offer vegetarian and vegan dishes and a "veggieday" should be standard'. There was no proposal for any legal ban against eating meat. But the 'veggieday' was presented by media as a limitation of individual freedom.

Energy transformation
One of the main achievements of the Greens was the decision by the Red-Green government of 1998–2005 to start phasing out nuclear energy.

However, when the Greens lost their seats in the government in 2005 this plan was cancelled. Then the nuclear disaster in Fukushima in Japan in March 2011 changed everything; in a very short time the power elite, including the political right-wing and big business, agreed that there is no future in nuclear energy. A huge Energiewende (energy transformation) was initiated. With the Energiewende it becomes clear that Green transformation includes a great deal of new production. In the May 2014 issue of the information magazine of the German Ministry of Foreign Affairs, the German Minister Sigmar Gabriel, also leader of the SPD, is asked the question: Why does an industrial nation like Germany go for a transformation to renewable energy? The reply: 'As an industrial nation we must phase out nuclear energy and increase the renewables.'[100] It is odd that the major industrial nation of Europe is making this switch towards Green energy without other European countries taking it seriously.

Green 'oligarchs'

What do politicians do when they are forced out of office? A couple of years ago the French monthly Le Monde diplomatique carried the headline 'M Joschka Fischer et les Golden Grünen' (Mr Joschka Fischer and the Golden Greens). The article reported that Joschka was earning millions of euros as a consultant for BMW, Siemens and the gas pipeline project Nabucco. Others of his colleagues from the period in government were becoming multi-million-aires by giving advice to producers of medicines, cigarettes, sweets and other hardly eco-labelled goods.[101] A similar report was published somewhat later in Der Spiegel.[102] The politicians who have managed to sell their experience in government for millions of euros are mostly SPD and CDU people, but also include Joschka Fischer (Beraterfirma Joschka Fischer Consulting).[103]

Die Grünen – a new CDU?

At its party congress in Hamburg in December 2014 Die Grünen officially erased the 'veggieday' from their programme and stated that they are indifferent towards what people eat. This statement, along with some other retreats, caused Der Spiegel to attack the party in an editorial: 'For a long time it wasn't enough for Die Grünen just to get elected, which distinguished them from the "club for electing a Chancellor" – CDU. Die Grünen had the ambition to change reality. But now the party doesn't even dare to recommend the Germans a meat-free day. The Green party is on the way to become a second CDU. It is on the wrong track.'[104] Der Spiegel is right in the sense that Die Grünen as a 'second CDU' has no raison-d'être. But most likely Der Spiegel is wrong in the sense that such a deterioration of Die Grünen seems utterly unlikely. However, the way Die Grünen treats the eternal tension between ideology and electoral tactics, between being defined out and being defined in, is a major factor in determining the role of Greens worldwide in the twenty-first century.

Sweden (1981)

Miljöpartiet de Gröna (Environmental Party – The Greens)
Founded 1981
Party leadership: co-presidents, one woman – Åsa Romson, one man – Gustav Fridolin
National elections 2014: 6.9%, 25 MPs
European elections 2014: 15.4%, 4 MEPs
(For information about the Red-Green government, 2014– , see Chapter 5)

http://www.mp.se

Miljöpartiet de Gröna was founded in September 1981.[105] A pivotal background was the referendum on nuclear energy in March 1980, where, after the Harrisburg incident in 1979, no established party dared to come out openly in favour of the nuclear option. The machinations of the power elite ended up with three formally anti-nuclear options: the first was supported by the right-wing party and the second by the Social Democrats and the Liberals, and both appeared on the front page of the ballot paper calling for a successive dismantling of nuclear energy. However, in order not to stand for the same option as the right-wingers, the Social Democrats added to the back page of option 2 a call for public ownership of nuclear reactors. Option 3 called for the rapid dismantling of the six existing reactors. Option 2 got 39.1%, option 3, 38.7%, and option 1, 18.9%. On this basis, the parliament decided that ongoing constructions and plans for new nuclear energy plants should continue (from 6 to 12 reactors), but that they should then be dismantled within 30 years (thus Sweden should have been nuclear-free in 2010). Large numbers of the population understood that this had been a sham play. Thus, the referendum not only put a major Green issue on the agenda, it also illustrated the ruthless power game of the established politicians. This was one reason for the emphasis the initiators put on creating new methods for the new party: gender balance, collective leadership, rotation and anti-cumulation rules.

The first political programme of 1981 stated that 'we, the living, have an implicit responsibility to safeguard the basic conditions of existence for ourselves, our children and coming generations'. Main priorities were listed, such as halting the destruction of soil, air and water; stopping wasting our natural resources; phasing out the use of nuclear energy; disarming and working for peace; and decentralising society. Most well-known Green concepts were invoked, such as spiritual and physical wealth; self-sufficiency;

meaningful work; gender equality; elimination of social and economic inequalities; small-scale activities; cultural variety and freedom of expression. It was emphasised that 'our goal is a small-scale, balanced economy with neither private nor public power concentration'. More specific demands were made for the recycling of non-renewable materials; self-sufficiency in basic food stuffs; agriculture totally free of poisonous substances; no cruelty towards animals; renewable energy instead of oil and nuclear; reduction of transports to a minimum; a six-hour working day; and a more tolerant immigration policy.

In its first election in 1981 Miljöpartiet got 1.8% of the vote, which was far below the 4% barrier, but above what any new party had got for decades. The figure for local elections, held the same day, was higher and Greens entered dozens of municipalities. In 1984 the collective leadership was replaced by two gender-balanced co-presidents, but the parliamentary election of 1985 was a disappointment, at 1.5%. However, the progress continued locally. In 1988 environmental issues were put on the agenda, partly by an illness among seals. The broadcasting commission assessed that there had been illicit discrimination by public radio and TV against Miljöpartiet during the election campaign in 1985. Thus, in 1988 Green representatives could take part in TV broadcasts. Polls predicted a flood of Greens into the parliament; it shrank to a river, but with 5.5% of the vote there were 20 Green MPs.

The Swedish Green Party had the same problems as Die Grünen when it came to working out how to act in a parliament in order to remain alternative and at the same time influence decision-making. When in 1990 the Social Democrat government temporarily lost support from the Left-Communist Party, which wouldn't accept an austerity package, the government resigned and talks were started with the Greens. However, the Social Democrats and the Greens spoke different languages; the Greens demanded the realisation of most of its programme for a sustainable society, while the Social Democrats offered some billion kronas for building railways. In the election of 1991 the Greens missed the 4% barrier and had to leave the parliament. Most observers thought that this was the end of the story. This author published a book in 1993, in which I proposed that the Green party should change its name to 'Kvinnopartiet – de Gröna' (The Women's Party – The Greens).[106]

Whether the behaviour during the governmental crisis in 1990 was the main reason for the electoral catastrophe is still open to debate. In its wake, a party executive replaced a number of committees and the ban on MPs being members of the party leadership was abolished. However the system of gender-balanced co-presidents, as well as rotation and other anti-cumulation rules, were retained. In the election of 1994 the Greens made a comeback, with 5% of the vote and 18 MPs. The election of 1998 was a major setback for the Social Democrats (down 30 MPs) and a minor setback for the Greens (down two MPs), but thanks to the victory of the Left Party, which doubled its support (led by a woman, Gudrun Schyman),[107] there was still a Red-Green majority. From 1998 the Greens initiated an organised cooperation with the Social Democratic government (as well as the Left Party), with common preparation of the state budget. Facing the elections of 2002 the Greens were caught in a crisis, down in the polls below the 4% barrier. One reason may have been the cooperation with the government, another that the male spokesperson Birger Schlaug, one of the strongest figures in the party, as well as his female colleague Marianne Samuelsson, had resigned according to rotation rules. The new spokespersons, Matz Hammarström and Lotta Hedström, had some difficulties being taken seriously by media. After internal deliberations they decided to resign. The mood in the party was desperate, and there even was a proposal to abolish the system of gender-balanced co-presidents in order to make the Green Star, Åsa Domeij, president of the party. It is true that Åsa had demanded this change in the leadership system herself, but she had explained that she only wanted to be *vice* president. When the party finally had to accept this, it preferred to elect a new pair, Maria Wetterstrand and Peter Eriksson. The result was slight progress, with the addition of one MP. After some hesitation the Greens decided to accept another four years of organised Red-Green cooperation without ministerial portfolios, but now with increased influence through Green experts employed in several ministries. Before the election of 2006 the Greens had decided that it was time for Green ministers. But the election was won by a right-wing alliance. Before an expected Red-Green comeback in 2010 a comprehensive common programme (including the Left Party) was agreed. The election saw a Green victory (reaching an all-time high of 7.3% and 25 MPs) but unfortunately also a Red setback. The right-wing four-party government remained in power.

In 2012 the popular spokespersons Wetterstrand and Eriksson had to resign according to rotation rules. The main achievement of the new pair, Åsa Romson and Gustav Fridolin, so far, is the entry of Miljöpartiet into a Red-Green government. Some critics allege that the party has adapted too much to power politics.[108] One example was the decision in 2008 to scrap the demand that Sweden should leave the EU. Probably the continued radical anti-EU position paved the way for the Miljöpartiet's major victory in the first Swedish EU election of 1995, when the party got four MEPs. However, more and more Swedish Greens felt uncomfortable with the exit demand. One reason was that they thought it better to try to exploit the EU for ecological purposes; another that the massive enlargement of 2004 made the EU 'the only show in town' for European cooperation; and a third that anti-EU rhetoric had been taken up by xenophobes. Thus, when spokesperson Maria Wetterstrand announced in 2008 that she would act in order to change the position of the party, she was also supported by veterans from the anti-EU struggle.[109] The decision to scrap the demand for exit was taken by internal referendum. According to a poll, May 2015, Miljöpartiet lost marginally since the election, down from 6.9% to 6.4%.

Ireland (1981)

Green Party (Comhaontas glas)
Founded 1981 as the Ecology Party, 1983 Green Alliance, 1987 Green Party. The Irish Green Party is an all-island party, with the Northern Ireland Greens as a region of the all-Irish party.
Leadership: A male leader, Eamon Ryan, with a female deputy, Catherine Martin.
National elections 2011: Less than 2%, all 6 MPs were lost.
Regional elections: 1 out of 108 seats in the Northern Ireland Assembly.
European elections 2014: 4.9%, no MEP.

www.greenparty.ie

The Comhaontas Glas adheres to basic Green principles: anti-growth, tougher legislation to control pollution, self-sufficiency, cooperation as more important than competition, peace, etc. Already in 1982 some Greens contested elections for the parliament (Dial) and got 0.2%. In 1984, in a letter to the Forum for a New Ireland, the Irish Greens presented some basic demands in order to solve the Northern Ireland issue: 1) Replacement of the British Army by an international body. 2) Secular coeducation. 3) Self-sufficiency of Northern Ireland. 4) Constitutional changes in the UK and the Republic of Ireland. 5) A multiple-choice referendum. At the local elections of 20 June 1985 one Green was elected with 7%. In a manifesto of May 1989, the Irish Greens stated: 'The policies of traditional Left, Right, and Centre have been abject failures. Their policies of unlimited growth, a technological "fix" for all our problems and universal affluence, are false.'

The first Green MP (Irish: Teachta Dála, TD), Roger Garland, was elected in June 1989. He donated his salary to the party. John Gormley was elected TD in 1997 (bringing the number of Green TDs to two). In 2002 the party reached a peak by getting six TDs. A veteran Green, Mary White, stated that these good results 'catapulted the party into the "big time"'.[110] From 1994 to 2004 there were two Green MEPs, Nuala Ahearn and Patricia McKenna.

During its first two decades, the Irish Green Party had different forms of collective leadership and only after lengthy debates was Trevor Sargent elected sole party leader in October 2001. He was replaced by John Gormley, who was elected with 478 votes against 263 for Patricia McKenna. In the 2007 elections the Greens gained some votes, from 3.8% to 4.7%, but still got six TDs.

For almost three decades the Irish Greens were 'eurosceptical' and opposed new EU powers in the several referenda held in Ireland. However, in 2009, a majority of party members decided to support the new Lisbon Treaty, but as the majority was less than the required two thirds the party didn't officially take the position. The result in the referendum was 'no', and after some renegotiations there was a second referendum at which the Green 'yes' supporters managed to win a majority of just over two thirds. This was the first time the Irish Greens had campaigned in favour of an extension of EU powers.

In 2007 the party joined a coalition government (see Chapter 5), but its ministers resigned in January 2011. In the following election all six MPs were lost. One major reason was popular disappointment with the government's handling of the severe economic crisis, another the absence of environmental issues from the election campaign. Also the abrupt switch of policy on the EU, from critical to supporting a new treaty, may have scared off some Green voters. The EU election of 2014, where the party came close to winning an MEP, may be a sign of recovery.

Portugal (1982)

Os Verdes (The Greens)
Founded 1982
Party leadership: one woman – Heloisa Apolonia
National elections 2011: Around 1%, 2 MPs (in a coalition)

www.osverdes.pt

Os Verdes identify as ecosocialist, left-wing, and agree with the Global Charter, but in a reply to the author say that they 'have some doubts on accepting the justified use of military force as it goes against our pacifist principles'. The party claims to be primarily anthropocentric and to belong to a left-wing trend. Os Verdes don't have gender quotas, but the national council has 16 women out of 35 official members. There are two MPs, one woman, one man.

Os Verdes didn't show up among other European Greens until a letter arrived to the CoEG in May 1987, in which the party asked for support in the upcoming elections in July, despite its coalition with the Communist Party in the 'Unitarian Democratic Coalition' (CDU), because 'CDU is the only political area that has not compromised with government and its policy of environmental, cultural and social degradation'. In June 1988 the CoEG received documents criticising Os Verdes' cooperation with the Communist Party from former Green MEP Antonio Gonzales and his assistant Isabel Moura, who were now members of MDP (Movimento Democrático Português, MDP, founded in 1969 and dissolved in March 1994). In a vote in the CoEG in 1988, both Os Verdes and MDP were accepted as members.

At its fourth congress, 1–2 April 1989, Os Verdes stated: 'An analysis of its aims, its structure, its relations with the rest of the world and its impact on the biosphere make us affirm that the EC is a non-ecological, non-democratic, non-solidary, aggressive and war-mongering organisation, in all contrary to development.' In the platform for the 2009 EU elections, Os Verdes called for 'Construir uma Europa para Todos. Não ao Tratado de Lisboa' (Build a Europe for all, no to the Lisbon Treaty).

Os Verdes has participated in all elections since 1987 on joint lists with the Communists. This has given the party two MPs in all elections. In June 2014 Os Verdes commented on the fact that another Portuguese party, Partido da Terra, had talks with the EGP by stating that 'we are by no means closed to cooperation and further conversations with the Partido da Terra'. Partido da Terra was founded in 1993 and stands for a liberal environmentalism. It has had representation in the Portuguese parliament and in the EU election of 2014 got two MEPs who are members of the Liberal Group in the European parliament.

Luxemburg (1983)

Dei Greng (The Greens)
Party leadership: co-presidents, one woman – Sam Tanson, one man – Christian
    Kmiotek
National elections 2013: 10.13%, 6 MPs
EU elections 2014: 15.01%, 1 MEP

www.greng.lu

Dei Greng was founded in 1983 and emphasises sustainable development, eco-taxes and renewable energy. It also supports equal participation of immigrants. The party got two MPs in its first election in 1984. However, it split in 1985 into the Green List Ecological Initiative (GLEI) and the Green Alternative Party (GAP). They won two MPs each in the 1989 elections. In 1994 they cooperated with a united list, which gained 11% and five seats. In the same year they got one MEP. In 1995 the two parties reunited as Dei Greng (The Greens). In 2004 the party increased its number of MPs to seven. Afterwards the Greens were invited as 'election winners' to coalition talks with Prime Minister Juncker, of the Christian Social Peoples Party, but nothing came out of it. In 2009 Dei Greng kept their seven MPs and single MEP. The local election of 2011 was a victory for Dei Greng, securing more than 30% of the vote in several communes. In 2013 the party saw a slight setback, losing one MP; but for the first time it joined a centre-left government coalition with the liberals and socialists (see also Chapter 5).

Dei Greng has been very 'pro-European'. However, the party protested against the EGP plans to nominate Green top candidates for the EU elections of 2014 because that would be biased in favour of the large countries. 'Just think of the benefit of, for example, a German EGP candidate in Southern Europe.'[111]

However the EGP carried out its plan, with a German woman, Ska Keller, and a French man, José Bové, as top candidates. And Dei Greng's MEP Claude Turmes was re-elected.

Netherlands (1983, 1989)

In the Netherlands there are two Green parties, both full members of the EGP.

De Groenen (The Greens) is the original Dutch Green party, founded in 1983. In the 2014 EU elections De Groenen got 0.23% of the votes. The party has not participated in parliamentary elections since 1998. It has a few local councillors. Party leadership: one man – Otto ter Haar.

www.degroenen.nl

GroenLinks (Green Left) was founded in 1989 as a merger of four small parties: PRP (Radical Political Party), the CPN (Communist Party of the Netherlands), the PSP (Pacifist Socialist Party), and the EVP (Evangelical Peoples' Party).
Party leadership: one male president – Rik Grasshof.
National elections 2012: 2.3%, 4 MPs
European elections 2014: 7%, 2 MEPs

https://groenlinks.nl

GroenLinks (GL) emphasises that it belongs to the freedom-loving tradition of the Left. GL was the only Dutch party to oppose the Gulf War in 1990–91. The Kosovo and Afghanistan wars caused a lot of internal strife. However, the US invasion of Iraq in 2003 was met with unanimous rejection by the GL.

In 1989 the GL got six MPs and gained 300 municipal council seats. In November 1990 the original parties dissolved, to make GL into a single coherent party. For the 1994 elections GL chose two co-leaders, one man and one woman. As the result was a slight setback the party switched to a single leader. In the 1998 elections, with one male leader, GL doubled its number of MPs to eleven. After 2002, when the xenophobic politician Pim Fortuyn was assassinated, leading Green Left personalities were harassed. Green Left has been the most anti-xenophobic of all parties. The leading GL MP, Frenke Halsema, declared the GL to be the 'last liberal party' in the country.

After the elections of 2006, GL took part in exploratory talks about forming a coalition government with the Christian Democrat, Labour and Socialist parties. However, Halsema declared that GL had to withdraw because the party had lost in the election and had little in common with the Christian Democrats. This started an internal debate about Halsema's leadership and the general strategy. However, in 2010 Halsema was re-elected party leader and got dispensation to stand for parliament a fourth time, and the party won 10 MPs, an increase of three. With this victory the party was ready for coalition negotiations. However, nothing came of it and – partly because of this failure, partly because of a general upsurge of xenophobic politics in the Netherlands – in 2012 GL lost six seats. Party leader Jolande Sap resigned and was replaced by Bram van Ojik. The EU election of 2014 was also a setback, with a reduction from three to two MEPs. The GL since 2011 has five Senators, members of the Upper House.

Switzerland (1983)

Die Grüne Partei der Schweiz, Parti Ecologiste suisse, Partito ecologista svizzero, Partida ecologica svizra (The Swiss Green/Ecological Party)
Founded 1983
Party leadership: two women – Adèle Thorens, Regula Rytz; some periods only one president.
National elections 2011: 8.4%, 17 MPs; 15 Chamber; 2 Senate

www.gruene.ch

The programme of the Swiss Greens has an emphasis on environmental protection, limits to truck traffic through the country, and similar Green demands. According to a survey conducted by the University of Lausanne in the 2000s, Green candidates were in favour of 'more state' rather than 'more market', and more for integration and public transparency than tradition and conservatism. The Greens are active in favour of immigrants, anti-NATO, for neutrality, and want more Swiss assistance to developing countries and limits to financial secrecy.

The first local Green parties won seats in local assemblies already in the 1970s. In 1979 a Swiss Green, Daniel Brélaz, became the first ever Green MP. However, the all-Swiss party wasn't established until 1983. Brélaz, like all Swiss MPs, was only part-time, and kept his old profession. He paid half his salary of 46,000 Swiss Francs to the party (2014 = 38,000€). During the 1970s there were sectarian struggles with the left-wing L'Alternative Socialiste Verte. In 1983 the Greens got four MPs (out of 200). The central office in Bern was, according to Brélaz, 'not more than a letter-box'. The party's main political demands were decentralisation, social solidarity, control over multinational corporations, and the struggle against nuclear energy and xenophobia. The Swiss Greens were staunchly anti-militarist and non-violent.

The referendum in 1992 around the EEA treaty (association with the EU) split the party; after the victory for the 'no' option, the Swiss Greens hit a low point with just above 5% of the votes. In 2007 a peak was reached with 9.6% and 20 MPs. This was followed by a slight setback in 2011 to 8.4% and 15 MPs. The Greens are the only major Swiss party which has never had representation in the collective government (Bundesrat). Referenda play a major role in Swiss politics. The Greens have successfully introduced several petitions, such as Green Economy and Regulated Nuclear Phase-out, both in 2012. In the autumn of 2006 (two years after the EU enlargement from 15 to 25 member states) the Swiss Greens made a statement in favour of joining the EU in order to transform it into a Green body.[112]

When on 27 April 2013 the Swiss Greens celebrated their thirtieth anniversary it was observed that the party was part of government in 10 out of 25 cantons. 'Much of what then seemed utopian is now part of everyday life', commented co-president Regula Rytz. 'Green energy and transport policies, the economical use of land and the protection of landscapes – these are now widely accepted.' But still there is much to do. The Greens want to phase out all nuclear plants, put more investment into sustainables, and make the banking system transparent.

Finland (1983/87)

Vihreä Liitto/Gröna Förbundet (The Green League)
Founded 1987
Party leadership: one man – Ville Niinistö
Presidential elections 2012: 18.8% (Pekka Haavisto), second round 37.4%
National elections 2015: 8.5%, 15 MPs
European elections 2014: 9.3%, 1 MEP

http://www.vihreat.fi

Finnish Greens first took part in parliamentary elections in 1983, running a handful of independent candidates. Two Green MPs were elected. In a presentation in 1984 one of them, Ville Komsi, wrote: 'I don't think that we ever will have a normal formal organisation ... nobody knows exactly how many Greens there are, but everybody knows that we exist. I think it's fine like that.' He listed the basic Green values: concern for environment, desire for peace and solidarity and social justice, non-violence, cultural diversity, rejection of ostentatious wastefulness, existential responsibility for one's own life, self-sufficiency, no to the 'hysterical' employment ideology which prevents reduction of working time, guaranteed income, no to nukes or dams or fossil fuel, taxes on energy and scarce materials. Komsi referred to the Koijärvi incident in the spring of 1979, a non-violent action against the drainage of a small bird lake, which became symbolic for Finnish Greens.[113]

In a chat with this author in 1986, the other Green MP, Kalle Könkkölä, admitted there were problems with not having a formal party. As an example he mentioned an incident when Pentti Linkola (considered eco-fascist) visited a Green meeting in 1985 and pleaded for violence against the enemies of environmental protection; he slapped a participant who protested. Then some Green women gave him flowers to demonstrate peacenik methods. But the media interpreted this as an approval of Linkola's opinions! With no party structure, how to publicise a negative appraisal of Linkola? Statements were made; some got many signatures, others fewer. Did the media understand? No. During the Stockholm congress of the European Greens in 1987, one leading Finnish Green, Osmo Soininvaara, complained that the Greens lost two million Finnish marks in state subsidies every year by not having a registered organisation. However Vihreä Liitto/Gröna förbundet was registered as a political party in 1988.

In a booklet from March 1988, 'The Greens in Finland', by the Finnish Green parliamentary group, it is reported that in late 1987 a splinter group led by Eero Paloheimo, MP, took the name Vihreät ry ('The Greens'). In a comment to the author, Heidi Hautala (former MP and minister, from 2014 MEP) writes: 'Eero Paloheimo and Erkki Pulliainen, two of our four MPs, were more eager than most others to found a formal party ... Furthermore they represented a more tough "dark Green" position, which highlighted the confrontation with those who also emphasised social and other issues. I belonged to the latter group, but could mediate with Paloheimo. They did not get enough support to register their party, but we got it ... Rather soon, however, most Greens were reunited.' Anti-Green commentators in the media ridiculed the Green internal strife and called them the gaudy (Vihreä Liitto) and the moss-green (the secessionists).

The local election of October 1988 saw a slight loss for the Greens. The day after, Heidi Hautala, then president of Vihreä Liitto, said: 'We must return to our original forms, not only citizens' actions (like Koijärvi) but also other efforts to awake the public opinion.'[114] When this author asked Hautala if there had been any more Koijärvi-like actions, she replied: 'No, I don't think so. We mobilised for the parliamentary elections in 1991 and more than doubled our seats, and for the first time had women as MPs, in 1991 we got 5 women and 5 men, in 1987 it had been four men only. One reason was that we had decided to have a hundred percent female leadership of the party, with me as president and three other women as vice presidents.' In December 1988 the Greens were attacked for supporting a right-wing taxation bill, by a left-wing MP, Esko Seppänen (later an MEP), who claimed that the Greens had been 'curtailed as radical movement' and now tried to 'make themselves acceptable as a government party'.[115] But the Greens in 1990 made it clear that they could not be part of a government which agreed to a fifth nuclear reactor in Finland.

Around 1989–90 Vihreät still had a pretty negative attitude towards the EEC/EU. In November 1989 Hautala demanded exceptions from EU rules that would allow 100% foreign ownership of Finnish firms.[116] The Greens also stated that the environment would be damaged by the EU Internal Market.[117] In 1994 about half the Finnish Greens were against joining the EU (while the party was in favour). Polls showed a Green majority against joining the EMU/euro, but the party was in favour. Since Finland's entry into the EU in 1995 Vihreät has always had a least one MEP.

In 1995 Pekka Haavisto became Minister of Environment and Development Aid in a broad rainbow coalition, under Social Democrat leadership. The Greens left the government over the nuclear issue. Again in 2007–2014 the Greens had several positions in the government, but left the government in December 2014 a second time because of a decision to build a nuclear reactor. *(For more on Vihreät's participation in governments, see Chapter 5.)*

The 2011 election was a defeat for the Greens (down from 8.5% to 7.3%, and 15 to 10 MPs). At this election the xenophobic and eurosceptic True Finns won a landslide victory, which has affected the political debate. At the local elections of 2012 the party got 8.5% of the vote; in Helsinki it became the second largest party with 23.5%. And in the presidential election in 2012 Pekka Haavisto had a great result (18.8%) and made it to the second round. In the parliamentary election of 19 April 2015, Vihreät progressed to 8.5% of the votes and 15 MPs.

France (1984)

Europe Écologie – Les Verts, EELV (Ecological Europe – The Greens)
Founded 1984
Party leadership: one woman – Emmanuelle Cosse
National elections 2012: 5.5%, 18 MPs (out of 577)
European elections 2014: 8.91%, 6 MEPs
Presidential election 2012: Eva Joly 2.31%

www.eelv.fr

Europe Écologie – Les Verts (EELV) has a radical programme for environmental protection, reduction of greenhouse gases, phasing out of nuclear energy, sustainable agriculture, and a moratorium for GMOs. Economically the party leans to the left, denouncing 'neoliberal productivism'. On social issues EELV is rather libertarian, in favour of same-sex marriage and adoption, euthanasia and legalisation of 'soft' drugs. It is also siding with 'sans papiers' (immigrants without papers), immigrants generally, and homeless people, demanding voting rights for foreigners, democratic reform and the abolishment of the accumulation of political positions.

France saw the emergence of a multitude of environmental organisations in the 1970s. In 1974 the agronomist and environmentalist René Dumont (1904–2001) was the ecologist candidate for president and received 1.32% of the votes. A nationwide Green organisation, Mouvement écologique, was established in 1974. In the EU election of 1979 a Green list got 4.4% but no MEP. In the presidential election of 1981 Brice Lalonde, former campaign leader of Dumont and president of Friends of the Earth, received 3.9% of the votes. In 1982 Confédération Ecologiste, CE, was established, but Lalonde chose to make it alone with Les Verts-Parti Ecologiste, while CE was transformed into Les Verts-Confederation Ecologiste. Lalonde's party was more environmentalist and centrally ruled (by Lalonde), while the Confederation was more ecologist and decentralised. In 1984 Les Verts-PE and Les Verts-CE joined into one party, but Lalonde remained outside to make his own race with Entente Radicale Écologique. This split prevented the Greens from getting any MEP in the EU elections of 1984.

The cantonal elections of 1984 were a minor victory for Les Verts, up from 0.47% in 1979 to 0.78% in 1984. But there were Green candidates only in 170 out of 2,200 cantons. The reason for this was that if a candidate did not reach 5% she/he would have to pay all costs, including for ballot papers, on average 3,000 French francs (about 250€). In fact the Greens got over 5% in over 100 districts.[118] The leadership (collège executive) in 1985 consisted of four national spokespersons: Didier Anger, Jean Brière, Yves Cochet and Solange Fernex (one woman/three men), plus seven other members, all men. In 1986 four new spokespersons were appointed since the previous four had signed a proposal that Les Verts should join a coalition with some small left-wing parties, which was rejected by the members. The new quartet was less left-wing and more environmentalist: Antoine Waechter, Andrée Buchman, Michel Delors and François Berthout (one woman/three men).[119]

In 1986 the party supported Waechter's neither-right-nor-left position and nominated him as its candidate in the presidential election of 1988, in which he received 3.8% of the vote. As a counter-measure the socialist Prime Minister Michel Rocard appointed Lalonde as Minister of Environment (a position he kept for three years). In an interview Lalonde declared that his view on nuclear power had 'developed', and he was now in favour of both military and civilian nuclear. This brought Bruno Boissière, French co-secretary of the CoEG, to initiate a 'protest against the attempt of Lalonde to discredit the ecologist movement in France and Europe'.[120]

The EU elections of 1989 were a success for Les Verts, which got two million votes, 10.6%, and nine MEPs. This led the Socialists once more to try to create a Green counter-force under their control, Géneration Écologique, with Lalonde as leader.

Les Verts split 50/50 over the Maastricht Treaty. In the referendum of 20 September 1992, the 'yes' voters won narrowly, 51–49%. In 1993 Waechter lost the majority support in the party, and Dominique Voynet rose into a leading role. There was a swing towards the left among party members. But the 1994 EU elections were a failure: Les Verts got no MEP, partly due to competition from Géneration Écologique. In the 1995 presidential election Voynet got 3.3%.

In 1997 Les Verts got their first four members of the French parliament (Assemblée Nationale), through cooperation with the Socialist Party (PS), which had understood that Les Verts could not be eradicated from the political scene. A Red-Green agreement was reached with some Green points: gender equality in politics (parité), a 35-hour working week, closure of the Superphenix fast breeder reactor, an end to the building of a Rhine-Rhone canal. According to the Green economist Alain Lipietz, more was gained for the Greens with this agreement than in 13 years of struggle outside the parliament. But at the same time Lipietz emphasised that 'between Les Verts and the Socialist Party two models of development collide'.[121]

Dominique Voynet became Minister for Environment and Territorial Planning *(see also Chapter 5 for more on Les Verts in government)*. The progress of Les Verts continued with success in the regional elections of 1998 and the EU elections of 1999 (10%, nine MEPs). In 2000 Les Verts got a second member of the government, Guy Hascöet, Secretary of State for Solidary Economy. Lipietz contends that until 2000 the participation in government was mainly positive. The Multilateral Agreement on Investment (MAI), considered a major threat by the anti-globalisation movement, was rejected by France. At the same time Voynet, despite being a minister, participated in demonstrations by illegal immigrants and homeless people. In 2001 she switched to become secretary general of the party, and was replaced as minister by Yves Cochet.

On 20 June 2001, Alain Lipietz was nominated by Les Verts as the candidate for the presidential election of 2002. But, according to Lipietz, most of the party bureaucracy preferred Noël Mamère, an ecologist who had joined the party only in 1998. When a statement by Lipietz about possible amnesty for Corsican terrorists was grossly misunderstood by the media and turned against him, Mamère's supporters saw their chance and took it. Lipietz was replaced by Mamère, who got a record result, 5.2%. But at the same time Jean Marie Le Pen of the xenophobic and populist Front Nationale came second. As the difference between the PS candidate Lionel Jospin and Le Pen was only 0.7%, Mamère's good result might have been one factor in Le Pen's relative victory. The parliamentary elections of 2002 were a disaster for the 'plurial left', including Les Verts, which got only three MPs.

In 2004 Les Verts celebrated its twentieth anniversary; the economist and geographer Cécile Duflot, 29 years old, emerged as a new star and was chosen as one of two spokespersons. In the regional elections of 2004 another 100 Greens were elected, but the EU election was a defeat, down from nine to six MEPs. The same year, Noël Mamère, in his capacity as mayor of a small town, Bègles, arranged the first ever marriage in France of a same-sex-couple. In 2005 Les Verts were divided over the EU Constitution. On 27 May 2005, the 'no' option gained by 54.7%. In 2006 Duflot advanced to become secretary general of Les Verts. In 2007 Voynet was nominated as presidential candidate for a second time, but she gained only 1.57%, the lowest score ever for a Green candidate. One main reason was the competition from the anti-globalist José Bové. The internal mood was low and Yves Cochet even suggested the dissolution of the party. Then Daniel Cohn-Bendit, a Green MEP since 1994, initiated an opening towards Bové, the TV ecologist Nicolas Hulot and other independent ecologists. The initiative was supported by Duflot, and Les Verts agreed to contest the EU elections under the banner of Europe-Écologie (EE) together with Bové, Hulot and others. This proved to be a success; EE received 16% of the vote and 14 MEPs. EE and Les Verts merged into EELV on 13 November 2010.

In the 2011 cantonal elections, EELV won 27 seats, 16 more than in 2004. In July 2011 Eva Joly, a Norwegian-born lawyer, won the nomination for the presidential election over Hulot with 58.16% of the EELV members' votes. In November 2011 she refused to promise that she would support the Socialist candidate in the second round of the 2012 presidential election, because she found the Socialist Party (PS) 'archaic'. Cohn-Bendit criticised her but she got support from Dominique Voynet and Alain Lipietz.[122] In the 2012 presidential election, Joly got one of the lowest scores ever by a Green candidate, 2.31%.

On 15 November 2011, EELV and the Socialist Party signed a coalition agreement. *(For more about the EELV in government, see Chapter 5.)* In September 2012 EELV (with 71% of the votes cast) decided to vote against French ratification of the EU Treaty on Stability, Coordination and Governance (TSCG), signed in March 2012, in which the EU members agreed to legislate to guarantee that their national budgets are balanced. The Federal Council of the EELV rejected the TSCG 'because it does not respond to the current crisis of the EU and constitutes an obstacle against ecological transition'. Despite the affirmation by the EELV leadership that it was in favour of 'more Europe' to solve the crisis, the 'Europeanist' Cohn-Bendit got into a fit of rage and declared that he put his membership of EELV between brackets. He declared himself an 'orphan' of the EELV and made crude attacks on Cécile Duflot.[123] When Eva Joly demanded a referendum on the TSCG Cohn-Bendit mocked her by asking her to demand a referendum on the euro in Norway.[124]

In September 2013 Mamère quit EELV because, he said, the party was ruled by a 'clan' around Cécile Duflot. One reason (which he didn't mention) may have been that he hadn't been chosen as president of the Green Group in the French parliament. The other Green MPs preferred two co-presidents (one woman/one man), François de Rugy and Barbara Pompili, to a one-man show by Mamère.[125]

In March 2014 the Socialist Party suffered major losses in the local elections, while the EELV had a more mixed result, including a Green mayor of Grenoble. But only a few days later the Green ministers chose to resign. For the municipal elections of March 2015, EELV split into three groups, cooperating with the Left wing, the Socialists or going autonomously. Officially EELV won 2.3%, 35 councillors; but Greens were also elected under other labels.

According to a French tradition most party members are affiliated to a specific faction (courant) inside the party. The factions propose general policy statements at party congresses, which delegates are asked to choose between. For example, at the congress in Caen in November 2013 there were no less than seven policy statements presented by different 'courants' to the delegates, from 'For an ecologist approach' to 'Objective Earth'. The winning one had the support of Cécile Duflot, and got 38.3% of the votes, which was less than expected.

One special aspect of the French Greens is their divisions over the European Union, with about half of all members supporting the 'no' option in the referenda of 1992 and 2005 and a clear majority rejecting the TSCG in 2013. It could be said that while one part gives priority to the form, the EU as such, the other part of EELV gives priority to the content and doesn't hesitate to oppose the extension of EU powers if that might threaten ecological considerations.

Austria (1986)

Die Grünen (The Greens)
Founded 1986 through a merger of Vereinigte Grüne Österreichs (United Greens of Austria, founded 1982) and Alternative Liste Österreichs (Alternative List of Austria, founded 1982) into Die Grüne Alternative (The Green Alternative). From 1993 Die Grünen/The Greens.
Party leadership: one woman – Ewa Glawischnig.
National elections 2013: 12.4%, 24 MPs
European election 2014: 14.5%, 3 MEPs

www.gruene.at

A Green citizens' list (Grüne Bürgerliste) won 5.6% and two seats in Saltzburg in 1977, 17.7% and seven seats in 1982. An important symbol for Austrian Greens was the referendum on the nuclear reactor Zwentendorf in November 1978, which the 'no' option won by 50–47%, thereby bringing nuclear energy in Austria to a halt. In 1982 two nationwide Green parties were established, Alternative Liste Österreichs (ALÖ), which was more ecologist, and Vereinigte Grüne Österreichs (VGÖ), which was more environmentalist. In the parliamentary elections of 24 April 1983, ALÖ got 1.36%, VGÖ 1.93% – which meant no MPs.

In a report to the CoEG in September 1984, co-secretary Sara Parkin reported that the ALÖ had 'shifted to the left via a Trotskyite take over, supported by Die Grünen, Germany'. In 1984 massive protests against deforestation in Hainburg became a Green symbol. At this moment Austrian Greens received important support from the Nobel Prize winner (Physiology, 1973), the ethologist Konrad Lorenz (1903–1989), as the figurehead of a Citizens' Movement to prevent the building of a power plant at the Danube. However, the social democratic Minister of Interior accused the Greens of being paid by Colonel Gaddafi.

Freda Meissner Blau, at the time the most well-known personality in the Austrian Greens, got 5.5% in the presidential election of 4 May 1986. In September 1986 a united Grüne Alternative Liste won 4.8% and eight MPs. A booklet by the Green Academy complained that 'one deficiency of the Austrian Greens is their lack of a detailed and comprehensive programme ... partly because of the very heterogeneous composition of the GAL'. Nevertheless, the booklet contains standpoints and actions on environment/pollution, nuclear power, peace, antifascism, social questions, minority rights, traffic and waste. The Green MP Walter Geyer protested against a law permitting increased air pollution with a nine-hour speech in parliament.[126]

During the 1980s and until the referendum in 1994 on EU membership the Austrian Greens were fiercely anti-EU.[127] A typical slogan was: 'Austria can remain neutral, but not in the EC'.[128] In a Europe manifesto of 1989 with the title 'No to EC, yes to Europe', a lot of Greens from other countries participated.[129] However, the 'no' option lost heavily, by 67% yes against 33% no, and the Austrian Greens immediately declared that they accepted the result. During the 1990s and 2000s the party has increased its votes, with only few and minor setbacks, culminating in 2013 with 12.4% of the vote and 24 MPs, and 14.5% in the EU elections of 2014 and three MEPs. However the Austrian Greens have been less successful in terms of securing national executive power. There have been some instances, especially during the presidency of Alexander van der Bellen (1997–2008), when talks about possible Green participation in a coalition government have been pursued, but until now there has been no result.

OTHER WEST EUROPEAN GREENS, AFFILIATED TO THE EGP

Here follows presentations of Green parties in Western Europe which were founded later than the beginning of the 1980s and are still weaker in terms of voters and political influence. These parties are members or associates of the EGP. (If the year indicated for membership of the EGP is earlier than 2004, it means that the party became a member of the EFGP in the given year. If the

year of membership is earlier than the year of the foundation of the party, it
means that a predecessor party became a member that year).

Andorra

Partit Verds d'Andorra (Green Party of Andorra)
Founded 2003
EGP 2010
Party leadership: one woman/one man – Isabel Lozano and Julio Fernàndez
    Blasi
National elections 2011: 3.35% (520 votes)
Local elections December 2011: one local councillor in La Massana in coalition
    with Ciutadans Compromesos.

http://bloc.verds.ad

In a ten-point basic programme the party outlines common Green principles,
but also, probably more than most Green parties, a wish to 'feminitzar la
societat' (to feminise society) and to guarantee 'llibertats sexuals' (sexual
freedoms), which means that all different sexual identities, homosexual, lesbian,
bisexual and transsexual, must be considered normal. Having failed at all
elections since its foundation to win a seat in the 28-member General Council
(parliament), for the elections of March 2015 the party joined a centre-left
coalition which got three seats.

Cyprus

The Ecological and Environmental Movement/Κίνημα Οικολόγων Περιβαλλο-
    ντιστών (Green Party)
This party represents only the Greek-Cypriot part of Cyprus.
Founded 1996
EGP 1998
Party leadership: one man – Giorgios Perdikis (plus a female general secretary)
National elections 2011: 2.21%, 1 MP
European elections 2014: The Greens joined a coalition with the Movement for
    Social Democracy; the coalition got 7.7% and one MEP, who however, joined
    the Social Democrats in the EP

http://cyprusgreens.org

The Cypriot Greens work according to a traditional Green programme for
sustainable development and protection of the environment. The party is also
active on animal rights. In the 2004 referendum on a UN negotiated peace

treaty, the Greens campaigned for the 'no' option, which won the majority among Greek Cypriots (65%); however a clear majority of the Turk Cypriots voted in favour (76%), but with a Greek Cypriot majority against nothing came out of it and the island is still divided. When some years later this author met with Cypriot Greens, some of them admitted that it had been a mistake not to grasp the chance of the UN-mediated peace treaty. However, in a letter of 2006 the Cyprus Greens protested against the Green Group in the European Parliament having held a meeting in North Cyprus, 'which is an illegal state'. But the party has also called for demilitarisation of Nicosia, together with the Turkish Cypriot New Cyprus Party. Thus, there are signs that the party is adopting a line closer to Green principles of compromise conflict resolution.

Denmark

In Denmark the original Green party, De Grønne, has been replaced by Socialistisk Folkeparti.

De Grønne (The Greens)
In the early 1980s two Green parties were established in Denmark, De Grønne (the Greens, G) in 1983 and Danmarks Miljøparti (Environmental Party of Denmark, EPD), in 1980. Both were very small, the EPD more environmentalist, with a traditional structure and mostly elderly men as members, G more ecologist, grassroots and democratic and with young members of both sexes. Despite some efforts they were unable to cooperate. In 1985 the Swedish Greens decided to choose G as their Danish partner, as did the Coordination of European Greens. Before the local elections of 1985 the Minister of Finance warned against the Greens, comparing them to the right-wing populist Fremskridtspartiet (Party of Progress). The Greens got 2.8% of the votes and ten seats in local councils. As the barrier for entry into the parliament is only 2%, this was a good sign. However in the parliamentary elections of 1987 and 1988 the Greens only managed to get 1.3% and 1.4%. In a report from the party congress in October 1989 a Swedish Green MP noted that De Grønne were 'very bohemic'. The congress discussed basic income, ecology, decentralisation. An opinion poll in the newspaper *BT* gave the Greens 3%, but at the elections of December 1990 the party only got 0.9%, and since then has never managed to fulfil the requirements to stand for elections. After this De Grønne never recovered; finally, in 2008, the party was expelled from the EGP.

Socialistisk Folkeparti (Socialist People's Party)
Founded 1959
EGP 2012 (associated), 2014 (member)
Party leadership: one woman – Pia Olsen Dyhr

National elections 2011: 9.2%, 16 MPs
European elections 2014: 10.9%, 1 MEP

http://sf.dk

After the disappearance of De Grønne the attention of the European Greens turned to the Socialist People's Party, which split from the Communist Party after the famous anti-Stalin speech of the Soviet leader Nikita Khrushchev in 1956, and stepwise adopted Green aspects into its programme. In 2004 the MEP of SF, Margrete Auken, joined the Green Group in the European Parliament and later the party became an observer at the EGP, from 2012 an associate member and from 2014 full member.

In 2007 SF got its best result ever in a parliamentary election, 13%, but in 2011 fell back to 9.2%. Despite this loss the party decided, for the first time ever, to join a government coalition, together with Social Democrats and Radicals (left liberals). SF got six ministers. However, the party quit the government in January 2014. *(For more about SF in government, see Chapter 5.)*

The SF's programme is a mixture of democratic socialism and Green considerations. Originally the party was opposed to Danish membership of the EEC/EU, but in the 1990s started to change position, which caused years of internal strife.

A breakthrough for Green thinking in Denmark came with the publication in 1978 of a book with the title *Oprør fra midten* (Revolt from the Centre), presenting a Green vision of a society in ecological balance, with a basic income for everybody.[130] The reception in Denmark was overwhelming; the book sold more than 100,000 copies (which is a lot in Denmark). A movement was formed to pursue the ideas of the book, and a follow-up book was published in 1982, but the Green upsurge was never transformed into a political party.

The first Danish Greens never managed to defeat their 'childhood disease' of too much grassroots democracy combined with too little efficiency in reaching voters. SF comes out of a different situation, having been for more than 50 years an established parliamentary party. Some Greens ask how deep the conversion of SF from Red to Green is. Until recently its closest Nordic partners have been non-Green left-wing parties in Sweden, Finland, Norway and Iceland, at the same time as their MEP has been a member of the Green Group in the European Parliament. At the EGP Council in Istanbul in November 2014, when SF became a full EGP member, its representatives assured the Council that the party is serious about its Green credentials. Facing fresh elections on June 18, 2015, according to opinion polls SF will fall down to about 6%, while the Red-Green Enhedslisten will gain and get about 9%. A new partly Green Party, Alternativet (The Alternative) seems to get around 3%, well above the 2% barrier.

Greece

Ecologist Greens (Οικολόγοι Πράσινοι, Oikologoi Prasinoi)
Founded 2002
EGP 1994
Party leadership: co-presidents, one woman – Magy Dousi, one man – Michalis
Tremopoulos

www.ecogreens.gr

Already in the spring of 1984 some existing European Green parties received invitations from the Ecologist Initiative to a meeting in Greece about a Green party 'independent from left and right'. And in a letter in 1985 to the CoEG, the EKO (Enalaktiki Kinisi Oikologon/Alternative Movement of Ecologists), presented itself as founded on 5 July 1985 with a programme that promised 'commitment to democracy on all levels of organisation, the rotation of posts and the recallability of all elected representatives ... equality of participation between the sexes ... consensus...'. The secretariat was described as a complicated Green web: '4 regular and 2 replacement members. Each member serves for 4 months, and every 2 months 2 members are replaced, having completed 4 months, by the replacement members'. Secretaries 'are selected by lot among the members'. In the national elections of 1990, the Greens won a seat in the Greek parliament, but internal strife, among other things, led the MP to leave the party.

Not much happened then until December 2002, when the Ecological Forum organised a conference in Athens which decided to establish the Ecologist Greens. The first congress was held in May 2003. In the local elections of 2006 the Greens won some 50 seats in local assemblies. The EG got its first breakthrough with one MEP elected in 2009. At the same time it got 2.5% in the national elections. In the June 2012 elections it got only 0.88%. The result in the EU elections of 2014 was almost the same.

The Greek Greens have had difficulties coping with the acute socioeconomic crisis of the country which has not left much room for Green considerations. In January 2015 the EG joined an election coalition with the new left-wing party Syriza, which resulted in one Green MP and one Green member of the new Syriza-led government, the Deputy Minister of Environment, Yannis Tsironis.

Italy

Federazione dei Verdi (Federation of Greens)
Founded 1990
EGP 1993
Party leadership: co-spokespersons, one woman – Luana Zanella, one man –
Angelo Bonelli

National elections 2013: no MPs, but since 2015, by party switch, one Senator.
http://www.verdi.it

Italy's Greens (I Verdi), like other Green parties, have deep roots in the anti-nuclear movement, which led to decisions by referenda in 1987 to abolish all nuclear power in Italy. However, the Green Party, despite this victory, never managed to grow strong in terms of votes, and after 1994 never gained parliamentary seats through its own strength. During the rest of the 1990s and 2000s, the Greens were part of left-centre alliances, which in 1996 resulted in 2.5% of the vote, 28 seats and two ministerial posts. There was a minor setback in 2001, and in 2006 the vote fell again, but the number of seats increased to 22. In 2008, however, that fell to zero, partly because of Italy's electoral system – a defeat from which Verdi has not recovered. *(For more on the Italian Greens in government, see Chapter 5.)*

In a report from Italy in September 1984, co-secretary of CoEG Sara Parkin remarked that 'after the EU elections 79 we hoped to cooperate with the Italian Radicals, they are very libertarian on sex, abortion, etc., but impossible to cooperate with, because of their chaotic style and Pannella (leader since 1962)'. For several years there would be attempts by Greens to cooperate with the Radicals; some leading Italian Greens had their political roots in Partito Radicale. It was possible to cooperate in the European Parliament on issues, but Partito Radicale had a male guru leader – Pannella – which was in total contradiction with Green ideals. There were two Green lists in the EU elections of 1989, which the pioneer and emblematic personality of the Italian Greens, the South Tyrolean Alexander Langer, characterised as 'non-understandable'.[131] Nevertheless the Greens made a breakthrough with 3.8% of the vote and three MEPs for 'The laughing sun'-Greens, and 2.4% and two MEPs for Arcobaleno (Rainbow). In 1996 Verdi for the first time joined a government, with Edouardo Ronchi as Minister of Environment and four secretaries of state. In 2000 Alfonso Pecoraro Scanio became Minister of Agriculture. *(For more about I Verdi in government, see Chapter 5.)* The following year he was elected president of Verdi, and in 2006 he became Minister of Environment. After the electoral disaster of 2008, when Verdi lost all their MPs, Scanio left the presidency. Since 2008 I Verdi have not managed to make a comeback, partly because of changes to the electoral system, partly because of the chaotic political situation in Italy. From the late 1980s until 2008 the Italian Greens managed to keep a considerable group of parliamentarians on all levels, despite never winning more than a little over 2% of the votes.

One of the most well-known figures in the Italian Greens, Carlo Ripa di Meana (born 1929), in a book in the late 1990s, written when he had terminated a turbulent period as president of the party from 1993 to 1996, describes his party as full of petty careerist kings (most often male). The book is dedicated to

Alexander Langer, who was for a long time the ideological inspiration for I Verdi. Unfortunately, Langer chose to take his life in July 1995 for unknown reasons.[132]

I Verdi have been pioneering in demanding full rights for gays and lesbians. During an animal rights campaign against fur coats, Ripa di Meana's wife, Marina, appeared on posters all over the country totally nude with the text: 'This is the only fur I wear.' Some Greens took it as a threat to the survival of the party. Ripa di Meana also affronted the Green mayor of Rome, Francesco Rutelli, when he joined a campaign together with Swedish and Greek Greens against the Olympic Games being held in either Stockholm, Rome or Athens (Athens got it, in 2004). Di Meana mocked Rutelli for having opposed the Olympic Games in Milan, but then supporting it coming to Rome.[133] When asked by the author in 2014 the current spokespersons of Verdi maintain that the disaster that befell the party in 2008 was a result of the long presidency of Alfonso Pecoraro Scanio and his mistakes. However, that hardly explains why there has been no sign of a comeback so far. It is true that the Italian Greens were never as strong as might have been assumed from the impression given by a rather large group of MPs and repeated participation in governments; however, other Green parties have collapsed, lost all their MPs, and yet still recovered.

In January 2015, for the first time since 2008, I Verdi got an MP when the senator Bartolomeo Pepe of the Five Stars party, led by Beppe Grillo, switched to the Greens.

Malta

Alternattiva Demokratika (Democratic Alternative)
Party leadership: one male president – Arnold Cassola
Founded 1989
EGP 1993
National elections 2013: 1.8%, but no MP (best ever result)
European elections 2014: 2.95%, no MEP (best result 2004: 9.3%)

http://www.alternattiva.org

Alternattiva Demokratika (AD) was founded in 1989 by scores of people coming from environmental and human rights NGOs together with two former Labour Party politicians, including Wenzu Mintoff, who retained his seat in parliament and was a kind of Green MP until 1992. In the elections of 1992 AD got 1.7%, and no MPs. When the election results did not improve in the 1990s Mintoff returned to the Labour Party and was replaced as chair person in 1999 by Harry Vassallo. AD took a position in favour of joining the EU in 1999, and was a foremost protagonist in the referendum on EU accession. In the 2004 EU election the party's score increased considerably to 9.3%, in favour of Arnold

Cassola, who narrowly failed to become an MEP. However, the results in the parliamentary and EU elections of 2008 and 2009 were meagre. In 2013 AD had its best result ever in a parliamentary election, 1.8%, but not enough to get an MP. Cassola was the secretary general of the European Greens 1999–2006 and a member of the Italian parliament 2006–2008. Since 2013 he has been the president of the party. AD has a few representatives in local assemblies. Three of 12 members of the party executive are women.

In the 2011 referendum on the introduction of divorce, AD campaigned in favour. The 'yes' option won by 53–46% and the possibility of divorce was introduced into the Maltese legislation. AD has been one of very few organisations to oppose the extensive spring hunting (all other EU countries ban hunting during the spring breeding season). After collecting signatures from around 14% of the Maltese electorate, and in collaboration with another 13 environmental NGOs, they secured a referendum, on 11 April 2015, which was narrowly won by the pro-hunting lobby, 50.4%–49.6 %, with 74.8% of voters participating. Subsequently the annual spring hunting season was opened, but rapidly closed again after incidents in which prohibited species of birds were killed. Greens and others in Malta hope that the country's adaptation to general EU hunting norms, despite the outcome of the referendum, will be just a matter of time.

Norway

Miljøpartiet De Grønne, MDG (The Environmental Party the Greens)
Founded 1988
EGP 1993
Party leadership: co-presidents, one woman – Hilde Opoku, one man – Rasmus
    Hansson.
National elections 2013: 2.8%, 1 MP

www.mdg.no

The Norwegian Greens agree with the Charter of the Global Greens. The party characterises itself as biocentric, and as being a part of a new alternative paradigm. Having once been as 'Eurosceptic' as the Swedish Greens (until 2008), the party now has no opinion in favour of or against Norwegian EU membership. However it believes the issue can only be settled by a referendum.[134] According to its statutes, each sex should have at least 40% representation in all party structures. There are some positions that cannot be held at the same time as certain others, and no position can be held more than ten years. For a period in the 1990s, under pressure from media, MDG introduced a one-person presidency, but as this neither helped to win more votes nor was felt to be Green, the system of two equal chairpersons was reinstated.

For decades MDG was relatively marginalised in Norwegian politics, which is odd, considering that Green thinking has had a prominent place in Norwegian public life through several thinkers, for example Arne Naess (founder of the 'deep ecology' philosophy) and Erik Dammann, who in 1974 founded the Green lobbying organisation The Future in Our Hands. However, opinion polls started to move upwards in 2009 and the party made a well-publicised attack on the Social Democratic government, accusing it of major environmental vices such as granting too many licenses for exploitation of oil, failing to use the financial crisis for a Green transformation, allowing increased over-fishing and not launching renewable energy projects. This may have convinced Norwegian voters that 'real' Greens are needed to move from words to deeds. In the local elections of 2011, MDG achieved a breakthrough and got 17 representatives in 16 different municipalities. In the 2013 elections it managed to win, for the first time, one seat in Stortinget (parliament).

Spain

There are two Green parties from Spain in the EGP, Equo (Spain except Catalonia) and Iniciativa per Catalunya Verds (Initiative for Catalonia – Greens)

Already in 1984 the CoEG received a letter from the ecologist Santiago Vilanova, representing Alternativa Verda, in which he asked for membership. In a report from the first congress of Los Verdes in February 1985, co-secretary of CoEG Sara Parkin observed that local police refused entry to some individuals who claimed to be Green. This author was present and remembers the consternation when one Green group called for the police to block entry for another one. Criticism from CoEG caused a vigorous rebuttal from Assamblea de los verdes alternativos de Madrid, full of scornful sneers against Sara Parkin, like 'we do not deny that the above report bears the charm of a delightful tourist description and displays, as such, a high narrative value equalling that of Charles Dickens' novels'. In July 1985 CoEG received a magazine[135] which claimed to be the official voice of Verde, which means Green but also should be seen as an acronym for Vertice Espanol Reivindication Desarollo Ecologica (Spanish top point demanding an ecological development). It was stated that Verde had been officially registered on 24 September 1982 and had a dozen regional offices all over Spain. Attached was a joint statement together with a Portuguese group on Unity of the Iberian Peninsula.[136] A further illustration of the extreme disintegration of the Spanish Greens in the 1980s is the following report on election results for Catalonia: Alternativa Verda-Movimento Ecologista de Catalunya 0.61%; Els Verds ecologistas 0.33%; Los Verdes 0.3%; Partido ecologista espanol – Verde 0.22%.[137] In a report at the third congress of Los Verdes in Benidorm, 3–5 December 1988, the party emphasised that 'we saw the necessity of developing an ideology learning of the mistakes of the traditional left parties … We are a different party, the alternative to the traditional parties.' A wish was expressed for electoral cooperation with the Confederation de los Verdes, another Green faction, which like Los Verdes was later accepted as member of the CoEG. The congress adopted resolutions against the celebration of the 500th anniversary of the 'conquest' of America, Spain's membership of the WEU, and the militarisation of women.

On 9 April 1989, an agreement was signed by Los Verdes and some members of the Confederation de los Verdes on a coalition for the EU elections. However, not until 2010 was a serious attempt made to bring the Spanish Greens into a united structure. These efforts led to the foundation, on 4 June 2011, of *Equo*, into which some 35 different Spanish Green parties decided to merge.

Equo
Founded 4 June 2011
EGP candidate member 2013
Party leadership: co-presidents, one woman – Rosa Martínez, one man – Juan López de Uralde.
National elections 2011: 0.9%, no MP
European election 2014: 1.9%, one 'half' MP

In a programme for the elections of 2011 point number 1 was a 'change of economic model' into a genuinely sustainable economy. There are also demands for renewable energy, rejection of nuclear energy and the dismantling of all Spanish reactors, social justice, no to GMOs, animal rights and the banning of bullfights (corridas), closing down of fiscal paradises, the introduction of a tax on financial transactions (Tobin tax), as well as non-violent resolution of conflicts.

On the eve of the general elections of 2011 Equo rejected a proposal to join ranks with the United Left (Izquierda Unida), because Equo wanted to offer Spanish voters a clear Green choice. Equo got 0.9%, but no MP. In regional elections in Galicia 2012, two Equo representatives were elected to the regional assembly. At the EU elections 2014 Equo won 1.92% as member of a coalition which gained one MEP seat, which Equo will take over on 1 January 2017.

Iniciativa per Catalunya Verds, ICV (Initiative for Catalonia-Greens)
Founded in 1987 (as a coalition of three parties)[138]
EGP 2006
Party leadership: co-presidents, one woman – Dolors Camats, one man – Joan Herrera
Regional (Catalonia) elections 2010: 9.9%, 10 regional MPs
National elections 2011: 8.1% in Catalonia, 2 MPs as part of coalition

European elections 2014: 1 MEP as part of coalition

http://www.iniciativa.cat

ICV is rather left than right, and ecosocialist. It rejects religion in politics and supports the right for Catalonia to decide its own status; in the referendum in November 2014, because of the limits of the Spanish Constitution, ICV did not give any recommendation. The co-president Joan Herrera declared that he would not vote. In 2005 ICV was fighting for a 'no' to the European Constitution. In February 2015 the ICV MEP Ernest Urtasun protested against plans from the Spanish government to limit the right to abortion, which he qualified as contrary to women's rights.

ICV has had representation in both the Catalonian and European parliaments for a long time, and since 2011 also in the Spanish parliament.

Turkey

Yeşiller ve Sol Gelecek Partisi, YSGP (Greens and the Left Party of the Future)
Founded 25 November 2012
EGP candidate 2012
Party leadership: co-presidents one woman – Sevil Turan, one man – Naci
    Sönmez

http://yesillervesolgelecek.org

In September 1989 a Swedish Green reported from a visit to Turkey that Yeşiller Partisi (the Green Party) had a nationwide organisation, which campaigned against pollution and military activity.[139] In December 1989 the CoEG received a message from a Green party in Bursa, protesting against a new power station. However, the establishment of a Green party in Turkey did not begin in earnest until November 2012, when the small Green Party merged with the Equality and Democracy Party to form the Greens and the Left Party of the Future.

The Turkish Greens identify as left-libertarian. In December 2013 the party celebrated its first anniversary. Sevil Turan, a young green activist, was re-elected as co-spokesperson, along with Naci Sönmez. A council of 75 persons (38 women) was elected. In October 2013 the Turkish Greens accused the Turkish government of neglecting 'the massacres and attacks in Kobanê' and affirmed that 'the Greens and Future Left Party remain at the side of the Kurdish population'. YSGP has recognized the Armenian genocide[140] and welcomed the Syriza government in Greece. The passing of the 10%-barrier by the opposition party HDP at the elections of June 7, 2015, was welcomed by the UK Greens as a 'win for the Kurds, the LGBP community and the Turkish Greens'.

WEST EUROPEAN GREENS OUTSIDE THE EGP

Iceland

There is no Green party in Iceland. However, the Women's List/Kvennalistinn, a feminist party founded 13 March 1983, participated in Nordic Green cooperation, and was sometimes considered as the Icelandic Green party in being. In the parliamentary elections of 1983 the Women's List got 5.3% and three MPs, up to 10.1% and six MPs in 1987. But in the 1990s the results started to drop off, with five MPs in 1991 and three in 1995. Thus in 1998 the Women's List decided to join three left-wing parties to establish the United Front. However, some of the members preferred to establish the Left Party–the Greens/Vinstrihreyfingin–grænt framboð. This party is a member of the Nordic Green Left, together with other left-wing parties in the Nordic countries, one of which is the Danish Socialistisk Folkeparti. The Left Party–the Greens hit a peak in 2009 with 14 members of parliament and became part of the government, but lost half of those MPs in 2013 and since then has been an opposition party. Out of the seven MPs left, five are women. Whether Vinstrihreyfingin–grænt framboð will follow the example of Socialistisk Folkeparti and approach the European Greens is too early to know.

http://vg.is

Liechtenstein

There is no Green party in Liechtenstein, but Die Freie Liste, FL (Free List), claims to be 'social, democratic and ecological'. FL was founded in 1985 and overcame the 8% barrier for the first time in 1993. In 2009 it got one seat (out of 25) in the parliament (Landtag), and three in 2013. The FL works for gender equality, integration of foreigners, environmental protection and social justice. The Executive (Vorstand) is made up of three women and two men.

http://www.freieliste.li

GREENS IN CENTRAL AND EASTERN EUROPE

Despite considerable differences, the Greens of the former Communist bloc have a common background which makes it appropriate to present them together here. Most of them are affiliated to the EGP, but not all.

Albania

Partia e Gjelbër e Shqipërisë or Të gjelbërit, PGJ (The Green Party of Albania) Founded 1 September 2001

EGP 2008
Party leadership: one man – Edlir Petanaj
National elections 2013: 0.12% (inside left-wing coalition Alliance for European Albania)
Local elections May 2011: 34 councillors in 8 municipalities and 26 communes.

http://www.pgj.al/index.html

The Albanian Greens identify as 'a left party in opposition, in coalition with the Socialist movement'.[141] The party has campaigned against GMOs, fossil fuel, nuclear power, and for bicycles and tree planting. It has protested against the building of a nuclear power plant in Shkoder, and against the destruction of a Botanical Garden. It won two seats in the local elections of 2003 and has since progressed on the local level, getting 34 councillors in 2011. However it has not had any success in parliamentary elections. As a result of seminars organised by the Swedish Green Forum more than 40% of the PGJ candidates in recent elections have been women.

Armenia

Social Ecological Green Party of Armenia
Founded 24 June 1998; re-registration 25 December 2000
Not an EGP member, but the party leader has been present at EGP Councils.
Party leadership: one man – Armen Dovlatyan.
MPs 2014: 0
National elections: boycotted elections in 2003 and 2007.

https://www.facebook.com/pages/Green-Party-of-Armenia

During 1990–92 a Green Party of Armenia was founded, but did not develop. In 1998 Armen Dovlatyan founded and registered the Social Ecological Green Party. This party has not been accepted as a member of the EGP because of difficulties in establishing some basic facts. In 2006 the Swedish Green Forum reported from a conference of Greens of South Caucasus: 'Since the Green party of Armenia is not functioning properly, and the reputation of the party with current leaders is rather weak, it was proposed by the Armenian participants to promote the establishment of a new Green party.' However, no new party was created and the Social Ecological Party appears in media reports on environmental actions in Armenia. For example, in November 2011, when the Armenian government scrapped a new hydroelectric project, a news agency reported that 'Green Party leader Armenak Dovlatyan said he would not be declaring victory until numerous unanswered questions were dealt with.' According to its programme the party is in favour of the creation and development of ecological and political governance systems, market economy, national unity and the safety of the nation, and the guaranteeing of human rights, liberty and political participation. The party 'accepts such a system of the ecology ruling which does not hinder progress'.

Azerbaijan

Azerbaycan Yasillar Partiyasi (Green Party of Azerbaijan)
Founded 2006
EGP observer 2008, associate 2012
Party leadership: co-chairman – Mayis Gulaliyev, co-chairwoman – Tarana Mamadova
MPs 0

https://www.facebook.com/pages/Azerbaycan-Yasillar-Partiyasi-Green-Party-of-Azerbaijan

The Green Party of Azerbaijan (GPA) has not been able to register because of the authoritarian regime in the country, which has even established a competing Green party to create confusion. According to its founder, Mayis Gulaliyev, the Green Party is the only political party in Azerbaijan which calls for a peaceful resolution to the Nagorno-Karabakh conflict and for the opening of borders between Turkey and Armenia. The party connects ecological problems with political and social problems, i.e. with the bad governance of Azerbaijan.

A book (in Azerbaijani) by Gulaliyev, with the title *The Great Satan or the Beginning of the End* (2007), includes chapters on: Anatomy of the US Empire, US Support for 'International Terrorism', NATO – final chord of US neo-colonisation, US-Israel Alliance is Global Danger. According to a promotional text in English by Gulaliyev, the book 'studies the essence of the US foreign policy and its impacts in the South Caucasus countries, including Azerbaijan'. GPA collected more than 44,000 signatures for the presidential elections of 2008. For the presidential election in October 2013, GPA established a political bloc with the 'Justice' Party and nominated its own candidate for presidency.

In March 2010, the twelfth EGP Council in Barcelona, Spain, stated that 'Azerbaijan has been in a downward spiral in terms of democracy and human rights for many years now.' EGP recalled that letters were sent twice to the Azerbaijan president asking for an explanation for the delay of the registration of GPA; however there has been no reply from the Azerbaijani authorities.

Belarus

Biełaruskaja Partyja 'Zialonyja', BPZ (Belarusian Party – the Greens)

Founded 1994
EGP observer 2007, associated 2013
MPs 0
Party leadership: one man – Oleg Novikov
Local assemblies: 0

http://www.belgreens.org/en

At the 20 year anniversary on 17 April 2014 in Minsk, party founder Oleg Gromyko said that the creation of the Greens in Belarus was caused by the Chernobyl nuclear disaster. Present party chair Oleg Novikov said that BPZ is different from other Belarusian parties because it takes decisions collectively. The party was practically absent from political life from 1996 to 2008, but was then the first in Belarus to take up a position in favour of the rights of gays and sexual minorities. It also uses an ecosocialist, anti-corporatist, anti-globalist rhetoric; it is anti-nuclear, in favour of social justice and workers' rights, non-violence, and grassroots democracy.

In May 2010 the BPZ presented its vice president Yurij Glushakov as candidate for the presidency of the republic, but he withdrew in October because of obstacles to his campaign. In October 2010 Novikov signed an agreement on the Establishment of the 'Eurasian Association of Green Parties' (EAGP), with the presidents of Green Party Rukhaniyat, Kazakhstan (S. Mambetalin), Russian Environmental Movement 'Greens', Russia (A. Panfilov) and Zeleny ('Greens'), Ukraine (A. Prognimak). Of these parties only BPZ has a formalised relation to the EGP. The three others are considered to be more or less 'fake' parties, supported by their governments. At a congress in November 2011 Novikov was re-elected president of the party with 29–5 votes. Campaigns were conducted against nuclear energy and the death penalty.[142]

In a statement on the Ukrainian conflict in May 2014, Novikov declared: 'There is no consensus in the Belarusian Green Party about the nature of the current political regime in Ukraine ... The Belarusian Greens support exclusively peaceful dialogue and an end to armed confrontation.'

Bosnia and Herzegovina

Zeleni Bosne i Hercegovine (The Greens of Bosnia and Herzegovina)
Founded 2004
No EGP relation
Party leadership: one man – Hasan Dalic
Positions: human rights, political freedoms, free market economy, protection of the environment, ecological standards for production, more local self-rule, EU membership.

Bulgaria

The EGP has two full member parties from Bulgaria: Zelena Partija Bulgaria, ZPB (The Green Party of Bulgaria) and Zelenite (The Greens)

Zelena Partija Bulgaria (The Green Party of Bulgaria)
Founded 1989
EGP 1993
Party leadership: female president – Marina Dragomiretskaya, 'govoritel' (spokesman) – Aleksandyr Karakachanov, male.
European elections 2014: 0.4%.

http://www.greenparty.bg

In the late 1980s and early 1990s Greens played a major role and got representation in parliament. ZPB was founded 28 December 1989 by environmental activists, several from the dissident Ecoglasnost. ZPB participated in the anti-totalitarian union UDF which fought for democracy. A major conflict of interests developed within the UDF and brought it to an ultimate split during the signing of the New Bulgarian Constitution when the Greens, lead by Karakachanov, chose to vote pro. From 1988–89 until the beginning of the twenty-first century, ZPB had representation in the parliament most of the time, in the framework of centre-left coalitions.

In the early 1990s ZPB shaped a political platform which stated that 'the opportunities for economic progress at the expense of the environment have been exhausted'. The party backed the country's membership of the EEC within 8–10 years, fought for the consolidation of civil rights and democracy, and criticised 'fabricated allegations and rabid agitation' against Bulgarian Turks. It acted in support of market economy, equality of all sorts of ownership, privatisation of farms, sharp reduction of taxes and campaigned to 'Save Bulgaria from its dangerous dependence on nuclear energy'.

ZPB has complained to the EU commission that land and forests have been given away free or at bargain prices to oligarchs. In September 2014 the EU commission declared that some of these swaps were contraventions of EU legislation.

In 2000 ZPB suffered a split and a competing Green party was formed, which was accused by ZPB of being the instrument of an oligarch. In 2008 there was a partial merger of Green parties, but ZPB did not participate in the parliamentary elections of 2009. In 2013 it was prevented from participation in the elections by the Central Election Committee for technical reasons. In the EU election of 2014 the party got 0.4% of the votes and no MEP. During the years 2006–2009, a representative of ZPB was Deputy Minister of Justice in a three-party coalition (see Chapter 5)

Zelenite (The Greens)
Founded 2008
EGP 2013
Party leadership: gender-balanced co-chairs: Anna Pelova, Petko Tsvetkov
National elections 2014: 0.61%, no MPs
European elections 2014: 0.56%

http://izbori.zelenite.bg

Zelenite emerged from a number of non-governmental organisations who felt, after years of work in the area of environmental protection, human rights, etc., that their work needed serious political backing if it was to have a lasting effect. Zelenite is a young party and decentralised in its structure (with two equal co-presidents). It claims to be 'the first to raise the topic of the citizens' direct participation in the government of the state', partly through more 'electronic government'.

Efforts to establish closer cooperation between the two Bulgarian Green parties, supported by EGP recommendations, have so far not led to tangible results.

Croatia

Zelena Lista (Green List), associated member of EGP since 2012, dissolved in the beginning of 2014 and its members joined ORaH, which was founded in December 2013.
Održivi razvoj Hrvatske, ORaH (Sustainable Development of Croatia). ORaH, is the Croatian word for walnut.
EGP candidate 2014
Party leadership: one female president, Mirela Holy, also MEP; the former leader of Zelena Lista Vlasta Toth is international secretary.
National elections: Zelena Lista 2011: 0.36%, no MP.
European elections 2014: 9.42%, 1 MEP (out of 11).

https://www.orah.hr

In the preamble of ORaH's programme, in addition to common Green environmental demands, it is emphasised that the economic development of the country is dependent on scientific findings and technological development; thus the party will promote bioorganic agriculture, sustainable eco-tourism, Green buildings, energy efficiency in building, heating, transport, and lighting, as well as Green technology.

Czech Republic

Strana Zelenych, SZ (Green Party)
Founded 1990
EGP 1997
Party leadership: one woman – Jana Drápalová
National elections 2013: 3.2%, no MP
European elections 2014: 3.8%, no MEP

http://www.zeleni.cz

One of the main goals of the SZ is to establish a new energy policy based upon renewables and to halt plans to build new nuclear reactors. It asks: 'Why do we live in two states, Czech and CEZ?', thereby attacking the influence of the major energy company, CEZ, partly private, but still with the Czech state as the main shareholder. Another issue on which the SZ is campaigning is to get more nursery and pre-school places.

SZ entered the parliament in 2004 with one seat in the Senate, and got a breakthrough in the elections of 2006 with 6.3% and six MPs. The victory led to an invitation to participate in a right-wing coalition government, from January 2007 to March 2009. However, internal quarrels erupted in the party, and the Green Minister of Education, Dana Kuchovà, was forced to resign in October 2007. At the party congress of September 2008, party leader Martin Bursik won re-election against Kuchovà, with 227–109 votes. But the Greens showed signs of falling to pieces and lost votes in elections to the Senate in 2008 and to the EU parliament in 2009. Bursik resigned after the failure at the EU elections. The elections in 2010 showed dissatisfaction among voters. SZ's vote share fell to 2.4% and it lost all its MPs. The national elections of 2013 and EU elections of 2014 may have been a beginning of a comeback. In October 2014 the party had three senators. *(See Chapter 5 for more details about SZ in government.)*

Estonia

Eestimaa Rohelised (Estonian Greens)
Founded 1989
EGP 1993
Party leadership: one man – Aleksander Laane
National elections 2015: 0.9%
European elections 2014: 0.3%

http://www.erakond.ee

Already in 1989 the CoEG was contacted by Tomas Frey of the Estonian Green Movement. He reported on heavy pollution, especially from oil shale and phosphorite mining, and added: 'Greens now fear the dangers of colonisation from the West.' In a programme from 1989 the Estonian Green Movement stated some basic points: 'Independent Estonia as a Green republic', nuclear-free Balto-Scandia, small farms, land to those who cultivate it, environmental security, local control of the economy. This was a considerably less free-market approach than was common among most other Eastern and Central European Greens at this time.[143] In the first free elections, while Estonia was still a Soviet republic, the Greens won eight seats in the Supreme Soviet. The party leader Tomas Frey was appointed Minister of Environment. But the first elections in independent Estonia were a disappointment, with only 2.6% Green votes and no MPs.

The Estonian Greens restarted in 2006, with a general assembly with 361 representatives. The election of March 2007 was a success, with 7.1% of the vote and six MPs. But in the elections of 2011 all six seats were lost. Between the successful and the failed elections there was internal strife. In 2010 the party expelled former leader Peeter Jalakas and some 20 other members.[144] Officially the cause was ideological, but according to a critical blogger 'this purge' was made in order to 'iron out a platform for next year's parliamentary elections'. In any case, the 2011 election was a disaster for the Estonian Greens.

In the election programme for the March 2015 parliamentary elections, the party gives highest priority to the eradication of poverty, which is said to hit 100,000 people. It promises that if it manages to enter parliament, it will give half of its state subsidies to charity. (It must be noted that the election programme is published on the website not only in Estonian but also in Russian). The election result was a disappointment, with only 0.9%.

Georgia

Sakartvelos mtsvaneta partia (Georgian Green Party)
Founded 1989
EGP 1993
Party leadership: one man – Gia Gachechiladze
MPs 1

http://www.greensparty.ge/en

The Georgian Green Party entered the parliament in 1992, during the Georgian liberation struggle, with 11 MPs out of 235. The leader during the first years was Zurab Zhvania, who also became co-secretary of the European Greens. However because of the chaotic situation, with civil war, Zhvania left the Green

Party and joined Eduard Shevardnadze. This damaged the party, which won only 0.55% of the vote in 1999. In 2001 Zhvania left the ruling party, becoming a leader of the Rose Revolution and then Prime Minister. The Green Party chose to cooperate with Shevardnadze for the 2003 election and the party president, Gia Gachechiladze, became an MP, but only for a few minutes – the inaugural session was disrupted by the entry of the Rose Revolutionaries, the parliament was dissolved, and in the elections of 2004 the Greens got no MP.

From the outset the Green Party warned that the new regime showed signs of disrespect for the rule of law. This criticism increased after the unexplained death of Zhvania in early 2005. On 28 April 2007 the Green Party held a congress in Tbilisi with 180 members from all over Georgia. Sofia Sakhanberidze was elected spokesperson, the male position remaining vacant; the former president of the party, Gia Gachechiladze, became general secretary. A short time after the congress the regime mounted a legally unfounded police raid against the party offices, which meant they had to find new headquarters.

The Georgian Greens make a clear distinction between the US and Europe. While being profoundly pro-European, the party prefers non-alignment to NATO membership. It also denounces violent means to reunite the country, while strongly criticising Russia for its interventions. In the elections of 1

Figure 16 Zurab Zhvania (right), founder of the Georgian Greens, at the party headquarters, 1993 (with unknown). Zhvania left the Greens and joined Eduard Shevardnadze. Later he was a leader of the Rose Revolution in 2003, and became prime minister in 2004. He was invited to give a keynote speech at the congress of the European Green Party in Rome, February 2004. He died in March 2005, officially from accidental carbon monoxide poisoning, but according to widespread belief in Georgia, as victim of an assassination. Photo: the author.

October 2012, Gia Gachechiladze was elected on the list of the opposition Georgian Dream coalition. Some of the ambitions of the Georgian Greens were the sharpening of environmental regulations, the re-establishment of the Ministry of Natural Resources, and improvement of human rights and respect for the law. In February 2014 Gachechiladze left the Georgian Dream parliamentary group over a disagreement on environmental and energy security issues. In the local elections of June 2014 the Greens had members elected in three sakrebulos (local assemblies): Mtskheta (9.86%), Tianeti (6.45%) and Mestia (4.67%).

Hungary

Hungary has two EGP-member parties: Zöld Baloldal Párt, ZB (Left-Green Party) which is a follow-up party to the original Hungarian Greens of the late 1980s, and Lehet Más a Politika, LMP (Politics Can be Different), which is a phenomenon of the twenty-first century. LMP is the main representative of Green politics today in Hungary, with representation in the European and national parliaments.

In 2009 the Zöld Demokratak joined the Feminist Initiative for an Alternative Europe (Európai Feminista Kezdeményezés Egy Másmilyen Európáért) and the Workers Party 2006 (Magyarországi Munkáspárt 2006) to establish the Left-Green Party (Zöld Baloldal Párt, ZB). This party (including its predecessors) has been a member of the EGP since 1993.

Lehet Más a Politika, LMP (Politics Can be Different)
EGP 2011
Party leadership: co-presidents, one woman – Bernadett Szel, one man – András Schiffer.
National elections 2014: 5.3%, 5 MPs
European elections 2014: 5%, 1 MEP

http://www.lehetmas.hu

The symbolic starting point for Green activity in Hungary was the struggle against the Danubian river dam project Gabcikovo-Nagymaros. The leading environmental organisation in Hungary was Duna Kör (the Danube Circle). At a meeting of a Green party in October 1989, 40 persons were present, a third of them women. A steering committee of seven was elected (four men, three women, including some leading Hungarian Green veterans: Szusza Beres, Andras Szekfü and Erszebet Schmuck), and it was decided that all Hungary's seven regions should have two representatives in a central board, one women and one man.[145] In December 1989 Erszebet Schmuck and Andras

Szekfü inaugurated the founding meeting of the 'Green Party of Hungary', rather than 'Hungarian Green Party' (which might have been interpreted as a party only for ethnic Hungarians). The event started with a very emotional film about a chicken emerging out of an egg. Several female speakers took the floor, but no quota was implemented when steering bodies were elected. Some of the participants maintained that the 'Greens are the only group which understands that the alternative to Communism is not the Western way but something new'.[146] In a letter to the Coordination of European Greens, Zsuzsa Bères affirmed that the Hungarian Greens had been registered and had a bank account. 'Whilst we are grappling with almost insurmountable difficulties and many of us are on the verge of physical exhaustion, we derive a sense of inspiration from the fact that this Green Party, small and frail as it still is, is taken seriously – by the government, the other parties, the media, the people.'[147]

The original Hungarian Greens never managed to achieve a political breakthrough. In 2006 the representative of the Hungarian EGP member party Zöld (Green) reported that a sponsor, Acs Laszlo, had given money and an office but had also hijacked the party. When the party congress didn't obey his directives, he established his own party, which created confusion.[148]

In May 2013, one of the founders of the LMP gave the following account of the history of the young party: 'We started our party Politics Can Be Different in 2007 ... We decided to participate in the 2010 elections, even though everyone thought it was impossible ... We got 7.5% of the vote ... That gave us a parliamentary group of 16 and allowed us to participate in Hungarian politics ... In the run-up to the 2014 parliamentary elections, LMP split. One part entered an electoral alliance with the Socialist Party to fight against the ruling party Fidesz. This group called itself Dialogue for Hungary. The other half kept the name LMP and vowed to maintain its independence.'

LMP broke the 5% barrier in the 2014 elections and got five MPs and one MEP, Tamás Meszerics. A former LMP member, representing Dialogue for Hungary, was also elected MEP and accepted as a member of the Green Group of the European Parliament. LMP has given high priority to the struggle against GMOs, a position enjoying wide support in Hungary. The EU accepted Hungary's anti-GMO regulations in 2005 and the constitution of 2010 declares Hungary GMO-free.

Kosovo

Partia e të Gjelbërve të Kosovës, PGJK (The Green Party of Kosovo)

A Green Party was founded in Kosovo in 1991, when Kosovo was part of Yugoslavia. The party contested the parliamentary elections of 12 December 2010 as part of the seven-party New Kosovo Coalition (Koalicioni për Kosovë të Re), which got 7.3% and eight MPs, however none of them was Green. PGJK has no formal affiliation to EGP.

Latvia

Latvijas Zala Partija, LZP (Latvian Green Party)
Founded 1990
EGP 2001
Party leadership: co-presidents, two men Viesturs Silenieks and Raimonds Vējonis
National elections 2014: 6 MPs (in a coalition framework)

www.zp.lv

There were three Greens in the last Supreme Soviet, 1990–93, but only one in the first freely elected Saeima of 1993–95. During the period 1995–98 there were four Greens, including Indulis Emsis, who became Minister of Environment from 1993 to 1998. From 1998 to 2002 there was no Green MP, but the Greens made a comeback in 2002 in the framework of the Union of Greens and Farmers, and got three MPs, one of them Emsis. Once again the party joined a government, with Raimonds Vejonis as Minister of Environment. In February 2004 Indulis Emsis became the first Green Prime Minister in the world. His minority government was forced to resign in the fall of the same year. A new coalition government took office, in which the Green Party was involved as part of the Union of Greens and Farmers.

It is remarkable how the Latvian Greens managed to avoid the long marginalisation that happened to most other Greens in the former communist bloc. It is likely that the personality of Indulis Emsis, a very keen environmentalist, suited the Latvian mood well. That he is highly respected is underlined by the fact that he was chosen as Speaker of the Saeima. The Latvian Greens have remained in parliament even since 2007, when Emsis (at the age of only 55) retired from politics.

The election of October 2014 was a considerable victory. The coalition (of which the Green co-chair Vejonis is the leader) increased from 12.2% to 19.5%, and from 12 to 21 seats in the Saeima, out of which the Greens got 6 (+2). The Greens also got a second minister (for health), Guntis Belevics. However, even if most signs are good, there is one big question mark: Why are the Latvian Greens so dominated by men? The Latvian Greens are the only Green party in the world which has two male co-chairs. All MPs, all members of the Board, and both ministers, are men. Most other positions in the party, with very few exceptions, are held by men.

Lithuania

Lietuvos žaliųjų partija (Lithuanian Green Party)
Re-founded 2011
Party leadership: one man – Linas Balsys
National elections: one MP

www.lzp.lt

There was a Green movement in Lithuania during the transition period. One of its leaders, Zigmas Vaisvila, even became Vice Premier. A Green party was established in 1990, but never managed to play any visible role, and was resurrected only in 2011. At a party congress in 2014 the president of the party, Linas Balsys, who is also its only MP (elected as independent), emphasised in an interview the importance of local economies. When the journalist tried to provoke Balsys by stating that while the Lithuanian Greens are liberal the Scandinavian Greens are 'kind of pro-communists', Balsys declared that 'we're set to get along with all the parties and movements in the spectrum'. For several years the greenest party in Lithuania was the Green and Peasants Party, LVZS, but now Balsys admits that the Greens do not agree with the LVZS on certain issues, like fodder and fertilizers. However, the MEP of LVZS has been accepted as member of the Green Group in the European Parliament. Balsys mentions Vaisvila as one of the Green pioneers. He deplores the fact that the government is 'giving up to the shale lobbyists' and demands that the 'nuclear project should be scrapped, as it is very detrimental to Lithuania's environment and security wise'.[149]

Macedonia

Demokratska obnova na Makedonija, DOM (Democratic Renewal of
    Macedonia)
Founded 2006
EGP: no formal relation, but the party leader has been present at EGP Councils.
Party leadership: one woman – Liljana Popovska
National elections 2014: 1 MP (as member of a 22-party coalition,
    VMRO-DPMNE)

http://dom.org.mk

DOM has a traditional Green programme, emphasising green jobs, renewable energy, human rights, democracy, ecology, tourism, eco-agriculture, women's empowerment, culture, and more funds for science and education. DOM has four priorities: Green Municipalities for a healthy life; Green economy and Green jobs; social justice and equal rights for all; tolerance, reason and cooperation. The party often uses activist methods like street actions using respiratory masks and bikes in order to promote eco-friendly transport as a way to reduce pollution. DOM also has a clear policy in respect of religious, cultural and sexual differences. In the elections of 2006, DOM won 1.9% of the vote and one (out of 120) seats in parliament. Since 2008 DOM has taken part in the ruling coalition VMRO-DPMNE. In elections in 2008, 2011 and 2014 it retained its one MP.

Moldova

Partidul Verde Ecologist (The Ecologist Green Party)
Founded 1992
EGP 2008
Party leadership: one man – Anatolie Prohnitchi
National elections 2014: 0.09%

www.greenparty.md

Partidul Verde Ecologist was founded in 1992 as the Ecologist Party of Moldova 'Green Alliance' (Partidul Ecologist din Moldova 'Alianța Verde', PEMAV). It got 0.4% of the vote in its first election in 1994, then did not contest again until 2009, with almost exactly the same result. In the following election the result was even lower. The party has never had any elected representative. According to Wikipedia the party is in favour of EU membership, despite a 'soft euroscepticism'.

Montenegro

Pozitivna Crna Gora (Positive Montenegro)
Founded May 2012
National elections 2012: 8.9%, 7 MPs
Party leadership: one man – Darko Pajovic

www.pozitivnacrnagora.me

The Green Party of Montenegro (Zeleni Crne Gore) was founded on 2 February 2002 at a meeting with 300 participants, and was officially registered on 21 March 2002. Its aim was to make Montenegro into an ecological state. Its role has been taken over by Positive Montenegro, which is a partly Green party but also has a high profile in favour of NATO membership, despite admitting that only 35% of the population is in favour.

Poland

Partia Zieloni (Green Party)
Founded 2003
EGP 2005
Party leadership: co-presidents, one woman – Agnieszka Grzybek, one man –
   Adam Ostolski
Parliament 2014: 1 MP (due to switch of party)
www.zieloni2004.pl

polskafair.pl (home page of Anna Grodska)

In October 1989 a Green party, Polska Partia Zielonych (Polish Party of
Greens) was founded. However, the official spokesperson of the Jaruzelski-
government, Jerzy Urban, publicly denied the existence of any Green party
in Poland. Unfortunately the party split and both factions called congresses
on 24 June 1989. A Polish Green bulletin explained that two congresses were
called 'because of controversial views of the spokesmen, each congress led by
one of the two spokesmen, Janusz Bryczkowski and Leszek Konarski'. In July a
German newspaper alleged that 'The Polish Greens are not green' and reported
differences over abortion, hunting and pesticides.[150]

After the internal struggles of the late 1980s, there was no active Green party
in the country until the present Polish Green Party was founded in September
2003 under the name 'Greens 2004' (Zieloni 2004) and formally registered in
February 2004. Zieloni was created by environmentalists, feminists, LGBT and
anti-war activists. The Green Manifesto, which was adopted by the founding
congress of the party, contains positions on social justice and solidarity,
civil society and reclaiming the state for citizens, environmental protection
and sustainable development, gender equality, respect for national, cultural
and religious diversity, protecting minority rights, and non-violent conflict
resolution. The party campaigned in favour of Polish membership of the EU, but
opposed the war in Iraq. Zieloni has contested national and European elections
in the framework of coalitions. The Green electorate has been minimal,
usually less than 1%. However, in 2014, Zieloni got one MP, Anna Grodzka,
a trans-woman who was elected on another list but switched to the Greens.
In December 2014 it was reported that Grodzka might become appointed
vice speaker of the Sejm, which triggered anti-transperson comments from
right-wing politicians.[151] She failed to collect the 100,000 signatures required
to stand as a candidate for the Greens in the presidential election of May 2015.

In an interview with the German Green Böll foundation in December 2013,
a member of the board of Zieloni, Bartłomiej Kozek, says: 'The year 2010 was
a breakthrough. Thanks to an electoral alliance with the SLD (Democratic Left

Alliance), we got our first five local councillors and two regional councillors in Silesia and West Pomerania.'[152]

Romania

Partidul Verde (Green Party)
EGP 1999
Party leadership: one man – Remus Cernea
National elections 2012: 2 MPs (as part of a coalition)
EU elections 2014: 0.35%

www.partidulverde.ro

In 1989 there were two Green formations in Romania, MER (Ecology Movement of Romania), which claimed to have 50,000 members and planned to take part in elections, and PER (Romanian Ecological Party).[153] A typical Romanian Green of this period was Marcian Bleahu (born 1924), a geologist and speleologist, who had a rather scientific attitude towards Green politics. He was MP 1990–92 and 1996–2000; in 1991–92 he was Minister of Environment.

The programme of Partidul Verde includes the usual Green principles, such as environmental protection, but also demands for more free market economics and the privatisation of state-owned enterprises. PV is in favour of same-sex marriage, LGTB rights, and action against homophobia.

Russia

There are several political parties in Russia claiming to be Green.

GROZA – The Green Alternative has been a member of the EGP since 1994. This is the remnant of the interregional Green party, established in the early 1990s. However, since its leading personality, Aleksey Kozlov, left Russia for Germany in January 2013, claiming that he expected to be jailed, GROZA has ceased functioning.

The Union of Greens, Russia (Green Russia) was established as a party in 2005 by Aleksey Yablokov, founder of Russian Greenpeace and adviser to president Yeltsin in the 1990s. However, the party failed to collect the necessary 50,000 signatures to register for elections. Thus, it accepted an invitation to join the liberal opposition party Yabloko as an internal faction. As of 2014 Green Russia had about 3,000 members; Aleksey Yablokov is president, with Alexander Nikitin and Olga Tsepilova as vice presidents. Despite the Yabloko party being a member of the European Liberal Alliance, Green Russia has been an associate member of EGP since 2013. However, one leading Russian environmentalist outside Green Russia characterises the Yabloko party as anti-ecological. (NB the similarity between Yabloko and Yablokov is coincidental).

http://rus-green.ru

The Russian Ecological Party 'The Greens' was founded in 1992 under the name of in the Constructive Ecological Party 'KEDR' (cedar), and in 2002 transformed into the Russian Ecological Party 'The Greens'. In 2007 it was denied registration because the Electoral Commission decided that too many of its signatures were fake. In 2008 it transformed into a social movement and recommended sympathisers vote for 'A Just Russia', which is close to the Putin regime.

http://www.greenparty.ru

The Alliance of Greens and Social Democrats/Green Alliance – People's Party was created in 2012 by the oligarch Gleb Fetisov, who was later jailed for alleged economic corruption. The party is based upon several small parties, among others the Green Alternative Movement (founded in 2009), whose chairperson Oleg Mitvol is the chairman of the new party.

http://russian-greens.ru

In the summer of 1989 a group of Swedish Greens toured the Soviet Union, visiting Moscow, Riga, Liepaja, Murmansk and Nikel, and met with leading Soviet environmentalists, including Sergej Zalygin (former editor of the literature magazine *Novyj Mir/New World*), Aleksey Yablokov and Angelina Guskova, chair of Soviet Doctors Against Atomic Weapons. The Swedish Greens found a growing environmental awareness. However, in 1993 the Russian sociologist Oleg Yanitsky concluded that, despite the fact that he estimated that about five million people in 1988 were involved in civic initiatives, there was 'an almost complete absence of civil society'; 'in Russia post-material values are cultivated only by an extremely narrow circle of people'.[154]

In 2003 it was reported that a coordination group had been created to try to organise a Green party of the Russian Federation. It had six male members and a female secretary. Nothing came of it.[155] According to a report by OSCE/ODHIR on the Duma elections of 7 December 2003, out of 23 listed parties, Greens got 0.42% (254,000 votes).

In 2004 Aleksey Yablokov wrote a paper about creating an 'Ecological Green Political Movement in Russia' in which he maintains that now is the time for a Green 'mass movement', which should have a leadership from all ecological organisations. He mentions 13 names for an 'initiative group' (including two women) and also 118 persons who might be members of the 'political council' (including 26 women).[156] The present author participated in a meeting with

Russian environmentalists in February 2004 and concluded: 'Russia is a very male society, a weakness. Russia is also very materialistic and militaristic. There is a need for an alternative.' In 2009 Oleg Yanitsky summarised the Green experience in Russia: 'It could be said that the green movement in the USSR never was politicised, and in the 1990s even took a distance from politics.' Many organisations were created by the West, and not adapted to Russian reality; small Green parties have remained marginal.[157]

To summarise: there is no real Green party in Russia in 2015. The EGP-member party is defunct; the associate party is not an independent party but a faction within a party that is not very ecological. Of the other would-be Green parties, one is defunct. Only a Green party controlled by a multi-billionaire oligarch, suspected of financial machinations, remains. Maybe that is the way it must be in the current 'steered' democracy of Russia. Why was no strong Green party established in Russia in the 1990s? The answer is probably that that decade was not only a period of new freedom, but also of humiliation and a dramatic drop in the material standard of living. In Russia a destructive revanchism has relegated Green concerns to the margin.

Slovakia

Strana Zelenych (Green Party)
Founded 1990
EGP 1995

http://www.stranazelenychpuchov.sk/sk

The Slovak Green Party was formed when Slovakia was still a part of Czechoslovakia. It then had a male president and a male vice president. As Gerhard Jordan remarked in a report to the European Greens in 1989: 'Like in many other East European Green parties only men were elected.' In 1990 the Slovak Greens got 3.5% of the vote and six MPs. During most of the 1990s they managed to retain one or two MPs, but slowly became marginalised. After many years at the margin of politics, in the local elections of 2010 the Greens got 58 councillors, two of them in the city council of Bratislava. However in the 2012 parliamentary elections the Greens got only 0.3% and failed to win a seat. This provoked a disappointed comment on the SZ homepage, in which it was observed that this was a victory of interest groups. Now SZ is mobilising for the elections of 2016.

Serbia

Zeleni Srbije (Greens of Serbia)
Founded 2007

Party leadership: one man – Ivan Karic
Elections: one MP

www.zelenisrbije.org

The present Serbian Green Party (ZS) was established on 14 September 2007. In 2008 and 2010 it won some seats in local councils. In 2012 it got its first MP (Ivan Karic) through a coalition with Choice for a Better Life. ZS is strongly against GMOs and nuclear energy, and in favour of environmental protection, social justice and solidarity, direct democracy, green economics, sustainability, respect for diversity and human rights, and prevention of all forms of violence.

In early 2014 the ZS signed a political cooperation agreement with the New Democratic Party and in February established the joint party New Democratic Party–Greens. But on 14 June 2014, the New Democratic Party split off and the Green label went back to the Greens of Serbia. There is an active Young Greens organisation which arranges an annual eco-festival over several days.

Slovenia

Stranka mladih – Zeleni Evrope (The Youth Party – European Greens)
Founded 2000
EGP 2006
Party leadership: one man – Igor Jurišič

www.sms.si

A Green party was founded in Slovenia in 1989. In the elections of 1990 the party got 8.8% of the vote and eight MPs. In 1992 it lost about half of its electorate, but still got five MPs. In 1996 it fell below the barrier of 4% and then continued to lose. It was still contesting the parliamentary election of 2004 but got only 0.5%.

Since 2006 the Youth Party has been the Slovenian member of the EGP. Among its political demands are basic income, environmental protection, sustainable development and abolishment of compulsory military service. In the elections of 2000 the party got four MPs, but lost them in 2004. In 2008 it entered a coalition with the Slovenian People's Party, which got five MPs. In 2011 the Youth Party got only 0.86% and no seat. At the local elections in October 2014 the party got eight local councillors in seven municipalities, which according to a comment by the party president showed that the party is 'alive and successful'.

Ukraine

Partija Zelenykh Ukrainy, PZU (The Green Party of Ukraine)
Founded 1990

EGP 1993
Party leadership: one man – Denis Moskal (since 2011), replacing a female –
    Tatiana Kondrachuk
National elections 2014: 0.24%

www.greenparty.ua

The PZU is a successor of the Green World Association (founded December 1987), which stood for the election in 1990 as part of the Democratic bloc. The Green World transformed into the PZU. The party was rather strong in the 1990s and reached a peak in 1998 with 5.5% of the vote and 19 MPs. One of the members, Serhey Kurikyn, became Minister of Environment (July 2001–November 2002) and was present at the Johannesburg Earth Summit in 2002. According to the historian Andrew Wilson, the party was more a kind of sanctuary for oligarchs than a real Green Party.[158] This is hard to estimate, but when this author in 1993 visited the office of the PZU in Kiev, the party president Vitalij Kononov (president 1992–2006) was keen to convince me to use his private firm to organise boat-tours for Swedish Greens on the Dnieper river. Maybe some oligarchs saw the Greens as a profitable project for the future, but got fed up when it appeared that PZU was not able to cope with the new situation after the orange revolution 2004–5.

In a fact-finding report on the situation for political parties in Ukraine in 2010, the EGP, following an application for membership by another Green party – Zeleni (The Greens) – gave the following picture: 'There is a common practice in the country for one businessman to create a party (perform all the registrations in the Ministry of Justice), wait until the party is legally capable to participate in the elections, and then sell it. Some examples of this practice could be "Front Peremen" (leader A. Yatsenyuk) and "Za Ukraynu" (leader V. Kyrylenko). The other trend shows the creation of "clones" of the Green parties before each election in the country with the aim of dispersing the Green vote. An example from the election campaign of 2006 is the political project of Sergey Taruta, one of the partners of the current leader of Zeleni, A. Prognimak, who invested in another political project "ECO+25" with Green ideology behind it. They didn't manage to get support.'

PZU was not able to maintain its results of 1998; in 2002 it got 1.3%, and in 2006 and 2007 failed to pass 1%. Still in 2012 it only got 0.35% and in October 2014 even less, 0.24%. However, the party claims to have more than 30,000 members, 26 regional and over 500 local branches.

On 22 February 2014, PZU president Denis Moskal demanded that separatists in Eastern Ukraine be brought to justice. He received support from the EGP which 'condemns the use of violence'. On 3 March 2014, PZU protested against the introduction of Russian troops into Ukraine, and on 17

March it warned that Russia planned to intervene anywhere in the country. In a strongly formulated message to the European Greens in August 2014, the PZU maintained that Ukraine is fighting a civilisational struggle against totalitarian aggression and asked for increased European support, including military-technological assistance as well as the toughest possible sanctions against the Putin regime; however, it also emphasised that it was not asking for foreign troops.

Facing the extremely complicated and dangerous situation in Ukraine, PZU has started to mobilise. Logically a party based upon a non-violent and multiethnic ideology should have a chance to play a role when a solution is sooner or later reached and implemented.

NOTES

(All online sources last accessed April 2015)

Introduction

1. Robert Sanders, 'Was First Nuclear Test the Start of New Human-Dominated Epoch, the Anthropocene?', UC Berkeley News Center, 16 January 2015, at https://newscenter.berkeley.edu.
2. Arnold Cassola and Per Gahrton (eds.), *Twenty Years of European Greens 1984–2004*, Brussels: European Federation of Green Parties, 2003.
3. Some recent overviews of Green politics are the following: Timothy Doyle (ed.), *Environmental Movements Around the World: Shades of Green in Politics and Culture*, Santa Barbara: Praeger, 2013; Donald Hughes, *An Environmental History of the World: Humankind's Changing Role in the Community of Life*, New York: Routledge, 2001; Mike Moon, *Green Ideology and its Relation to Modernity, Including a Case Study of the Green Party of Sweden*, Lund Studies in Human Ecology, 2008; Mianda Scheurs and Elim Papadakis, *Historical Dictionary of the Green Movement*, 2nd edition, Lanham: Scarecrow Press, 2007; Dustin Mulvaney (ed.), *Green Politics: An A-to-Z Guide*, London: SAGE, 2011.

Chapter 1

1. Peter Øvig Knudsen, *Blekingegadebanden* (The Blekinge Street Gang), Copenhagen: Gyldendal, 2008.
2. Daniel Cohn-Bendit, *Forget 68*, Paris: Éditions de l'aube, 2008.
3. Henry David Thoreau, *Walden*, Las Vegas: Empire Publishing, 2013 (originally published 1854).
4. Aldo Leopold, *A Sand Country Almanack*, New York: Ballentine, 1986 (originally published 1949).
5. Vladimir Vernadsky, *The Biosphere*, Göttingen: Copernicus, 1998 (originally published 1926).
6. Alvin Toffler, *Future Shock*, New York: Bantam, 1970.
7. Jean-Jacques Servan-Schreiber, *Le defi mondiale*, Paris: Fayard, 1980.
8. Andrew Dobson, *Green Political Thought*, London: Routledge, 1990.
9. John Button, *A Dictionary of Green Ideas*, London: Routledge, 1988.
10. LGBT is used in most languages as an acronym for Lesbian, Gay, Bi- and Transsexual; however there are some exceptions, such as Sweden, where HBTQ is used, for Homo, Bi, Trans and Queer.
11. *Novaya Gazeta*, 8 October 2014.
12. Jared Diamond, *Collapse: How Societies Choose to Fail or Survive*, New York: Viking Press, 2005.
13. Kelly Knauer, *Disasters That Shook the World: History's Greatest Man-made Catastrophes*, New York: Time Magazine, 2012.

14. Gary Haq and Alistair Paul, *Environmentalism Since 1945*, London: Routledge, 2011.
15. St Thomas More, *Complete Works*, vol. 4, New Haven: Yale University Press, 1997.
16. Charles Fourier, *Manuscrits*, 4 vols., Paris: Librairie Phalanstérienne, 1851–1858; *Œuvres complètes*, 6 vols., Paris: La Phalange, 1841–1845.
17. Ernst Callenbach, *Ecotopia*, New York: Bantam, 1975.
18. Quoted from Wikipedia, retrieved 12 October 2014.
19. Karin Bradley and Johan Hedrén (eds.), *Green Utopianism: Perspectives, Politics and Micro-practices*, London: Routledge, 2014. Bradley and Hedrén have been members of the board of the Swedish Green think-tank Cogito.
20. Karl Mannheim, *Ideologie und Utopie*, Bonn: Cohen, 1929.
21. Ernst Schumacher, *Small is Beautiful: Economics as if People Mattered*, New York: Harper Perennial, 1989 (originally published 1973); *Times Literary Supplement*, 6 October 1995.
22. Colin Hines, *Localisation: A Global Manifesto*, London: Earthscan, 2000.
23. Caroline Lucas and Michael Woodin, *Green Alternatives to Globalisation: A Manifesto*, London: Pluto Press, 2004.
24. René Dubot and Barbara Ward, *Only One Earth: The Care and Maintenance of a Small Planet*, New York: W.W. Norton, 1972.
25. Claus Offe, *Strukturprobleme des kapitalistischen Staates* (Structural Problems of the Capitalist State), Frankfurt am Main: Suhrkamp, 1972.
26. Robert Merton, *Social Theory and Social Structure*, New York: Free Press, 1957. See also my PhD thesis Per Gahrton, *Riksdagen inifrån*, Prisma 1983 (with an English summary).
27. Jürgen Habermas, *Legitimationsprobleme im Spätkapitalismus* (Problems of Legitimacy in Late Capitalism), Frankfurt am Main: Suhrkamp, 1973.
28. Claudia Roth, *Das politische ist privat. Erinnerungen für die Zukunft* (The Political is Private. Memories for the Future), Berlin: Aufbau Verlag, 2006.
29. Anna Bramwell, *The Fading of the Greens: The Decline of Environmental Politics in the West*, New Haven: Yale University Press, 1994.

Chapter 2

1. Haq and Paul, *Environmentalism Since 1945*.
2. Alf Hornborg, *Myten om maskinen* (The Myth of the Machine), Göteborg: Daidalos, 2010.
3. Alf Horborg, 'Why Solar Panels Don't Grow on Trees', in Bradley and Hedrén, *Green Utopianism: Perspectives, Politics and Micro-practices*.
4. James Lovelock, *The Revenge of Gaia*, London: Allen Lane, 2006.
5. George Herbert Mead, *Selected writings*, ed. A. J. Reck, New York: Bobbs-Merill, 1964.
6. Barry Commoner, *The Closing Circle: Nature, Man and Technology*, New York: Random House, 1971.
7. See http://en.wikipedia.org/wiki/Uncertainty_principle.
8. Fritjof Capra, *The Tao of Physics: An Exploration of the Parallels between Modern Physics and Eastern Mysticism*, Berkeley: Shambala, 2010 (originally published 1975).
9. Miriam Kennet, *What is Green Economics?* January 2009, available at http://www.greeneconomics.org.uk/page550.html.

10. Herman Daly, *Toward a Steady-state Economy*, New York: W. H. Freeman, 1973.
11. Kenneth Boulding, 'The Economics of the Coming Spaceship Earth', in H. Jarrett (ed.), *Environmental Quality in a Growing Economy*, Baltimore: Johns Hopkins University Press, 1966.
12. Hazel Henderson, *The Politics of the Solar Age: Alternatives to Economics*, New York: Doubleday, 1981.
13. The 9th International Conference of the European Society for Ecological Economics, Istanbul, 14–17 June 2011.
14. 'Learning from Turkey: Degrowth to What?' Paper presented to the 9th International Conference of the European Society for Ecological Economics, Istanbul, 14–17 June 2011.
15. See www.esee2011.org.
16. Cornucopia = horn of plenty.
17. Daniel Bell, *The Coming of Post-Industrial Society*, New York: Basic Books, 1973; Herman Kahn, *The Year 2000*, New York: Collier McMillan, 1968.
18. Tim Jackson, *Prosperity Without Growth*, London: Routledge, 2009.
19. Jorgen Randers, *2052 – A Global Forecast for the Next Forty Years*, White River Jct: Chelsea Green Publishing, 2012.
20. Julien Morel, *Beyond GDP Use* (Master of Science thesis), Stockholm: Royal Institute of Technology, 2012.
21. Nicolas Georgescu-Roegen, *The Entropy Law and the Economic Process*, Cambridge MA: Harvard University Press, 1971.
22. Jeremy Rifkin, *Entropy*, New York: Viking Adult, 1980.
23. Émile Durkheim, *Suicide: A Study in Sociology*, New York: The Free Press, 1951 (originally published in French 1897); *Les règles de la méthode sociologique*, 13th edition, Paris: Presses universitaires de France, 2007.
24. R. A. Easterlin, 'Does Economic Growth Improve the Human Lot? Some Empirical Evidence', in Paul A. David and Melvin W. Reder (eds.), *Nations and Households in Economic Growth: Essays in Honor of Moses Abramovitz*, New York: Academic Press, 1974.
25. Carol Graham, *Happiness Around the World: The Paradox of the Happy Peasants and the Miserable Millionaires*, Oxford: Oxford University Press, 2009.
26. R. A. Easterlin et al. 'The Happiness-income Paradox Revisited', *Proceedings of the National Academy of Sciences* 107:52 (2010).
27. Garret Hardin, 'The Tragedy of the Commons', *Science*, 13 December 1968.
28. Elinor Ostrom, *Governing the Commons: The Evolution of Institutions for Collective Action*, Cambridge: Cambridge University Press, 1990.
29. See www.bhutanstudies.org.bt, www.grossnationalhappiness.com.
30. Alan Weisman, *The World Without Us*, New York: Virgin, 2007.
31. Charlene Spretnak and Fritjof Capra, *Green Politics*, Boulder: Paladin, 1985.
32. Dobson, *Green Political Thought*.
33. Françoise D'Eaubonne, *Le féminisme ou la mort* (Feminism or Death), Paris: Pierre Hory, 1974.
34. Carolyne Merchant, *Death of Nature: Women, Ecology and the Scientific Revolution*, New York: HarperOne, 1980.
35. Arne Næss, *The Ecology of Wisdom*, Berkeley: Counterpoint, 2008.
36. Murray Bookchin, *Remaking Society*, Montreal: Black Rose Books, 1989. Other important early books by Bookchin are *Postscarcity Anarchism* (1971) and *Toward an Ecological Society* (1980).
37. Dobson, *Green Political Thought*.

38. Henry Salt, *Animals' Rights: Considered in Relation to Social Progress*, New York: Macmillan, 1894.

39. Peter Singer, *Animal Liberation*, New York: Ecco Press, 2001 (originally published in 1975).

40. Dobson, *Green Political Thought*.

41. William Catton, *Overshoot: The Ecological Basis of Revolutionary Change*, Chicago: University of Illinois Press, 1982.

42. R. Wetering and J. B. Opschoor, *Towards Environmental Performance Indicators Based on the Notion of Environmental Space*, Rijswijk: Dutch Advisory Council for Research on Nature and Enviroment, 1994.

43. 'Towards a Sustainable Europe', Wuppertal Institute, 1994.

44. Mark Satin, *New Age Politics*, Vancouver: White Cap, 1978.

45. Marilyn Ferguson, *The Aquarian Conspiracy*, Los Angeles: Jeremy B. Tarcher, 1980.

Chapter 3

1. Sara Parkin, *Green Parties: An International Guide*, London: Heretic Books, 1989.

2. For the full text see http://www.globalgreens.org/globalcharter-english.

3. 'L'homme et Nature en Afrique', *Polititique Africaine N-053*, January 1994.

4. First African Green University held in Morocco, 17 July 2009, report by Mike Feinstein, International Committee of the Green Party of the United States.

5. In an email to the author 2 June 2014.

6. La Fédération des Verts africains affiche ses premiers succès, published 1 May 2012, http://www.novethic.fr/empreinte-sociale/droits-humains/isr-rse/la-federation-des-verts-africains-affiche-ses-premiers-succes-137260.html.

7. Per Inge Lidén in a report (in Swedish) to Green forum.

8. See http://www.africangreens.org/news/declaration-establishing-eastern-africa-greens-federation.

9. AGF homepage, 12 June 2013, http://www.africangreens.org.

10. In my mimeographed report, *Greens in North America: A report from a five week trip to the USA and Canada, Dec 89–Jan 90*, I concluded that my experience among the North American Greens 'together with the emergence of Greens on all continents, at the same time as Greens are expanding into Eastern Europe, brings me to the conclusion that time is becoming ripe for the launching of the World Greens'. For the full report see www.gahrton.dinstudio.se.

11. Stewart Jackson (University of Sydney) and Alex Bhathal (Curtain University), *Barriers to the Development of Green Politics in the Asia-Pacific*, paper for the APSA conference, Perth, 30 September–2 October 2013, http://www.auspsa.org.au.

12. Eko Priyo Purnomo (University Muhammadiyah, Yogyakarta); Klaus Hubacek, (University of Maryland – Department of Geography); Megandaru Widhi Kawuryan (Institute Pemerintahan Dalam Negeri), *The Critical Comparison of the Green Parties' Phenomena between Indonesia and Thailand*, 4 April 2011, http://papers.ssrn.com/sol3/papers.cfm?abstract_id=1802541.

13. *Guardian* and *The Times*, 23 March 1985.

14. In an email to the author.

15. Campaign for Peace Year, *From Two Blocs Towards One World*, with contributions from the Green Party, UK; Les Verts, France; Miljöpartiet de Gröna, Sweden; Comhaontas Glas, Ireland; Ecolo, Belgium; Die Grünen, Germany, Brussels: The Coordination of European Greens, 1986.

16. In an email to the author.
17. In German, 11 December 1986.
18. In German, 5 December 1987.
19. A mini-congress, made up of representatives from the regions/Länder.
20. In a letter to 'Green, alternative and radical parties in Europe', 12 March 1987.
21. BAG Internationalismus, 8 April 1987.
22. Compiled by Jürgen Maier, 20 September 1988.
23. 'Da zum gleichen Zeitpunkt ein Treffen der realpolitischen Grünen (Realos) stattfinden wird, an dem ich unbedingt teilnehmen möchte', 31 July 1987 (letter in the archive of the author).
24. Staes left the Belgian Flemish Greens in 1994, after he was not nominated for a third term as MEP, and joined a Conservative party, giving his version in an aggressively critical book, *De zachgekookte eitjes, een politieke vertelling over het Groene Fabriekje* (The Soft Boiled Egg: A Political Account of the Green Factory), Groot-Bijgaarden: Scoop, 1996.
25. *Frankfurter Allgemeine Zeitung*, 31 August 1987: 'Ein erster schritt zu einer Grünen international'.
26. *Frankfurter Rundschau*, 31 August 1987: 'Eine Grüne international soll es nicht geben'.
27. *NRC Handelsblad*, 31 August 1987: 'Groenen blijeven verdeeld over hun strategie'.
28. *Guardian*, 31 August 1987.
29. *Die Grünen* 38, 19 September 1987: 'Keine Grüne international, Entwicklung der nationalen Alternativparteien zu unterschiedlich'.
30. The representativity must not be overstated (there were 72 replies, 32 from Swedish Greens, 30 from members of other Green parties and ten unidentified).
31. Bundeshauptausschuss, 22 April 1989.
32. The fourth was held in Antwerp in 1988, with a concentration on local politics.
33. *Le Monde*, 1 June 1989: 'L'enquête: preparation du scrutin du 18 juin – La Saga des Verts Européens'.
34. Coordination of European Greens, minutes 24–25 June, 1989.
35. The proceedings of the Rome congress were extensively covered by the bulletin of the European Greens, *Update*, no. 1, February 2004.
36. 'Les ecolos et la communauté européenne – une erreur historique', *24 heures*, 11 November 1988, 'Absage der Grünen an Europa-Binnenmarkt', *Schaffhauser Nachrichten*, 11 November 1988.
37. *Bulletin Vert*, Le Journal romand des Verts, no. 2, September/October 2006.
38. *Soldarité et force – l'avenir de l'union Européenne*, Böll Stiftung and the Green European Foundation, 2011.
39. *Le Monde diplomatique*, October 2012.
40. Alain Lipietz, *Green Deal. La crise du libéral-productivisme et la réponse écologiste* (Green Deal: The Crisis of Liberal-productivism and the Ecologist Reply), Paris: La Decouverte, 2012.
41. Alan Lipietz, *L'Audace ou Enlisement* (Audacity or Downfall), Paris: La Decouverte, 1984.
42. Gerhard Jordan, *Grüne in Mittel- und Osteuropa – ein wechselvoller Weg* (Greens in Central and Eastern Europe: A Changing Way), Wien: Grüne Partei, 2010.
43. See http://gef.eu/home and http://www.greeneuropeanjournal.eu.
44. Wolfgang Rüdig, *Explaining Green Party Development*, Glasgow: Strathclyde Papers on Government Studies, no. 71, 1990.

45. Russell J. Dalton, *The Green Rainbow: Environmental Politics in Western Europe*, New Haven: Yale University Press, 1994.
46. Elizabeth Bomberg, *Green Parties and Politics in the European Union*, London: Routledge, 1998.
47. John Burchell, *The Evolution of Green Politics*, London: Earthscan, 2002.
48. Gene Frankland, Paul Lucardie and Benoit Rihoux (eds.), *Green Parties in Transition: The End of Grass-roots Decmocracy*, Farnham: Ashgate, 2008.

Chapter 4

1. This is an updated and much developed version of my contribution to *Is There a Need for a Green Ideology?* (published by Cogito in English, Spanish and Swedish in 2008). Thus it might happen that an individual quotation refers to a programme that has been changed or a party that has ceased to exist.

2. My database consists of what can be found on the web. Altogether I have been able to find programmes and platforms from about 50 Green parties. I do not claim to have made a scientifically rigorous content analysis. The following material has been used: Albania: The Program of the Green Party of Albania (English). Andalusia: Estatutos de los Verdes de Andalucia, revisados, modificados y aprobados el 14–5-2006 en el XII Congreso (Spanish). Australia: Take Action, Green Action, Green Policy Initiatives, Federal election 2007 (English). Austria: Grundsatzprogramm der Grünen, Beschlossen beim 20. Bundeskongress der Grünen am 7. und 8. Juli 2001 in Linz (German). Andorra: Verds d'Andorra – Declaració de principis, fevrer 2003 (Catalan). Belgium/Wallonia: Une terre plus verte, un monde plus juste, ECOLO présente ses priorités de campagne pour les élections du 10 juin 2007 (French). Belgium/Flandres: De toekomst begint nu, programma Groen! voor de federale verkiezingen van 10 juni 2007 (Dutch). Bénin: Le contrat d'avenir pour les béninois proposé par les VERTS du Bénin, Juin 2005 (French). Brazil: Programma do Partido Verde – PV, Convenção Nacional, Brasilia/ DF, 2005 (Portuguese). Bulgaria: Програма на Зелената партия, 01 февруари 2007 (Bulgarian). Canada: Green Party of Canada Platform 2006 (English). Chile: Sobre el Partido Ecologista Nosotros / 06 de Mayo de 2007 (Spanish). Croatia: Greens for Zagreb, Programme, Principles, Accepted and proclaimed at the Constituent Assembly on 29 December 2004 (English). Czech Republic: Volební program Strany zelených 'Kvalita života' pro volby do Poslanecké sněmovny 2006 (Czech). Colombia: Código de Ética del Partido Verde Oxígeno, 15 de diciembre de 1997 (Spanish). Denmark: De Grønnes Ideprogram, no date (Danish). Finland: Manifesto of the Green League, Approved by the Annual Party Congress on 28 May 2006 (English). France: Le monde change avec les Verts – changeons le monde, L'écologie/Les Verts 2007 (French). Germany: Ein für alle: Das grüne Wahlprogramm 2005 (German). Greece: Ecogreens – programmic proposals – general elections 2007 (English). Iran: Green Party of Iran Platform, no date (English). Ireland: Manifesto 2004 European and Local elections, Green Party/ Comhaontas Glas (English). Italy: Statuto – Titolo I, Principe, Art.1 Dichiarazione sui principi ispiratori, no date (Italian). Japan: Ecolo Japan – Five Basic Principles of Our Group, no date (English). Latvia: Programme of Latvian Green Party, August 2002 (English). Luxemburg: La déclaration de principe du parti Déi Gréng, no date (French). Malta: Alternattiva Demokratika – Our Principles/Il-Principji taghna, no date (English/Maltese). Mexico: Declaracion de Principios, el Partido Verde

Ecologista de Mexico, no date (Spanish). Moldova: Declaraţia Politică a Partidului Ecologist 'Alianţa Verde' din Moldova Adoptată de Congresul III din 25.12.2004 (Moldovian). New Zealand: The Green Charter, the founding document of The Green Party of Aotearoa New Zealand, no date (English). Netherlands: Groei mee, programma van GroenLinks, Tweede-Kamerverkiezingen 22 November 2006 (Dutch). Norway: Miljøpartiet de Grønnes manifest 2005–2009, vedtatt av landsmøtet 2005 på Hafjell, endret av landsmøtet 2006 i Trondheim (Norwegian). Philippines: Green Phil's platform 2000, greenphilippines.org (English). Poland: Zielony Manifest. Kluczowe tezy programowe Zielonych 2004 (Polish). Portugal: Os Verdes – Programa Aprovado na IX Convenção Nacional Ecológica 16 e 17 de Maio de 2003 Casa do Artista Lisboa (Portuguese). Quebec: Nous sommes tous verts, Plate-form du Parti Vert du Québec 2007 (French). Romania: Party Profile, European Green Party (English). Russia: Проект Программы политической партии "Союз зелёных России" ("Зелёная Россия"). В редакции Федерального Политсовета партии от 6 сентября 2005 г. (Russian). Scotland: The Principles of the Scottish Green Party, no date (English). Slovenia: Guiding principles of the Youth Party of Slovenia (English). Somalia: About the History of Somalia Green Party, by Eng.Ahmed Haaji, MSc (Enviromentalist), Director International Relations, Somalia Green Party (SGP), no date (English). South Africa: Web presentation of The Green Party of South Africa, also known as The Government by the People Green Party, no date (English). Sweden: Miljöpartiet de Grönas partiprogram, antaget av kongressen 2005 (Swedish). Switzerland: Eine andere Welt ist möglich, Manifest der Grünen Schweiz, verabschiedet von der DV am 24 August 2002 (German). Taiwan: History of Green Party Taiwan, 20 December 2000 (English). Turkey: Ten Basic Principles of Yesiller, Discussed and adopted in Bodrum meeting, 20–23 April 2002 (English). Ukraine: Electoral Progamme of the Party of Greens of Ukraine, no date (English). UK: Green Party of England and Wales – Statement of Core Principles, Updated 18 May 2001 (English). USA: Platform 2004, as adopted at the National Nomination Convention, Milwaukee, Wisconsin, June 2004 (English). Venezuela: ¿Qué es un Movimiento Ecológico Venezolano o Movimiento Verde?, no date (Spanish).

3. Paul Ehrlich, *Population Bomb*, New York: Ballentine, 1968.
4. Tom Chivers, 'Paul Ehrlich Still Prophesying Doom, and Still Wrong', *Telegraph*, 26 April 2012.
5. Sandy Irvine and Alec Ponton, *A Green Manifesto: Policies for a Green Future*, London: Optima, 1988.
6. 'Endgültigen Ausstieg aus dem Atomkraft', *Der Spiegel* 38 (2011).
7. The Swedish Greens won a major victory when in February 2015 the new Red-Green government, officially labelling itself 'feminist', decided not to extend an agreement for military cooperation with Saudi Arabia. The decision was met with wide support from Human Rights and feminist organistions all over the world, but also with diplomatic reprisals from Saudi Arabia and the Arab League.
8. André Gorz, *Critique of Economic Reason*, London: Verso, 1989.
9. In Finnish: *Hyvinvointivaltion eloonjäämisoppi*, 2004.
10. 'Is Finland Ready for a Basic Income?', *Helsinki Times*, 17 July 2014.
11. See http://www.basicincome.org.
12. *A Third Sector - Green responses to privatisation of welfare services across Europe*, Green European Foundation, 2014.
13. Jean Marie Perbost, *Work More? Work Less?*, Green new deal series, vol. 8, Green European Foundation, December 2011.

14. Julia Hailes and John Elkington, *The Green Consumer Guide*, London: Gollancz, 1988.
15. Sandy Irvine, *Beyond Green Consumerism*, London: Friends of the Earth, 1989.
16. Kirkpatrick Sale, *Dwellers in the Land: The Bioregional Vision*, San Fransisco: Sierra Club, 1985.
17. Dobson, *Green Political Thought*.
18. See http://www.gdrc.org/icm/lets-faq.html.
19. However, as of 2015, the economic crisis has almost turned the profit-based money-lending system upside-down by pushing some Central Banks to establish interest rates close to, or even below, zero. It is nevertheless doubtful whether a zero interest rate established as the result of a crisis in the dominant productivist market economy could be exploited for Green economic purposes. In any case, it is a challenge for ecological economists.

Chapter 5

1. This chapter is a considerably revised, enlarged and updated version of a report by Angela Aylward and Per Gahrton for the Green European Foundation and the Swedish Green think-tank Cogito in 2010 (in English and Swedish), updated by Cogito in 2014 (only in Swedish). It can be found at www.cogito.nu.
2. The concepts *individual co-optation, resilience creating, necessity-based* and *legitimacy-creating* participation in government are invented by the author, after inspiration from his wife, Drude Dahlerup, professor of political science at Stockholm University.
3. A. Sikk and R. H. Andersen, 'Without a Tinge of Red: The Fall and Rise of the Estonian Greens', *Journal of Baltic Studies* 11 (2009).
4. For the Georgian experience, see Per Gahrton, *Georgia, Pawn in the New Great Game*, London: Pluto Press, 2010.
5. Benoit Rihoux and Wolfgang Rüdig, 'Analysing Greens in Power, Setting the Agenda', *European Journal of Political Research* 45 (2006).
6. Wolfgang Rüdig, 'Between Ecotopia and Disillusionment: Green Parties in European Government', *Environment* 44 (2002).
7. Pierre Serne, *Des Verts a EELV, 30 ans d'histoire de l'écologie politique* (From the Greens to EELV [Europe Ecologie, Les Verts], 30 Years of History of Political Ecology), Paris: Les Petits Matins, 2014.
8. Cécile Duflot, *De l'interieur – voyage au pays de la disillusion* (From Within – A Journey in the Country of Disillusion), Paris: Fayard, 2014.
9. Wolfgang Rüdig, 'Is Government Good for Greens? Comparing the Electoral Effects of Government Participation in Western and East-Central Europe', *European Journal of Political Research* 45 (2006).
10. Roberto Biorcio, 'The Italian Greens Between Government and the Anti-globalisation Movement', 2nd ECPR General conference, Marburg 2003.
11. There is an abundance of literature on the German Red-Green government, 1998–2005. Some examples: C. Egel and R. Zohlnhöfer, R, *Ende des rot-grünen Projekts. Eine Bilanz der Regierung Schröder 2002–2005* (The End of the Red-Green Project: An Evaluation of the Schröder Government 2002–2005), Wiesbaden: Vs Verlag, 2007; A. Radcke, *Das Ideal und die Macht, das Dilemma der Grünen* (The Ideal and the Power: The Dilemma of the Greens), Berlin: Henschel, 2001; J. Raschke, *Die Zukunft der Grünen. So kann man nicht regieren* (The Future of the Greens: In This Way it is Not Possible to Rule), Frankfurt: Campus, 2001.
12. 'Zurück and den Wurzeln' (Back to the Roots), *Der Spiegel* 14 (2008).

13. Ludger Volmer, *Die Grünen, von der Protestbewegung zur etablierten Partei* (The Greens, From a Protest Movement to an Established Party), München: Bertelsmann, 2009.
14. See http://www.wahlrecht.de/umfragen.
15. In Belgium the Dutroux case of the paedophile killing of several girls caused a major uproar against the authorities, manifested in the White March of October 1996 in Brussels with 300,000 participants.
16. Christian De Bast (ed.), *Ecolo, l'épreuve du pouvoir* (Ecolo, the Test of Power), Bruxelles: Luc Pire, 2002; P. Delwit and B. Hellings, 'Ecolo et les élections du 18 Mai 2003, du paradis au purgatoire ou a l'enfer?', *L'Année sociale* (2003).
17. P. Delwit and E. van Haute, 'Greens in a Rainbow: The Impact of Participation in Government of the Green parties in Belgium', in Kris Deschouwer (ed.), *New Parties in Government: In Power for the First Time*, London: Routledge, 2008.
18. M. Hooghe and B. Rihoux, 'No Place at the Table: Green Parties in the 2007–2008 Political Crisis in Belgium', *Environmental Politics* 17 (2008).
19. Pauline Dumoulin and Marc Jacquemain, 'Les militants Ecolo: quels changements suite a la participation au gouvernement federal? Etude comparative de deux générations de militant Ecolo', Université de Liège, 2007.
20. J. Paastela, 'Finnish Greens' Exit From the Government', 2nd ECPR General Conference, 2003.
21. She was elected to the EU parliament in 2014.
22. J. Sundberg and N. Wilhelmsson, 'Moving from Movement to Government: The Transformation of the Finnish Greens', in Deschouwer, *New Parties in Government*.
23. *Irish Independent*, 28 September 2009.
24. Pat Flanagan in the *Mirror*, 26 August 2009.
25. Mary Minihan, *A Deal With the Devil: The Green Party in Government*, Dunboyne: Maverich House, 2011.
26. Rihoux and Rüdig, 'Analysing Greens in Power'.
27. P. Dumont and H. Bäck, 'Why so Few, and Why so Late? Green Parties and the Question of Governmental Participation', *European Journal of Political Research* 45 (2006).
28. Deschouwer, *New Parties in Government*.
29. M. Pedersen, 'Towards a New Typology of Party Lifespans and Minor Parties', *Scandinavian Political Studies* 5:1 (1982).
30. Nicole Bolleyer, 'The Organisational Costs of Public Office', in Deschouwer, *New Parties in Government*.
31. 'Ecolo dans d'eventuelles participations gouvernementales: principes', 16 July 2009.
32. Rihoux and Rüdig, 'Analysing Greens in Power'.
33. Rüdig, 'Is Government Good for Greens?'.
34. F. Müller-Rommel and T. Poguntke (eds.), *Green Parties in National Governments*, London: Routledge, 2002.
35. Bolleyer, 'The Organisational Costs of Public Office'.
36. Jim Jepps, 'How Three Green Parties Went Wrong', 5 June 2010, at http://jimjay.blogspot.com/2010/06/those-right-wing-greens.html.
37. Rüdig, 'Between Ecotopia and Disillusionment'.

Chapter 6

1. The Greek Greens made an electoral agreement with Syriza and as a result gained one MP and one portofolio in the new government in January 2015.

2. Samuel Huntington, 'The Clash of Civilsations', *Foreign Affairs* 72:3 (1993).
3. Diakonia press release, 15 January 2015.
4. *Forskning och framsteg* (Research and Progress) 9 (2014).
5. *Le Monde*, 6 December 2014.
6. *Der Spiegel* 25 (2012): 'Raubbau im Amazonasgebiet schreitet voran. Naturschützer wurden von Mordkommandos bedroht'.
7. *Le Monde*, 15 December 2012.
8. WHO, *Global Status Report on Noncommunicable Diseases 2014*, January 2015.
9. 'Har vi rätt att äta ihjäl oss?' (Do we have the right to eat ourselves to death?), *Svenska Dagbladet*, 20 January 2015.
10. *Nature* 461 (2009).
11. *Dagens Nyheter*, 24 June 2012.
12. *Green Leaves*, published by the Greens in the European Parliament, September 1992.
13. *Science*, vol. 335, no. 6074, 16 March 2012.
14. Swedish Green weekly *Miljömagasinet*, no. 51/52, 19 December 2014.
15. Arrhenius, Svante, 'On the Influence of Carbonic Acid in the Air upon the Temperature of the Ground', *Philosophical Magazine and Journal of Science*, Series 5, vol. 41, April 1896.
16. *Late Lessons From Early Warnings: The Precautionary Principle 1896–2000*, EEA: Environmental Issue Report, no. 22, 2001.
17. *Late Lessons From Early Warnings: Science, Precaution, Innovation*, EEA report, no. 1, 2013.
18. Rachel Carson, *Silent Spring*, Boston: Houghton Mifflin, 1962.
19. *Global Mail*, 16 April 2013.
20. See http://www.rightlivelihood.org.
21. Quotations here are from the ceremony in 2009.
22. Robert Michels, *Zur Soziologie des Parteiwesens in der modernen Demokratie. Untersuchungen über die oligarchischen Tendenzen des Gruppenlebens* (Political Parties: A Sociological Study of the Oligarchical Tendencies of Modern Democracy), Leipzig: Klinkhardt Verlag, 1911.
23. Thomas Mathiesen, *Det uferdige* (The Unfinished), Oslo: Pax, 1971.
24. Jonas Anshelm, *Kampen om klimatet, miljöpolitiska strider i Sverige 2006–2009* (The Struggle About the Climate: Fights About Environmental Politics in Sweden 2006–2009), Stockholm: Pärspektiv förlag, 2012.
25. Serge Latouche, *Le pari de la décroissance* (The Challenge of De-growth), Paris: Fayard, 2006.
26. Gösta Ehrensvärd, *Före – efter, en diagnos* (Before – Afterwards, a Diagnosis), Stockholm: Aldus, 1971.
27. Lasse Berg, *Gryning över Kalahari, Hur människan blev människa* (Dawn Over the Kalahari: How Humans Became Humans), Stockholm: Ordfront, 2005.
28. James Howard Kunstler, *World Made by Hand*, New York: Atlantic Monthly Press, 2008.
29. Diamond, *Collapse: How Societies Choose to Fail or Survive*.
30. John Elkington, *The Green Capitalists: Industry's Search for Environmental Excellence*, London: Victor Gollancz, 1987.
31. Daniel Tanuro, *L'impossible capitalisme vert* (The Futility of Green Capitalism), Paris: La Decouverte, 2009.
32. Immanuel Wallerstein, 'The Structural Crisis Middle-Run Imponderables', *Commentary*, no. 345, 15 January 2013.

33. Derek Wall, *The Rise of the Green Left*, London: Pluto Press, 2010.
34. Derek Wall, *The No-nonsense Guide to Green Politics*, London: New International, 2010.
35. John Bellamy Foster, *The Ecological Revolution: Making Peace with the Planet*, Oakland: Monthly Review Press, 2009.
36. Erik Damman, *Verdirevolusjon* (Revolution of Values), Olso: Flux förlag, 2014.
37. Roland Inglehardt, *The Silent Revolution*, Princeton: Princeton University Press, 1977, and *Culture Shift in Advanced Industrial Society*, Princeton: Princeton University Press, 1989.
38. Edward Abbey, *The Monkey Wrench Gang*, New York: Harper Perennial, 2006 (originally published 1975).
39. Dave Foreman, *Ecodefense*, California: Ned Ludd books, 1985.
40. *Miljömagasinet*, no. 49, 5 December 2014.
41. Dobson, *Green Political Thought*.
42. In the capacity of Member of the European Parliament.
43. See http://www.tni.org/article/ten-years-later-challenges-and-proposals-another-possible-world.
44. Report of the World Commission on Environment and Development, UN 1987.
45. Interview in Danish *Information*, 13–14 November 2010, about his new book: Marc de Vos, *After the Meltdown: The Future of Capitalism and Globalisation in the Age of the Twin Crises*, London: Shoehorn Media, 2010.
46. PEW Research Center, *Environmental Concerns on the Rise in China*, 19 September 2013.
47. Jonathan Waters, *When a Billion Chinese Jump*, New York: Simon and Schuster, 2010.
48. Joy Zhang and Michael Barr, *Green Politics in China: Environmental Governance and State-Society Relations*, London: Pluto Press, 2013.

Appendix

1. Ram Ouedraogo, *Ma part de bilan* (My Part of the Result), Burkina Faso, 2010.
2. *L'intelligent d'Abidjan*, 10 January 2014.
3. http://lepays.bf/ram-ouedraogo-president-du-rdeb-jai-ete-ministre-detat-jai-les-dossiers-monde/lepays.bf.
4. http://lepays.bf/ram-ouedraogo-president-des-verts-propos-de-depart-de-blaise-compaore-blaise-compaore-dehors-constitue-un-danger-pour-le-burkina-faso.
5. Letter by the Greens of Chad to the Greens of Ivory Coast, 13 June 2008.
6. Nevine El Shabrawy, 'Does Egypt Have a Green Party?', *Al-Masry al-Youm*, 18 January 2010.
7. Electronic newspaper *Gerida 25 janair*, 17 July 2011.
8. *Sharq al-Awsat*, Arabic edition, 20 July 2011.
9. 'Is Egypt Ready for a New Political Green Party?' *Al-Masry al-Youm*, 24 October 2011.
10. http://www.greenprophet.com/2012/01/arab-spring-egypt-green-party.
11. http://egypttoday.com/arabic/2014/12/15/green-party-elections-2014.
12. Olivia Marsaud, 'En Guinée, l'écologie c'est la protection de la vie humaine', 20 April 2001, http://www.afrik.com/article2635.html.
13. Information found at the home page of Ivory Coast Greens, http://parti-ecologique-ivoirien.org.

14. *Presentation et activités du Parti vert hasin'i Madagasikara 2009–2012*, a summary of Green Party activities, supported by a large number of press cuttings.

15. http://www.orange.mg/actualite/election-hery-rajaonarimampianina-parti-vert-reagit.

16. 'Madagascar: l'état de droit selon Hery Rajaonarimampianina', 4 April 2014, http://www.madagate.com/politique-madagascar/dossier/4043-madagascar-letat-de-droit-selon-hery-rajaonarimampianina.html.

17. *Radio France International*, 24 August 2013.

18. 'Manifestations et grève de la faim pour la compensation', *Le Mauricien*, 2 February 2012.

19. http://lesahel.org/index.php/2011–07–25–15–57–34/item/1471–3eme-congres-extraordinaire-du-parti-de-rassemblement-pour-un-sahel-vert-rsv-niima--volonte-de-preserver-lenvironnement-pour-un-developpement-durable.

20. *Le Sahel*, 6 August 2013.

21. Information supplied to the author, autumn 2014.

22. *Radio Senegal*, APS, 11 May 2014.

23. Infosrewmi.com, 23 December 2014.

24. Seneweb.com, 28 December 2014.

25. 'Naissance d'un nouveau parti politique', Pa-lunion.com, 15 October 2011.

26. *La voix de la nation*, 13 November 2012.

27. *Savoir News*, 12 February 2014.

28. 'Politique: Tunisie Verte dénonce l'hégémonie de Hamma Hammami sur le Front populaire', http://www.kapitalis.com/politique/22338-politique-tunisie-verte-denonce-l-hegemonie-de-hamma-hammami-sur-le-front-populaire.html.

29. 'Tunisie Verte: Le parti écologiste qui a refusé de s'inféoder à la dictature', *Le Quotidien Tunisien*, 13 February 2011.

30. http://www.virgin.com/unite/leadership-and-advocacy/africa%E2%80%99s-first-green-party-enters-zambian-politics.

31. http://www.lusakatimes.com/2014/04/07/green-party-legalise-cultivation-marijuana-export-market.

32. http://www.theguardian.com/environment/2014/nov/14/can-zambia-save-its-environment-with-marijuana.

33. https://www.facebook.com/tousbeninois/posts/213434442009839.

34. https://groups.google.com/forum/#!topic/greenmng/S-4OT1rg2vE.

35. 'Time for a Green Party in Nigeria', *Daily Trust*, Abuja, 22 May 2013.

36. 'Green Will Not be Voters' Favourite', http://www.timeslive.co.za/thetimes/2014/03/25/green-will-not-be-voters-favourite.

37. Olivia Marsaud, 'Un parti écologiste en Mauritanie: l'idée folle de Ould Dellahi', http://www.afrik.com/article2670.html.

38. *Plan de gobierno*, gestion 2014–19.

39. Tibor Rabóczkay, *Repensando O Partido Verde Brasileiro*, São Paulo: Ateliê Editorial, 2004.

40. *Update* (Bulletin of the European Greens) no. 1, February 2004.

41. David McRobert, 'Green Politics in Canada', *Probe Post: Canada's Environmental Magazine*, October 1985.

42. Claudia Chwalisz, 'Canada's Left Voters Face a "Traffic Light" Choice', *Policy Network*, 26 February 2015, http://www.policy-network.net/pno.

43. In a report to the Coordination of European Greens, 'Brief Remarks on the Humanist Party', 7 December 1988, Jürgen Maier, Die Grünen, stated that Humanists had infiltrated Greens not only in Latin America, but even in Spain

and Italy, and to some extent in Britain, France, West Germany, Spain, Denmark, Iceland, Holland and Portugal. Sara Parkin a year later (30 September 1989) reported that the Humanists followed the teachings of a guru, 'Silo', a pseudonym for the Argentinean writer Mario Luis Rodríguez Cobos, who was superficially Green, but basically fascist. Some Eurogreens believed that the 'siloistas', supported by anonymous financial power groups, aimed at the destruction of the Greens. However the problem disappeared in the 1990s as the Greens became stronger. Silo withdrew in 2002 and died in 2010.

44. Ingrid Betancourt, *Même le silence a une fin* (Even the Silence Has an End), Paris: Folio, 2012.

45. Almoment.net, 23 February 2015, http://almomento.net/dice-responsables-ataques-contra-leonel-han-unificado-al-pld.

46. *Los Angeles Times*, 19 March 1996.

47. Al Gore received the Nobel Peace Prize in 2007 for his environmental campaigning. However, the headline of an article he wrote in 2010 (with David Blood) gives a hint that Gore may not be Green in the Green party sense: 'Toward Sustainable Capitalism', *Wall Street Journal*, 24 June 2010.

48. Wall, *The Rise of the Green Left*.

49. *Le Parisien*, 26 May 2014.

50. David Hetherington, 'Is the Party Over for Australia's Greens?', *Policy Network*, 26 February 2015, http://www.policy-network.net/pno.

51. Posted on APGF homepage, 28 October 2014, written by Suresh Nautiyal, Member of the APGF committee, and Convener of UKPP.

52. http://www.theage.com.au/world/india-closer-to-first-green-party-20090921-fykb.html#ixzz32XvlfZUK.

53. 'India's Green Party Maverick', 5 January 2011, http://inthesetimes.com/article/6742/indias_green_party_maverick.

54. http://www.party.ind.in/contact.htm.

55. http://www.hindustantimes.com/StoryPage/Print/1217100.aspx?s=p.

56. Mukul Sharma, *Green Saffron: Hindu Nationalism and Indian Environmental Politics*, Delhi: Permanent Black, 2011.

57. On Indian environmentalism, see also Ramachandra Guha, *How Much Should a Person Consume? Environmentalism in India and the United States*, Berkeley: University of California Press, 2006.

58. 'The Critical Comparison of the Green Parties' Phenomena between Indonesia and Thailand', by Eko Priyo Purnomo, University Muhammadiyah Yogyakarta; Klaus Hubacek, University of Maryland – Department of Geography; Megandaru Widhi Kawuryan, Institute Pemerintahan Dalam Negeri, 4 April 2011, http://papers.ssrn.com/sol3/papers.cfm?abstract_id=1802541.

59. Koji Sonoda, 'Japanese Green Party Forms With an Eye on National Politics', 30 July 2012, http://ajw.asahi.com/article/0311disaster/fukushima/AJ201207300010.

60. Yuji Kanamaru, Wayo Womens University, 'Challenge and Difficulty of Local Network Parties in Japan, New Political Parties in the Crisis of Representative Democracy', IPSA Conference, Fukuoka, 2006.

61. 'Green Party Expels Pro-alliance Chairman', english.news.mn, 18 February 2011.

62. http://www.infomongolia.com/ct/ci/3125.

63. Press release by New Zealand Greens, 6 June 2014.

64. www.greenpartywatch.org/2009/05/18, 18 May 2009.

65. www.greenpartywatch.org/2010/04/20, 20 April 2010.

66. Serhat Ünaldi, *From Grassroots to Government: A Study of Recent Green Party Building in the Philippines*, School of Politics and International Studies, University of Leeds, September 2009.
67. George Carcasson and Paul Ekins, *Ecology Past and Present: A Short Historical Note*, London: The Ecology Party, 2nd edition, 1983.
68. http://www.carolinelucas.com/latest/yes-to-a-referendum-and-yes-to-a-better-europe.
69. Paul Webb, 'Britain's Green Wave', *Policy Network*, 26 February 2015, http://www.policy-network.net/pno.
70. For the early history of Ecolo, see B. Lechat, *Ecolo, la democratie comme projet, Tome 1, 1970–1986, du federalism à l'écologie*, Bruxelles: Etopia, 2014.
71. *4 ans d'action politique*, Bruxelles: Ecolo, 1985.
72. *Ecolo-info*, 1 September 1984.
73. *Ecolo-info*, December 1988, Assemblée Generale Europe.
74. Jacky Morael, *Generations vertes, Regards croisés sur 30 ans d'écologie politique* (Green Generations, Different Views on Thirty years of Political Ecology), Bruxelles: Etopia, 2014.
75. *Die Grünen, Das Buch*, Die Zeit Magazin, 2011.
76. *Washington Post*, 14 February 1982.
77. *Der Spiegel* 8 (1983).
78. *Sydsvenska Dagbladet*, 9 March 1983.
79. Letter to the parliamentary group of Die Grünen, 9 January 1984.
80. Letter to the parliamentary group of Die Grünen, 14 February 1984.
81. Alice Schwarzer, *Eine tödliche Liebe, Petra Kelly und Gert Bastian* (A Deadly Love: Petra Kelly and Gert Bastian), Köln: Ki-Wi Taschenbuch, 1993.
82. Sara Parkin, *Life and Death of Petra Kelly*, London: Rivers Oram Press, 1994.
83. Some examples: Joachim Fischer, *Von Grüner Kraft under Herrlichkeit* (From Green Strength and Might), Reinbeck: Rowohlt, 1984; Antje Vollmer, ...*und wehr Euch täglich! Bonn, ein grünes Tagesbuch* (And Defend Yourselves Daily: A Green Diary from Bonn), Gütersloh: Verlagshaus Mohn, 1984; Monika Sperr, *Petra K Kelly, Politikerin aus Betroffenheit* (Petra K. Kelly, Politician by Compassion), Berlin: Rowohlt, 1985; Tomas Eberman and Reiner Trampert, *Die Zukunft der Grünen, ein realistisches Rezept für eine radikale Partei* (The Future of the Greens: A Realist Recipe for a Radical Party), Hamburg: Konkret, 1985.
84. Bundesversammlung 13–15, December 1985 in Offenburg.
85. Michael Schroeren, *Chronologie der laufenden Ereignisse*, papier der Grünen Partei, 13 October 1988.
86. Joschka Fischer, 'Zwischen Wiedervereinigungsillusionen und NATO-Austrittfiktionen' (Between Illusions About Reuniting Germany and Fictions About Exit from NATO), speech in Berlin, 20 November 1987.
87. Erklärung der Grünen Partei, Berlin, 25 November 1989.
88. Jürgen Schreiber, *Meine Jahre mit Joschka, Nachrichten von fetten und mageren Zeiten* (My Years With Joschka: News From Fat and Slim Years), Berlin: Econ Verlag, 2007.
89. 'Zurück zu den Wurzeln', *Der Spiegel* 14 (2008).
90. Christian Schmidt, *Wir sind die Wahnsinnigen, Joschka und seiner Frankfurter Gang* (We Are the Mad, Joschka and his Frankfurt Band), Berlin: Econ Verlag, 1998.
91. Joschka Fischer, *Die Rot-Grünen Jahre, Deutsche Aussenpolitik, vom Kosovo bis zum 11. September* (The Red-Green Years: German Foreign Policy, From Kosovo to September 11), Köln: Kiepenheuer & Witsch, 2008.

232   GREEN PARTIES, GREEN FUTURE

92. Joschka Fischer, *I Am Not Convinced, Der Irak-Krieg und die Rot-Grünen Jahre* (I Am Not Convinced: The Iraq War and the Red-Green Years), Köln: Kiepenheuer & Witsch, 2011.

93. 'Helmuth Markwort: Joschka Fischers beste Nummer', *Focus* 9 (2011); 'Joschka ist der einzige Popstar, Interview mit Dany Cohn Bendit', *Welt am Sonntag*, 8 June 2003; 'Triumph der Wut, about "Joschka und Herr Fischer"', *Der Spiegel* 19 (2011).

94. Jutta Dithfurth, *Krieg, Armut, was sie reden, was sie tun, Die Grünen*, Berlin: Rotbuch, 2011. Another famous fundi who was disappointed early was the East German dissident Rudolf Bahro who was deported to West Germany in 1979 because of the book *The Alternative*. He joined Die Grünen, which he explained in *From Red to Green* (London: Verso, 1984), only to leave the party in 1985, taking a distance from party politics and pursuing a more spiritual path.

95. *Der Spiegel* 25 (2012).

96. Roth, *Das politische ist privat*.

97. *Der Spiegel* 20 (2013).

98. Daniel Cohn-Bendit, *Der grosse Basar* (The Great Bazaar), München: Trikont, 1975. As a well-known figure Cohn-Bendit has been the object of several fierce attacks, for example in Paul Ariés and Florence Leray, *Cohn-Bendit, l'imposture* (Cohn-Bendit, the Fraud), Paris: Max Milo, 2010.

99. 'Das grüne Gedächtnis', *Der Spiegel* 39 (2013).

100. *DE Magazin Deutschland*, May 2014.

101. 'Enquête chez les Verts allemands', *Le Monde diplomatique*, August 2011.

102. 'Politik lohnt sich doch – vom Staatsdiener zum Grossverdiener' (Politics is Profitable – From Public Servants to High-income Earners), *Der Spiegel* 17 (2012).

103. One of the buyers of the services of Fischer's consultancy bureau was the EGP, for its common election campaign in 2014, according to the homepage of the EGP.

104. *Der Spiegel* 47 (2014).

105. This author was one of the initiators, partly through a book, Per Gahrton, *Det behövs ett framtidsparti* (There is a Need for a Party for the Future), Stockholm: Prisma, 1979. I have told the story of the first 30 years of the Swedish Greens, from my perspective, in another book, *Det gröna genombrottet, mina trettio år med Miljöpartiet* (The Green Break-through: My Thirty Years With the Green Party), Stockholm: Carlssons, 2011.

106. Per Gahrton, *Låt mormor bestämma 2000-talet* (Let Grandmother Decide the Twenty-First century), Stockholm: Bonniers, 1993.

107. Gudrun Schyman is a phenomenon in Swedish politics. She was leader of the Left Party 1993–2003, but was ousted from the leadership for alleged mismanagement of an income tax return. She initiated Feminist Initiative in 2005, which in 2014 got one MEP, but narrowly failed to cross the 4% barrier at the parliamentary elections the same year.

108. One strong critic is Birger Schlaug, spokesperson 1985–88 and 1992–2000, who has quit the Greens.

109. This author was one of them, the arguments being developed in a book, Per Gahrton, *Befria EU* (Liberate the EU), Stockholm: Ordfront, 2009.

110. Dan Boyle, *A Journey to Change: 25 Years of the Green Party in Irish Politics*, Dublin: History Press, 2006.

111. Letter to the EGP committee, May 2013.

112. *Bulletin Vert*, Le Journal romand des Verts, no. 2, September/October 2006.

113. 'Who we are', by Ville Komsi, 21 January 1984.

114. *Hufvudstadsbladet*, 19 October 1988.

115. *Hufvudstadsbladet*, 12 December 1989.

116. *Finska Notis Byrån*, 26 November 1989.

117. *Hufvudstadsbladet*, 6 January 1990.

118. *Combat Nature* no. 68, May 1985.

119. *Eurogreens Newsletter* no. 4, November 1986.

120. *Le Figaro*, 5 November 1988.

121. Alain Lipietz, *Refonder l'esperance, lecon de la majorité plurielle* (Refound the Hope: Lessons of the Plural Majority), Paris: La Decouverte, 2003.

122. http://www.france24.com/fr/20111124-france-eva-joly-europe-ecologie-verts-parti-socialiste-politique-presidentielle-2012.

123. *Le Monde*, 23 September 2012.

124. *Liberation*, 22 August 2012.

125. www.lefigaro.fr/politique/2013/09/25/01002-20130925ARTFIG00084-noel-mamère-seul-contre-la-firme-eelv.php.

126. Booklet, in English, by Green Academy, 1989.

127. The tough anti-EU position was vividly represented by Johannes Voggenhuber, leader of the party in the parliament, MEP 1995–2009; as a member of the EU Convention in 2003 which proposed an EU constitution he converted to a more federalist pro-EU position.

128. Österreich kann neutral bleiben, in der EG nicht.

129. *Impuls Grün*, Grüne Bildungswerkstatt, February 1989; among the contributors were Andras Sekfü, Hungary; Friedrich Wilhelm zu Baringdorf, Germany; Alexander Langer, Italy; Lucius Theiler, Switzerland; Pekka Haavisto, Finland; and Per Gahrton, Sweden.

130. The authors were a professor of technology, Niels I. Meyer, a former liberal member of the government, Kristen Helveg Petersen, and a well-known author, Villy Sørensen.

131. Nach der Europawahl, *Kommune*, June 1989.

132. The present author worked with Langer in the Committee for Foreign Affairs in the European Parliament. Once when a reporter asked me to organise an interview with Langer, he looked at his agenda, which was divided into quarter-hour blocs. Could he find one quarter for my journalist? Langer took upon himself a moral duty that was inhuman. See also 'Wie Judas im Olivenhain, über den Selbstmord eines grünen Politikers' (As Judas in the Olive Garden: About a Suicide of a Green Politician), *Der Spiegel*, 28 August 1995.

133. Carlo Ripa Di Meana, *Sorci Verdi* (Green Mice), Milano: Kaos Edizioni, 1997.

134. The Norwegian voters have twice, in 1972 and 1994, rejected membership agreements proposed by the political elite.

135. *Verde*, year II, no. 3.

136. Signed 1 June 1985 by José Luis Barceló, 'Presidente del comité ejecutivo permanente' (President of the Permanent Executive Committee) of Verde, and Ezequiel Saragoca, 'portavoz' (spokesperson) of FLFP.

137. *El Periodico*, 31 May 1988.

138. PSUC, Partit Socialista Unificat de Catalunya (Unified Socialist Party of Catalonia), PCC, Partit dels Comunistes de Catalunya (Catalan Communist Party), and the Entesa Nacionalista d'Esquerra (Left-wing Nationalists Agreement).

139. Christan Schickardt, report, Turkey 17 September–1 October 1989.

140. *Armenpress*, 11 November 2014.

141. *Update* (Bulletin of the European Greens), 3 June 2006.

142. http://eozp.info/?menu=info&id=14&lang=en.

143. CoEG minutes, 16–17 December 1989.
144. 'Estonia Needs a Postmodern Green Party', *Baltic Report*, 20 May 2010.
145. Gerhard Jordan, 'Die Grünen in Ungarn', 5 October 1989.
146. Per Gahrton, 'A Green Party in Hungary' (a report to the CoEG), 15 December 1989.
147. Szusza Beresz, in a letter to the CoEG, 17 December 1989.
148. Görgy Droppa in the newsletter of the EGP, *Update*, 3 June 2006.
149. 'Green Party Takes Root', *The Baltic Times*, 5 November 2014.
150. *TAZ*, 18 July 1989.
151. *Huffington Post*, 3 December 2014.
152. 'The Polish Green Party and the Upcoming Elections: An Interview with Bartłomiej Kozek – European Integration', *Böll Foundation*, 3 December 2013.
153. Gerhard Jordan, in a report to CoEG, December 1989.
154. Oleg Yanitsky, *Russian Environmentalism: Leading Figures, Facts, Opinions*, Moscow: Mezhdunarodnyje Otnoshenija Publishing House, 1993.
155. Draft Report, Russian Greens dialogue, Moscow, 11–12 January 2003.
156. Aleksey Yablokov, 'Ecological Green Political Movement in Russia', presentation in Russian, 5 February 2004.
157. O. N. Yanitskij, *Environmentalist Dossier, Draft for Intellectual Biography* (in Russian), Moscow: Sociological Institute of the Russian Academy of Science, 2009.
158. Andrew Wilson, *Virtual Politics: Faking Democracy in the Post-Soviet World*, New Haven: Yale University Press, 2005.

INDEX

Note: References for specific national Green parties can be found under the name of the relevant country. The exceptions are Miljöpartiet of Sweden, and Die Grünen of Germany, which are under their party names as they are most commonly referred to this way in the text. Page numbers in *italic* refer to figure captions.

In line with standard practice, individuals are included in the index only when there are significant passages about them in the text. Other individuals can generally be found by looking in the sections on their national party.